Unfinished Rabbi

UNFINISHED RABBI

SELECTED WRITINGS OF

Arnold Jacob Wolf

Edited by Jonathan S. Wolf

With a Foreword by

EUGENE B. BOROWITZ

IVAN R. DEE
Chicago 1998

UNFINISHED RABBI. Copyright © 1998 by Arnold Jacob Wolf. All rights
reserved, including the right to reproduce this book or portions thereof in any
form. For information, address: Ivan R. Dee, Inc., 1332 North Halsted Street,
Chicago 60622. Manufactured in the United States of America and printed on
acid-free paper.

Library of Congress Cataloging-in-Publication Data:
Wolf, Arnold Jacob.
    [Selections. 1998]
    Unfinished rabbi : selected writings of Arnold Jacob Wolf / edited by
Jonathan S. Wolf ; with a foreword by Eugene B. Borowitz.
        p. cm.
    Includes index.
    ISBN 1-56663-183-1
    1. Judaism—20th century. 2. Judaism—Doctrines. I. Title.
BM565.W572 1998
296'.09'045—dc21   97-36236

CONTENTS

I try to walk the road of Judaism. Embedded in that road are many jewels. One is marked "Sabbath" and one "Civil Rights" and one "*Kashrut*" and one "Honor Your Parents" and one "Study of Torah" and one "You Shall Be Holy." There are at least 613 of them, and they are of different shapes and sizes and weights. Some are light and easy for me to pick up, and I pick them up. Some are too deeply embedded for me—so far at least, though I get a little stronger by trying to extricate the jewels as I walk the street. Some, perhaps, I shall never be able to pick up. I believe that God expects me to keep on walking Judaism Street and to carry away whatever I can of its commandments. I do not believe that He expects me to lift what I cannot, nor may I condemn my fellow Jew who may not be able to pick up even as much as I can. . . .

I do not "accord status" to the commandments. I do not feel permitted to rate them in advance of performing them. In principle, no commandment is inferior to any other. But some are in fact unavailable to me, some are dependent on a land in which I do not live, some on a world that is not my world. Some are just too heavy for me to lift. That is no reflection on them or, perhaps, even on me; it is just so. Any Orthodox insistence that every Jew must do the same thing at the same time in the same way is oblivious of human differences. Liberal subjectivism that lets every Jew be his own god forgets our deepest need to become what we are not yet by serving a very great Master. Neither Orthodox nor liberal, I try to be a Jew.

[*Commentary* Symposium, August 1966]

Franz Rosenzweig [the early-twentieth-century German-Jewish theologian] refined our understanding of liberalism and the law by accepting in principle the whole of traditional *halakhah* but living only that portion of it that he could conscientiously perform. He would answer for those details of the law that he could not himself enact by pleading "not yet." I have described this view in recent years as "walking along Jew Street picking up all the packages of *mitzvot* that one can handle and leaving those that are, for the time, still too heavy." This view has the advantage of not identifying the whole tradition with that portion of the tradition that we find personally congenial, and yet leaving us not feeling guilty about that portion of it that we simply cannot live with in our time and place. And, as long as we have not eliminated parts of the *halakhah* from the Jewish agenda just because we find them too difficult or remote, there may come a time when we, or our descendants, will recover those portions.

[*Moment*, September 1983]

PREFACE

THIS SELECTION of the writings of Rabbi Arnold Jacob Wolf contains articles written over many years and a generous sampling of the almost weekly columns which Arnold, as the rabbi, contributed to the temple bulletins of Congregation Solel and of KAM Isaiah Israel. The book is thus a record, over four decades, of an active and sensitive mind. It is intended as a tribute upon Arnold's retirement, a testimonial of the love, admiration, and respect of his friends, his congregations, his students, and his family, all of whom contributed to its production.

But a collection of Arnold's writings can be only a partial portrait of a great rabbi, because Arnold is not, foremost, a writer. He is an orator, perhaps the finest orator of our generation. This is a talent which must be heard to be fully appreciated . . . but there are no recordings of sermons, or even of lectures or classes, in this volume. Were there sermon transcripts they would not suffice, nor would even an audio CD tucked into the back cover. Such a tape might capture the musical cadence and the prophetic timbre of Arnold's voice, but it would miss the presence, the physical sense of his compelling us to attend and listen. The CD would not let us see how a man surrounded by a giant ark and *bimah* still looms large by the power of his moral conviction. It would also fail to convey the moment when the sermon ends and Arnold turns away from the congregation and slowly walks back, leaving us to accept and respond to the challenges he has put before us.

Arnold's writings only partially express his greatest strengths, because Arnold is not simply a thinker. He is a teacher, whose genius must be experienced in encounter, dialogue, and provocation. His skill as a teacher is measured not primarily in what he has put down on paper but in what he has inspired and brought out in those lives he has shaped and transformed. His life work is not centrally in what he has written but in what his students—all of us—have lived.

This volume, then, is an incomplete picture. And yet, for all its imperfections, it constitutes a vivid record of what, in the second half of the twentieth century in America, it was possible for a rabbi to be and to achieve. The portrait includes all the appropriate elements: discussions of theology, *halakhah*, ritual, *mitzvot*, Israel, ethics, congregation. It also includes plenty of Freud, of family, and of fun; of humor, irreverence, and the White Sox. Beyond this, it records Arnold's lifelong passionate engagement with the defining political issues of our time: race, Vietnam, the Middle East, poverty, injustice, intolerance. This record is extraordinary for the breadth of Arnold's involvements, and it reflects a man living out the metaphor he himself formulated: trying to pick up as many of the precious jewels on Jew Street as he can carry, and then some. He reminds us that although that path is broad and secular rather than narrow and sectarian, it is for this reason no easier.

This book has been produced by KAM Isaiah Israel Congregation, seeking a fitting way to honor its rabbi on his retirement. It was Arnold's son, Jonathan, who gathered and pruned all of Arnold's writings, organizing and editing them. From the rich manuscript he assembled, a committee of the congregation (Nikki Stein, Rona Brown, Lee Haupt, Jerry Podell, Charlotte Podell, Tom Meites, and Howard Helsinger) made the final selection.

In many ways this book resembles one of Arnold's sermons: informal, intellectually challenging, humorous, intensely serious, topical, rooted in and pervaded by *Torah*. As Arnold relinquishes the *bimah* and leaves us to reflect on and react to the challenge he has issued, those of us who have learned so much from him fondly exclaim: *Yasher Koach!*

HOWARD M. HELSINGER
THOMAS R. MEITES

August 1997 / Av 5757

EDITOR'S NOTE

THIS BOOK would never have happened without the initiative, persistence, and talents of its author's wife, my stepmother, Grace W. Wolf. She determined that the book was needed and should be published now, and she overcame myriad obstacles to see it to completion. In this as in so many other ways, she has brought joy and fulfillment to my father's life and to all of us.

The congregation he has served for the past seventeen years, KAM Isaiah Israel, made this book possible. The committee of members who worked with me to create and shape it, chaired by Nikki Will Stein, made numerous contributions, especially those of Howard Helsinger. The Temple office, overseen by the masterful Vicki Goldwyn, provided indispensable assistance. Linda Turner typed the manuscript with dedication and skill. My brother, Benjamin Wolf, was of great help and encouragement. Ivan R. Dee and his staff did a marvelous job of designing and editing.

Manifold thanks are due to those of my father's colleagues and students who read portions of the manuscript and made comments and contributions: Rabbi Larry Kushner, Reverend Krister Stendahl, Albert Vorspan, Professor Norbert Samuelson, Rabbi Tsvi Blanchard, Carolyn Toll Oppenheim, Kathy Kurtzman Lawrence, and the late Henry Schwarzschild, z"l.

During the years in which this book was being prepared, my wife, Kathy Goetz Wolf, and I were becoming engaged and married. She contributed immense practical, intellectual, and moral support and played a major role in the book's completion. I am, as always, in her debt.

In reading this material over and over, refining it and putting it in place, I have become ever more convinced of what an important and singular thinker my father is. The reader will note many strands of thought continuing throughout the book, twisting together, connecting and illuminating one another. These represent perhaps one-eighth of what he has written over forty years. Yet this selection makes clear how far ahead of his time he has been on a wide range of issues. It is astonishing how consistent his style, his convictions, and his fervor have been over the decades. In these pieces he is by turns outraged, affectionate, wistful, stalwart, discouraged, insistent. But his fundamental outlook has never changed: the future is in God's hands, but we must do *our* work, with a faith and determination that is neither liberal nor right-wing, neither Orthodox nor Reform, but eternally, messianically hopeful.

It has been a privilege and a labor of love to toil in this vineyard, and I hope the fruits will reach and inspire many, as my father's ideas and voice so richly deserve.

J. S. W.

FOREWORD
Eugene B. Borowitz

FOR DECADES Arnold Jacob Wolf has been the finest English stylist in the American rabbinate. Were he an author of fiction, or of the impressionistic vignettes that some other rabbis write, my praise would already be high. But Arnold's flashing style has been at the service of ideas, the abstractions we employ to give self-consciousness to faith and underlying justification to politics. In the diverse fields that have engaged him, he has written with unique clarity, penetration, belief, and sophistication. He disdains academic turgidity and religious sentimentality, cant, or evasion. His writing, as the *Midrash* says of Revelation, "smashes against the ear." Even in the stillness of reading him, one can hardly miss his uncommon quality as a rabbi and a person. Yet the style, for all its virtues, is not the man; neither is its content the whole of his person or his rabbinate. His riches of person have decisively shaped his way of being a rabbi, since he is a Jew to his utter depth; and his Jewishness, focused in the rabbinate, has shaped his eventful life.

Arnold came to rabbinical school as the scion of an extended German-American family proud of its long record of Jewish service and centered on the scholar-rabbi Felix Levy. Arnold not only knew the Reform rabbinate from inside but identified serious Jewishness with the outstanding mind, heart, and person. That quickly isolated him from the many then (and since) who were satisfied with lesser standards. Relishing the give and take of argument, congenitally provocative, Arnold related to his fellow students in a way that anticipated his future relations with colleagues—and to some extent with the community as a whole.

Arnold's early otherness came partly from his depth of faith. Almost every student knew that something needed to be done to give Reform services new life, if only to make them "more Jewish." Even so, most students resigned themselves to the existing conventions, preferring passivity to the pain and peril of change. Arnold, however, cared about making God manifest in life, so he (with a few others) experimented as best he could with prayer and ceremony (long before "spirituality" became a generation's rallying cry). This boldness of faith was threatening to many who were secretly deeply ambivalent about belief.

Arnold balanced his elitism of excellence with an utterly uncommon respect for students and congregants. They too had something important to contribute to our ever-developing Reform Jewish practice. So he scorned teachers who just lectured or rabbis who acted as if they had all the worthwhile wisdom. Using the University of Chicago method of teaching by discussing, he confronted high school kids with Jewish sources or human situations and had them think things through among themselves (with the help of a leader). This led to students' creating their own services. Immediately following ordination (1948), he helped to develop the NFTY Camp Leadership Institutes model for member-directed youth groups. Later the extraordinary creativity of Congregation Solel— its member-written prayer books, the earliest synagogue Holocaust weekend commemoration, its rousing theopolitical discussions— grew out of this continuing faith in what people, with some guidance, could bring to Judaism. His was no self-serving elitism but the empowerment (another then unknown term) of anyone willing to reach for high Jewish standards.

Over nearly five decades of Jewish service, it seems clear that from early on Arnold was determined to give new meaning to that increasingly empty motto "Prophetic Judaism." When Jews cared largely about validating their participation as Jews in the general society, Prophetic Judaism essentially meant stressing Judaism's universally human teaching (explicating its ethics in a neo-Kantian way). Just as many Jews found Ethical Culture (if they were humanists) or Unitarianism (if they sought the cover of the least unbearable church) preferable to Reform Judaism, there were also within the Reform movement itself, as Arnold saw it, their fellow reductionists—those who condensed Prophetic Judaism to social betterment or to the imitation of upper-class Protestant church style. He considered their narrowness of focus a travesty of prophets who spoke only because God said they must and whose message was God's own. The prophets had addressed the Jews about their communal obligations and failures, seeking to make them better Jews, not just fine people-in-general. Intuitively Arnold saw what was needed and set about living and articulating it. More important, he began challenging congregants, students, colleagues, and the community with his radical message: they were not being true to their avowed standard. Only a radical politics grounded on a rich Jewish piety and practice deserved being called "Prophetic Judaism" or, in fact, "Judaism."

Despite the contribution he made by this critical stance, it carried a high social price. The prophet is necessarily an outsider. He cannot become an insider and continue speaking from the Divine perspective, whether in condemnation or comfort. Arnold, of course, never claimed to be a prophet, only—but what an "only"!—a rabbi. He has lived as a Jew inside Jewish institutions, not as one who disdains ordinary folk responsibilities while criticizing the community from its margins. He has given synagogues (and a Hillel Foundation) a leadership conscious of budgets and programs, participated in rabbinic organizations, and done his member's duty there and elsewhere. It sounds like an eccentric manner of renewing Prophetic Judaism until one remembers Martin Buber's teaching: the rabbis of the Talmud were the true successors of the prophets. We see this most clearly in the way they used their genius for routinization and democratization to sanctify the everyday. To be sure, as with all human enterprises, structure tends to become an end in itself, in the Talmud's case by sanctifying a bureaucratization that can suffocate the soul. Then the Jewish spirit must renew itself as it so amazingly always has. Arnold, it is now evident, has sought in our ever-turbulent times to model Buber's rabbi, the one in whom the prophetic impulse lives within the community.

Perhaps no event in his near-half century of service better epitomizes the dialectics of the prophetic rabbinate than his presidency of Breira in the mid-1970s. (Actually he was the national "chairperson," as befit those heady, antihierarchical, antisexist days). It was a time of widespread intolerance of some Jews by other Jews. The established organizations were solidly against any criticism of the State of Israel within the community. A group of idealists—academics, rabbis, lay people—rejected the common wisdom that Israel could not take first steps toward peace, and said there was indeed a choice, a *breira*. They publicly called for the establishment of a Palestinian state as the only long-range political solution to the Arab-Israeli struggle and the only Jewishly just alternative to incessant conflict.

Breira encountered indignation and outrage. B'nai B'rith was pressured to fire Arnold from his post as Hillel director at Yale, and many a rabbinic colleague shunned him for years. All this and much more because of what by then might have been considered a most gentle kind of political action: founding an organization and issuing a statement. Even in the early 1980s, when most major American Jewish organizations were themselves publicly endorsing responsible Diaspora criticism of the State of Israel, some in the Jewish community still bitterly condemned Arnold for having violated the consensus a few years before.

He had not sought to head Breira, though he had long espoused a position similar to the one it took. He certainly did not seek its special pains, for Breira fell apart after about a year, as much from internal dissension as from the implacable community campaign against it. Arnold bore the contumely with simple dignity but with an absolute refusal to renege on what he knew was his ethical, that is, his Jewish, duty. He felt Jewish responsibility required him to dissent from an uncommonly united community but not to withdraw from the give and take of Jewish life.

Anyone who has known Arnold for any length of time soon learns that what might seem provocative or self-serving behavior in others is Arnold's natural way of trying to respond—and get others to respond—to what he hears as a Sinaitic categorical imperative. He plays with kids and teases teenagers with that same intense devotion; he once wrote funny skits and plays, and was no mean performer of them. His kind of prophetic rabbi knows one can make demands only when they are structured by love; and any love without demands demeans the lover as well as the beloved. It is a hard if mature Torah.

Two other paradigmatic acts express his kind of contemplative devotion to the God of Israel. First, his theological pioneering: in 1965 Arnold put together *Rediscovering Judaism*, a collection of essays by the diverse adherents of a nascent theological movement later called Covenant Theology, and its first major articulation. Some of these ideas had already surfaced in articles by Reform and Conservative thinkers as well as at meetings of the Central Conference of American Rabbis. Arnold's book broke new ground not only in giving dimension to the new thinking but in transcending all denominational divisions to show the pluralistic commonality of Judaism as it struggled for a new self-understanding. Most of its authors had been at one or another of the several small meetings of like-minded theological seekers at the UAHC's camp in Oconomowoc, Wisconsin, a group Arnold helped inaugurate. (A few years later a larger group, this time under modern Orthodox auspices, met for several years in Canada, laying the groundwork for the present Hartman Institute in Israel.) *Rediscovering Judaism* prefigured much of the theological development of the following decades. Later Arnold made his contributions through inimitably insightful and judgmental reviews and articles. Unlike the academics who produce most such pieces, he has had to focus on practical Jewish concerns other than the mind.

He made another contribution through a daring experiment in Jewish observance (which is, of course, the twin of Jewish thought).

In the 1970s Arnold decided to act on his mounting concern about the erosion of disciplined Jewish living, specifically about the fate of Jewish law, *halakhah*. He felt compelled to accept it, that is, to live by its strictures, at least as defined by Conservative Judaism. He therefore joined the Conservative rabbis' association (while maintaining his membership in the Reform CCAR). He appreciated the Conservatives' Jewish style and pattern of observance, but his prophetic side quickly drove him to their margins. Wanting more change than they were ready for, he found himself among their *halakhic* left, and, those being the days of Breira, he was also one of the small number of their radical *political* left. Among the CCAR colleagues, a number of whom were more sympathetic to his politics, the challenge of his lifestyle—the implicit insistence that Jewish observance involved far more than ethics—relegated him to the tiny Reform far right. He had too rich a Jewishness for either group, but neither could easily ignore his presence as message.

Like all contemporary Jewish theologians, he still struggles with the fundamental non-Orthodox conundrum—how can "objective" Jewish law channel the free spirit without violating it? Rosenzweig resolved the issue simply by positing the primacy of the law in this ultimate dialectic of the modern and the Jewish. Arnold appears to offer his own version of that stand, but the puzzle remains for him, as for most others, work in progress. One can do much worse than to stand with so noble a thinker as Rosenzweig in pondering this mystery of Jewish faith.

When we were students fifty-plus years ago, we dearly wanted to edit the student publication called (when we arrived) the *HUC Monthly* (soon reduced to the *HUC Quarterly*). Three times we ran for that office, and three times we lost. If memory may be trusted, the last time (or was it the last two times?) we lost by one vote. It hurt and, in some secret way, still does. No doubt our prophetic eagerness was so overlaid with elitism and ego as to bring about our colleagues' rejection of our leadership. But something else might have been at work. Despite the mellowing effect of years and psychotherapy, Arnold is still not trusted by colleagues to speak the accepted words and observe the conventions of safe rabbinic leadership. They worry lest he say one of those things that tears the cover from our religious compromises and forces us to confront the duty we know we should do but evade. Yet for that very reason many a colleague and congregant loves and reveres him as our generation's incomparable instance of the prophet become rabbi.

All this says much too little about Rabbi Arnold the person. No appreciation of style, of acumen, of stance can take the place of that extraordinary creation, the living Arnold Jacob Wolf. He has inimitably fulfilled this era's new commandment: to create oneself. Gloriously alive and involved, profligately scattering sparks of true being, he is that utter rarity: person and Jew as one, and no less real in either aspect for being so much the other. No foreword can properly describe that. But let it at least be noted that only in the enigma of human becoming can one meet Arnold's true greatness.

Unfinished Rabbi

PART ONE

Rabbi and Congregation

THE RABBI IS A TEACHER

NOBODY BELIEVES ME, least of all my own congregation, but the fact is that I only work here. Rabbis are not, in my view, spiritual leaders, bosses, administrators, organizers, fund-raisers, or PR types. We are teachers, hired to teach and *only* to teach. If we really teach, we have little time for anything else. I teach regular classes in the congregation *every* week in *Talmud* and *Midrash*, modern Jewish thought, the concept of *mitzvah*, the portion of the week with commentaries. Every week I teach pre–Bar Mitzvah families, confirmands, groups of adults, converts, college students—a veritable *erev rav* (mixed multitude). I also teach, much more informally, officers, board members, social-action people, and many varieties of worshipers. That, my friends, is a full-time job. I also try to teach Judaism, really to teach, at dinner parties, Israel support groups, in bulletin columns and counseling sessions, funerals, weddings, conversations, and holiday celebrations. I prepare for all these events, so I have no time left to politick, to romance, to publicize, or to "outreach."

Some people think I am this active because so many people want to come and learn from *me*. Well, some do and some don't. But the real point is, Jews want to learn from all rabbis. They no longer seek intrusive spiritual imperialists or political sages or pulpit magicians. They want facts, texts, problems, serious attention on a regular basis to serious issues; maybe not all of them do, but more do than we think, and more and more of them all the time. My successes, and they are real successes, are not personal victories. My defeats are more often the result of personal inadequacy. But I triumph, when I do, by reading the signs of the times. Nothing succeeds like Torah!

It is the only merchandise we have, and to sell it does not require much charisma, salesmanship, or brilliance. It does require consistency, diligence, and a combination of modesty and guts.

I have worked for years with young suburbanites on the way up, with college students at the busiest time of their lives, and now with an urban mixture of people from eighteen to eighty: college professors and high school graduates, black and white, traditional and humanist, the interested and the preoccupied.

In each case I have discovered that they are allergic to superficial one-shot lectures and to halfhearted generalities. They want to keep at something Jewish, something classical and not necessarily "relevant" in any obvious way. But Jewish texts are relevant, of course, if they are read carefully, much more relevant than the trendy and the modern that may still pass for important, but less and less frequently.

If the rabbi is a teacher and not a coach, a leader, or a performer, that leaves the congregation free to do its job. The membership is released to be Jewish without the rabbi's substituting for them or directing their Jewish destinies. In that sense, too, the rabbi is an employee, a perfectly respectable but humble *melamed* (elementary teacher), a *meshamesh hatsibur*, one who works for the community. When rabbis used to be superstars and the congregations basked in their reflected glory, the congregation did just that: basked, but did not perform. It watched and applauded but did not act. It criticized and denounced but did not collaborate. Ours is an era of diminished rabbinic visibility in the service of lay leadership, what Eugene Borowitz prophetically called *tsimtsum* (self-limitation). Even God had to pull into Herself in order to leave space for people to act in freedom.

Jewish people will, of course, not always do the right thing, as the rabbi sees it. If they are free to decide serious issues, they will often decide against his view. They must do what they think best, even when that violates his convictions. I defend to my death their right to be wrong.

Often they will not be wrong at all. If they have the sense that they are in charge, that the future of our small Jewish world is in their hands, they will be free to imagine, to innovate, to choose wisely, and, most important, to learn how to choose. In recent months our people have created a food pantry, a new plan for the Shabbat education of older children, a lecture series that features other views and other learning than the rabbi's, and a great many other programs, large and small. The *Shabbat minyan* is their creation. The Purim *seudah* (meal) and *Megillah* reading belonged to them and to their children; the school is their responsibility; reacting to Reaganomics, with its contempt for the underprivileged, is largely their responsibility; welcoming new Jews and new members is their responsibility. My responsibility is to help them see their responsibility.

And my responsibility is to be the best Jew I can. I must learn in order to teach. I must learn every day if I will have enough to teach every week. I must work out my own religious way, which will not always be the same as the way in which most members of my congregation work out theirs. If they are truly free, then so am I. My destiny is not in their hands any more than theirs is in mine. I can be more observant without making them feel guilty, more critical of Israel without making them anti-Zionists. I am bound to, but distanced from, the very community in which I work and live and, so help me, love. But they can and someday will live without me, and I can and someday will live without them. We are brothers and sisters, but we are not surrogates for each other, neither enemies nor intimates, neither victims nor masters, neither exactly the same nor wholly different.

Being a rabbi is, I suppose, easier said than done. But what that is valuable is not? And, while difficult, it is not at all impossible. Rabbis, demythologized, and congregations, empowered, often can and do work together. In the end, it is God alone who establishes or undermines the work of all our hands. But it is upon us to begin.

[*Sh'ma*, May 14, 1982]

WHAT IS A RABBI? TWO GENERATIONS' VIEWS

UNTIL I READ Dr. Abraham Feldman's straightforward, unself-conscious presentation of his rabbinic style in his new book, *The American Reform Rabbi*, I did not realize how very much the American rabbinate has changed. I should like to record my own, perhaps not wholly atypical, divergences from Dr. Feldman's stated recommendations. It is both impossible and unnecessary to defend these differences here. They are offered with neither apology nor pride, but only to suggest what one suburban rabbi does that is different from a colleague of his some thirty years or a generation older. For convenience I shall chart some of our divergences. The page numbers noted are citations from Rabbi Feldman's book. My comments are in italics.

7. "I have not found anyone in any walk in life with whom I would swap places."
I have, but I did not think I was permitted to "swap."
29. "I put very much stock in the Confirmation."
I put almost none. Especially in the kind of sentimental, formalistic charade described in the appendix. Eschewing many traditional, commanded forms, Rabbi Feldman introduces many other private and new ones of doubtful taste. Why?
35. "I shamed the parents through their children."
!!!!!?????
41. "I am chairman of the Ritual Committee."
Then there is no Ritual Committee! The only hope for serious and un-

fettered reconsideration of congregational ritual is for the rabbi to release laymen, convince laymen that Judaism is theirs, mostly by letting them make their own mistakes and assume their full responsibility.

42. "I came to Reform Judaism as a matter of conviction. I chose Reform."

I didn't. I was born into a family of several generations of Reform. That may be why I am much less afraid than Dr. Feldman is of criticizing, reformulating, indeed of reforming Reform. It seems to me that most of our younger Reform Jews are more like me than like him.

44. "When strangers enter my Temple I want them to recognize it as a Reform Temple."

When strangers enter my (?) Temple, I am delighted to find they know it is a synagogue but are not always certain what kind.

46. "[The wearing of hats] is a pagan custom which came into Jewish life rather late."

So is the belief in immortality. Dr. Feldman repeats the old Reform confusion between origins and validity. He uses history as evidence for his own quite unhistoric preferences. If the covering of the head is only a minor incursion, why not do what most Jews do?

46–47. ". . . Especially in the case of *bar mitzvah*, I would not be unhappy if I could do away with it altogether."

So—do away with it! Your people can be convinced of its utter uselessness and irrelevance as even my less mature Jews were. Why be exercised at the yarmulke and lose your nerve when it comes to Bar Mitzvah?

48. ". . . This whole business of "halakhic practices" which they throw at me is just poppycock! I have discovered that *halakhah* is only what the individual Orthodox and/or Conservative rabbi wants it to be."

I have found that honest Orthodox and Conservative rabbis, who seem to me the vast majority, take the problems of law very seriously. I wish we Reformers knew that Judaism without halakhah, however mediated to us, is empty and solipsistic.

48. "On *Yamim Noraim* I skip a good deal."

I never skip part of the service. If I do not feel obligated by the Mahzor, who will?

49. ". . . I rather think that my announcing the sermon topic for next week just gives it a little extra punch."

I never announce my topics in writing or at services. Reform Judaism has dangerously emphasized sermons over prayer, I fear.

50. ". . . The *attoroh* [fringeless stole] is simply a part of a pulpit uniform rather than a *tallis*."

That's what is wrong with it. It is ceremonialism run amok, neither classically austere nor Jewishly authentic. When Reform romanticizes instead of Judaizing, it becomes gauche and coy.

65. ". . . If a rich person dies and his family wants to bury him in a bronze, hermetically sealed casket, why should I as a rabbi step into the picture . . . ?"

You are in the picture. Rich men, also, need instruction. Funerals instruct.

83. "[The Torah service] is a very impressive sight."

Reform has almost gone blind on "impressive sights."

112. ". . . They [the laymen] take care of the business affairs of the congregation, and I take care of the educational and spiritual affairs. I do not meddle in their affairs; they keep out of mine."

An incredible dichotomy! If I had to make a choice (sometimes I do), I would care more about the fiscal policies of the congregation than about their "spiritual" decisions. Nothing is more "spiritual" than money to me.

114. ". . . The rabbi shall, by virtue of his office, have the privilege to attend meetings of the Board of Trustees."

Rabbi Feldman fought for this privilege. I have fought (unsuccessfully, on the whole) for the right to be absent when the board does its work. They can use the freedom, and I could use the night.

120. "Several of the rabbis, as we were kibitzing among ourselves, whispered to each other that brotherhoods are nothing but 'pains in the neck.' I disagree with that."

I disagree with the disagreement. Any Jewish group that is not for the purpose of study, prayer, or acts of faithfulness can only be a dangerous diversion. What Men's Club is?

132. "Jewish unity, so-called, might be had at too costly a price."

Jewish unity, "so-called," is above price.

136. "I am known as one who believes in *shtadlonus*—in working quietly behind the scenes, seeing the right people, bringing pressure to bear, and getting what we want that way. . . ."

The only reason you can get what you want "that way" is that you do not want enough.

138. "I eat what is served."

I eat only what is (biblically, anyway) kosher.

147. "Rotary, Kiwanis, or Lions. Don't sneer at these."

I may not sneer, but I surely won't become a Rotarian like Dr. Feldman, even to meet someone he considers "top man in his category."

148. ". . . The more favorable exposure you have, the more civic contacts you have, the more useful you are as a Jewish representative."

Poor Amos! Poor Akiba! Poor Baal Shem Tov! Poor Einhorn!

150. "Some men feel strongly about some causes and want to indicate their interest and enthusiasm. But that is a matter of personal taste."

Personal taste is just what I think it is not. Civil rights, for instance, is either our obligation or becomes a dangerous self-assertion.

152. "By and large, the rabbi should keep out of politics—it is not his field."

By and large, God's world is his "field."

159. "'The rabbi is not a "square"' [is] neither complimentary nor recommendation."

It is if it means he is not a stuffed shirt. "Square" Judaism seems to me blasphemous.

159. "I see nothing wrong in a rabbi's indulging in a sociable card game."

I see batlanut *("sociability") as one of the rabbinate's enemies. Some great rabbis have bid away their usefulness at the bridge table. Luckily, I was never very good at bridge.*

160. "The Rabbi should always be *the Rabbi* to all, and never Abe or Jake or Sam to anyone."

There is certainly a phony, artificial, first-name informality in the suburban synagogue. But it is possible to be a rabbi, even to those who must call you by your first name. As time goes on, they will begin to call you the rabbi, but you must give them time, I think.

161. "The Rabbi is always on call; he is always on duty."

Like God?

172. "Q. Would it be wise to develop a confidante in another rabbi? . . .

"A. I wouldn't, I wouldn't. You may fall out next week, and some rabbis are more human than others."

A rabbi must have a colleague whom he trusts, loves, and confides in. K'ne L'cha Haver. ["Acquire yourself a friend"—Pirkei Avot]

186. "Q. If you were looking for a new assistant and you came to interview the graduating students at Hebrew Union College, what would you look for in a candidate?

"A. You are putting me on a spot, are you? The fact is that I may have to come. What do I expect of my assistant? I expect him to be a gentleman—a gentleman in the social sense of the word and also a gentleman in relation to the senior rabbi. . . ."

The "Jewish gentleman" Rabbi Feldman seeks seems to me too bland, too careful, too suave to serve a community in crisis.

188. "We have four lecturers, 'visiting firemen,' whom I invite, each of whom speaks on some particular theme, with a discussion following. On alternate weeks, the rabbis conduct adult classes. . . ."

Education means study of a text throughout many years with a teacher who is intimately acquainted with the spiritual life of the student. Rabbi Feldman seems to be playing the adult education game, not really teaching.

191. "I teach them the Judaism that I know and that I believe in; they can take it or leave it."

Unlike Dr. Feldman, I also strive to teach the Judaism I do not (yet?) believe in. I fill my staff with teachers of diametrically opposed views. Learning of Judaism must be dialectical, not apodictic, and Reform is stultified by conformity to any rabbi's idiosyncratic theologizing.

202. "Remember that whatever formal Jewish theology we have in Jewish life has been given by Reform."

I think almost the opposite in this case. Whatever we have now is a re-

action against (classical) Reform. Nearly all the serious religious thinking in Judaism today is an attempt to recover or to reconstruct what Kaufmann Kohler and Abraham Geiger left in shambles.

221. "So far as I know, there is no antagonism between the Hebrew Union College and the Union of American Hebrew Congregations. There are occasional misunderstandings between people who work for the Union and people who work for the College. . . ."

Conflict can easily be reduced to personalities, but it only becomes creative tension when it is honestly explored and not soft-pedaled.

227. "I am more hopeful today than I was thirty years ago."

Hope is, of course, a theological category, but if his has been extrapolated from present-day Judaism in America, I do not know what Rabbi Feldman is so hopeful about.

I would be wrong to leave the impression that I am in total disagreement with Dr. Feldman. Indeed, I am with him more often than against him. I agree with his views on the personal God, sermonics, suicides, *schnorrers*, the rabbi's family, study, funerals, and mixed marriages. I honor his candor, his grace, his character. But I cannot escape the distinct impression that we live in two different rabbinic worlds. And I fear that the future will be more like mine than like his.

[*Reconstructionist*, November 12, 1965]

BUILDING THE NEXT GENERATION OF JEWISH LEADERS

SYNAGOGUES AND Jewish organizations cry desperately for new leadership. They claim they both need and want younger, fresher men and women to inherit the duties that tired old men unwillingly (or incompetently) are still forced to perform. If only young leadership would present itself, it would immediately be handed the baton and offered all rights and privileges appertaining to nascent *macher*-ship. This is the myth; the reality is at least somewhat different.

The Jewish bureaucracy communicates a quite contradictory message. It shows, not by what it says but by what it does, that it likes things very well the way they are, or at least does not propose to risk rocking the boat by changing leadership in what is a perpetual midstream. It needlessly complicates discussion of the problem of transitional leadership out of all rational proportion. It endlessly studies how and what it should do in order to find new, qualified synagogue officers and Federation board members. But simple demystification points to a quite straightforward solution: give people power and responsibility and they will, with help, often come to live up to it. Leaders can be trained only on the job; there is no other school. They can only be tested by being tested *in situ*. Jews can only become Jews by acting like Jews, leaders by acting like leaders.

Historically the synagogue has played a purposefully diminishing role. The great community (*kehillah*) enterprise of European Jewry shrunk early on in America to a mere congregation. Later the synagogue itself often became just another American church.

Nathan Glazer speaks of "the desire of prosperous laymen to acquire a religious service [more] in keeping with their social status," thus reminding us that the function of our religious institutions was always closely geared to the assimilating needs of an upwardly mobile middle class. The *embourgeoisement* of the American synagogue, successively Reform, Conservative, and Neo-Orthodox, was a choice. The purpose of our institutions was significantly to assist the process of our acculturation; it got the leaders that it both wanted and needed to forward that goal.

Jewish community institutions were created or redesigned to meet the needs, on the one hand, and the threat, on the other, represented by the East European immigration at the turn of the century. We can no longer even imagine how frightening to newly Americanized Jews were these hordes of doctrinaire socialists, Orthodox fanatics, Zionists. One solution was to build Jewish structures that would contain, instruct, and reform the new immigrants. The leaders of such organizations had to be, above all, responsible, discreet—in a word: Americanized. No wonder that many of us have ended up, in Glazer's words, with a "stubborn insistence on remaining a Jew, enhanced by no particularly ennobling idea of what that means."

Jewish institutions normally select rabbis, presidents, and leaders according to quite visible criteria: suavity, wealth, decorousness, reputation. Our institutions become larger and more impersonal as their tasks proliferate, thereby requiring more specialized direction, more professionalism, less democracy. The tasks require hard-line accounting by standards sometimes less ethically nuanced than those in one's personal affairs. Leaders must be willing to cut corners when necessary, and people who can't must be superseded. There is no room for the finicky or the ethically scrupulous at the American Jewish top.

In order to proceed without assumed or covenanted tasks, conflict must be avoided at all costs. Hence leaders are likely to be bland, conventional, dependable at least in their mediocrity. The stuffed shirt is preferable to the as-yet-unsocialized young, which is at least one reason why so much Jewish leadership is senescent. Programming is dull, not accidentally but because excitement often polarizes and controversy is believed to reduce contributions. The brightest among us are driven away by a level of tasteless irrelevance that has its own raison d'être but nonetheless selects out for a lower intelligence and a less sensitive palate among leadership. Leaders tend to be alike, alike in their backgrounds, needs, and limitations. We get the "leadership" we want, despite what we say to the contrary.

Since real leadership demands responsibility, it will not be satisfied with "Mickey Mouse" alternatives. For years women (and, more often than not, men too) have been given busywork by synagogues and community organizations: petty fund-raising, empty and invidious bazaars, sports events, undisguised trivializing. Obviously these make-work tasks bore the gifted and fail to inspire even the less intelligent. They say, more clearly than words: this is what we think of you and of what you can do. They were and are a way of keeping Jews away from real Jewish responsibilities and entitlements. But the people must be empowered if they are ever to be asked to lead.

People are willing to work, to do even small ungrateful tasks regularly and willingly. But these tasks, however mundane, must have a direct relationship to real needs. If possible they should be physically close to those larger needs: teaching as well as sitting on a board of education, personally meeting Russian Jews as well as petitioning the Soviet government, chanting the Torah as well as hiring a cantor. Federations can no longer content themselves with dull reports at second and third hand cleared through self-defensive executives. The problems as well as the successes of each group must be shared with all its supporters. And they must not only have but also know they have the power to do something specific about those problems.

The role of the professional must, in any case, be clearly circumscribed if lay leadership is to emerge. Rabbis cannot now be "spiritual leaders"; administrators cannot be "executive directors." Lay boards must decide, and professionals should only clarify what is to be decided, and help their decisions to be effected. Rabbis and educated laymen who work for Jewish organizations must, above all, be teachers who share Torah, skills, and commitment, but who do not insist ever on representing those whom they help. Professionals are not surrogates but only servants. Good Hillel directors reject the title "Director of a Foundation" in favor of being a university rabbi, and the change has been more than semantic. If students plan programs, sign checks, and hire personnel (including the rabbi), they will know who is boss, and they will likely be willing to raise some of the money, lead some of the services, and share with their community of peers all of the nitty-gritty decisions. But not otherwise. The model for congregational or community organizing should no longer be the corporate board with its officers, directors, and executive-suite employees. More fluid models are now common, especially among student and young adult *havurot*. They all manifest what Eugene Borowitz has called *tsimtsum*, the intentional contraction of Jewish professionals, who consciously withdraw from power in order to leave space for new, lay leadership. Rabbis and executives do not need lackeys, much less competitors; what we all need are disciples.

New leadership cannot be manipulated but only taught. Handling agendas to eliminate failure, selection of leaders (often by professionals themselves, directly or indirectly) for their malleability, a total absence of self-criticism—all ensure that lay leaders will do anything but lead. On the other hand, frankness and dialogue do produce concern. We can only pray that our Jewish establishment learns to level with us Jews, telling us neither what we want to hear nor what is likely to make us more obedient, but what seems to be the truth. The truth is, of course, debatable, so it must be sought from many differing sides.

Why need we go to offbeat groups like Breira for a dissenting view on Israel, or to Nahum Goldmann for a dissenting view on Soviet Jewry? Why cannot we build into our own decision-making process alternative possibilities and minority opinions, as all democratic groups must? An anti-Zionist Communist can sit in the Israeli Knesset but could hardly have a place on a congregational or Federation board, though his opposition itself might clarify the views of all. Jewish intellectuals are used to controversy (or used to be used to it) and find Jewish unanimity suspicious and boring. Our young insist on a platform for those who hear a different drummer, if they are to dance at our weddings themselves. Official Jewish propaganda must give place to data, debate, and deciding, if new leadership is ever to come.

Young leaders are also put off by the narrow parochialism of our Jewish institutional structure. Once it may have seemed permissible for Jewish groups to compete with each other to meet the Pope or hear Golda, or teach the young, but it is too late and too expensive for that now. Young Jews often do not understand, and do not wish to understand, why it is so important to be a "Reform" or a "Conservative" or a "Reconstructionist" Jew; even the Orthodox, whose separateness seems to have some inevitability, have trouble keeping their lines distinct. Partly under the influence of the Holocaust, where Jews died without benefit of modifying adjectives, partly because nineteenth-century distinctions mean as little in the twentieth to us as differences among Protestants or blacks do to them, we are fast becoming impatient of such pettiness. The very claim of Federation to represent all Jews without distinction is its most powerful attraction to our young, who then are disappointed to find it as parochial as any *schul*. Most of us just want to be Jews, and we wish the Jewish organizations would let us be.

There are examples of the new style of leadership in congregations and communities around the country. *Havurot* within and without synagogues; *batim* where young Jews live and create together; women's groups no longer content simply to raise consciousness; universities where lots of young Jews are learning more than the Jewish establishment would have liked them to know; free Jewish schools of the Buber-Rosenzweig Frankfurt model, and all possible American versions of a *Lehrhaus*; Young Leadership experiments which promise a generational if not also an ideological revolution up the road. Some of these new-style Jewish groups are narcissistic and self-serving. They are places where Jews do their own things, heedless of the needs of others. But many are deeply responsive to commandment and covenant, to what their brothers lack and what their own comrades still need to learn. They care nothing for divisions between "religious" and "secular" organizations, between old German and newer East-European, between rich and poor Jews, between the dissident and the conventional. They only know that the establishment can no longer meet all possible Jewish needs, and they are no longer satisfied to wait their turn. They know how bad things often are, but the knowing is not intolerable. They are centered far outside their own small circles, and some know that God is the center of any circle at all. They are no longer mere followers; but they will never be leaders unless soon they start to lead.

[*Sh'ma*, May 2, 1975]

PART TWO

Beliefs

ON JEWISH FAITH

THE QUESTION "What is a Jew?" is both un-Jewish and unproductive. I can think of many better questions, for example: "What must I do?" "What can I become?" "What does God promise or seek?"

Jewish theology is the critical analysis of questions more than it is the presentation of answers. And I fear that Jewish theology, at least as I see it, must derogate from the kind of question that the phrase "criteria for being a Jew" implies. One of the greatest problems of modern Judaism is that we have the wrong problems: "Is there a God?" instead of "What does God want?" "What is a Jew?" instead of "How can I become a Jew?"

But, you might object, one cannot possibly become a Jew unless he knows *ab initio* what a Jew is. Really? Is it not more probable that one finds out what a Jew is only by becoming one? That one finds out what a man is only by becoming human? Liberal Judaism has assumed with nineteenth-century Idealism that essence always precedes existence, but the fact is that facts precede meanings. A Jew, says Rabbi Zalman Schachter, is someone who Jews. . . . The Hebrew Bible consistently prefers narrative to ascriptive theology with good reason. God is what God does (at least as far as man is concerned). The Jew is as the Jew does (at least as far as God is concerned).

This view has practical consequences. It lifts "practical theology" above "systematic theology"; Judaism really knows only practical mysticism, practical psychology, surely only practical theology. Theology for us is the art of *mitzvah*-making; it is the poetry of Jew-ing. This does not imply any chaotic anarchy in Jewish thought. The *Yad Hachazakah* (Maimonides' code) is no more chaotic—or less philosophical—than the *Moreh Nevuchim* (Maimonides' theology). A truly philosophical theology of modern Judaism would cast suspicion on much of what passes for Jewish religiosity (the Bar Mitzvah, the public relations, racism, denominationalism); not everything that calls itself Jewish is. . . .

In a poignant aside, Franz Rosenzweig remarks how German Liberal Judaism had produced so many wonderful principles and so few actual consequences (to us it may look like rather many as compared with our paucity of results), many fathers with few children, many chiefs and few Indians. It is time for us to begin with specific Jewish tasks (Sabbath, *tzedakah* [charitable giving], learning) and to let our theology be a precise examination of those tasks. A Jew, then, is someone who does something, not someone who is (or was) something. A Jew is a human being whose humanity is refracted by Jewish history and the Jewish task and the Jewish people.

A Jew must do whatever he can for God. The assumption is that there is a God, that there is a God who cares about what we do, that some of what God cares about that we do is "Jewish." I do not think that "Jewish" means only peculiar to Jews, otherwise keeping kosher would be a higher *mitzvah* than loving one's neighbor. The point is that the Jew helps God by loving *and* by eating. In our post-Freudian age we know how closely eating and loving are linked, how profoundly they interpenetrate. None of us would be able to say with Jesus anymore, "Not what goes into the mouth defiles a man, but what comes out of the mouth, this defiles a man." What goes in comes out!

Distinctions between "ethical" and "ritual" commandments are invariably premature if not downright useless. Religion is not only a matter of being a good boy; in fact, being a good boy is a lot harder than it looked to early Reform Judaism. The country of Kant and Hermann Cohen produced the murder camps. Everyone knew what was good, all right, but very few Germans risked doing it. The problem of religion is not saying good things but changing people. *Kashrut* may be as relevant to that task as *tzedakah*; they are finally inseparable.

More profoundly, the need of our time is the ethicizing of the apparently ritual and the ritualizing of the ethical. *Pesach*, prayer, piety are full of human, that is, ethical, consequences. But these must be recovered in the modern age. Where classical Reform fell prey to the philosophic trap, modern (romantic) Reform falls into a sociological pit. Thus Passover (!!—do we call *Shavuot* "Weeks"?) once was reduced to a kind of Freedom Charade. Now it is more likely to be manipulated into a children's bribe or a nostalgic exercise in culinary Judaism. But *Pesach* remains an ethical religious, that is, an existential, possibility. *Pesach* is a time of revolution in which the Jewish man can find his obligation to all the enslaved including himself; *Pesach* is more than I can say it is.

The Sabbath is the supreme ethical-religious moment. It is full of doing, remembering, discovering. Prayer, food, study, Exodus, community, social justice, children are all interwoven. Turn it and turn it, everything is potentially *Shabbosdik*. But Shabbat requires a good deal of preparation and concern, at least as much as a congregational membership campaign or a TV program. It takes one's thought and one's will and one's time. It has its own choreography and its own tempo. It is unmodern and therefore supremely important to modern Jews. Our fathers' fathers could have done without Shabbat; we dare not try. But who of us could say whether it is an "ethical" or a "ritual" commandment?

The apparently "ethical," on the other hand, requires ritualizing. The best example of this I know is civil rights. When it was a matter only of saying nice things or doing easy ones, we Jews were all ethical. But once the chips were down and civil rights came to mean the Negro Revolution (against, *davke*, us), Black Power, and the radical left, our Jewish liberals fled in unseemly hurry and panic. They did not have, we do not have, stamina for ethics in an urban setting. We are not willing, perhaps not even able any longer, to give up our old presuppositions, our bourgeois biases, just because they are wrong. But that means, of course, that we are no longer authentic Jews even if we think we are Orthodox.

A real Jew would have ritualized the ethical problem of equality. He would have made his moral commitment not on the basis of self-interest or emotional attachment to the suffering Negro or of his view of American self-interest. He would be with the underdog against the oppressor (even when he himself *is* the oppressor) for exactly the same reason he doesn't give a party on Friday night or eat bagels on *Pesach*—the only possible good reason being to do something for God.

Being good is largely a matter of being guilty in the right way and having the stamina to deal with one's guilt. These are both classical ritualistic problems. Reform was wrong to derogate from the sacrificial system the fasts and the confessionals. We need all the help we can get to rid ourselves of deep, corroding guilt. But we also need the *halakhah* (or at least an *halakhah*) to tell us how to channel our proper responsibility, to ritualize our personal duty. In other words, we desperately need to be commanded, and by a Commander worthy of the name.

The conventional Orthodox response to the question of religious authority is the assertion, despite all evidence to the contrary, that the Torah (Pentateuch? Bible? Commentary? Talmud?) is the literal Word of God. The conventional liberal response is to assert that the Hebrew Bible (with or without commentary) is the highest achievement of the human spirit in its attempt to reach God. I think both of these views are indefensible.

I cannot fault the Orthodox assertion that God could, if He wished, deliver over to us His concrete will. He could also, if He wished, appear to me personally in all His glory and tell me exactly what to do. But if He did I would disappear. God can only protect my integrity by keeping His distance from me. This is implied in each prophet's initial rejection of the Word, and by Israel's recurrent rebelliousness against the God Who appears to them at Sinai and in the Land. God's direct, immediate Presence is too much for man to face. A literal Torah would be the end of Judaism, not its beginning.

A God who completely revealed Himself would convert me, but only by destroying me in the process.

But that does not mean that the Torah is nothing more than a very, very good book—something like Tolstoy, Blackstone, and Dr. Spock all rolled into one. Nor does it mean that the only standard we are left with is our own selves as we construe the tradition. If Judaism is whatever we think it is, there is nothing ever against us, nothing for us to grow toward or to become because we are not yet. I believe that to interpret chosenness as Jewish superiority (especially superiority in "spiritual" matters) is both unbiblical and phony. I believe that the Bible is both more and less than the national epic of Israel, that it both discloses and represses the will of God.

How then do we come to know what pleases God? By personal relationship with Him in prayer, study, and doing. Relationship is not precisely revelation, but revelation only emerges from relationship. By being a father (as fully as I can learn to be), I discover what a father must do to father. My child does not tell me; I do not tell myself; the relationship tells me. But it tells me only if I attend to its subtle, insistent commands.

The Bible is not in and of itself a relationship. It is certainly not a univocal statement of God's will. But it is a record of the Great Relationship. It is the ground rules for the God-Man game. It is a paradigm, a poem, a prayer. It is (and all of Judaism also is) indispensable. While the Bible does not tell us what God wants *tout court*, it tells us how to find out what God wants. If Judaism does not always create in us a clean spirit, it is yet our Way, our Truth, and our Life.

God does not hide from me, nor does He, I believe, obliterate me. He meets me. He meets me in everything I do and am, in everything my people has seen or told. When He meets me, I always have *mitzvot* to perform: hearing (O Israel), cleaving, loving (with all my heart and soul and mind). He does not find me only in the privacy of my own conscience (which itself turns out to be far less private than our first Reformers believed) but in the interplay of human dialogue, in the abrasive contact of *halakhah* and in the saga of Israel insofar as that incorporates myself.

The conclusion of the matter (far less than all having been heard) is: I must do for God whatever I can do. He will not leave me alone in the dark. He will not force me. But He will love me and teach me Torah. And nothing in His Torah must be offensive to me. I must study it all, try it all, and add to it whatever comes out of my own meeting with Him. I will not be an Orthodox Jew if that means demanding the same automatic (compulsive?) response from every Jew every day. I will not be a Reform Jew if that means doing whatever I think is right just because I think so. I will be a Jew, a Jewish human being, myself as a Jew. I will be open to the wind of instruction that blows in every tree, every word, every hour. But I may not absent myself from Sinai, nor seek to evade my Jewish humanity. I will go for help to Him from whom all help comes, but I will not expect Him to do my work for me. I will try to love my crooked neighbor as I love my crooked self. I will not pretend that the "standards" issue from me or that I am alone in the world.

The *mitzvah* is firm, demanding, and resolute. But what, after all, is more full of the possibility of joy?

[*Dimension*, Winter 1967]

REMEMBER TO REMEMBER

MEMORY IS as Jewish as chopped liver, even more Jewish since Sephardic Jews remember too. Everyone knows that Judaism is about keeping our past vividly in mind. What they may not know, however, is that remembering is not just a nice tradition; it is a commandment. When Judaism gets most serious it does not speak the language of custom or convenience; it talks about *mitzvot*, obligations communicated by God through the medium of Torah. And memories definitely qualify as *mitzvot*.

There are many events and meanings that Jews should recall occasionally or even often. But, according to the *Talmudic Encyclopedia*, the Torah specifically commands six memories. Each of these is to be brought to our attention purposely and not accidentally, daily and not once in a while, orally and not merely mentally, and finally intentionally and not by chance or at random. Some Jewish prayer books list these six so that every Jew may give them attention during his daily devotions. Some of them are key events in the history of our people, but some seem to be strange and eccentric choices, at least at first glance. It is natural to recall the revelation at Sinai; but who among us can describe accurately Miriam's sin? Still, both are on our list, and both must be brought to our attention every day if we are to fulfill the command of Torah's God.

I

First, we must remember the Exodus.

"Remember this day on which you came out of Egypt, out of the house of bondage, for with a strong hand did He bring you out of there; no leaven shall be eaten" (Ex. 13:3).

The whole of Passover, and especially the *Seder*, is a mnemonic for the Exodus. That is why we do not eat leaven. That is why we ask questions, serve special foods, and every year gather together in familiar surroundings for a journey to far away and long ago.

But the Exodus is not remembered only at *Pesach*. Every holy day is a "remembering of the going forth out of Egypt." And every day we are obligated to bring to our consciousness the experience of deliverance from slavery in Egypt, too. Some rabbis say that even after the Messiah comes we will still be required to remember Egypt. The daily Sh'ma includes not only our proclamation of God's unity and of our obligation to love Him with all our heart and mind and self, but also the story of how He delivered us from Egypt, how we came to know there can be no god like Him.

But we do not remember Exodus only by speaking about it in prayer. We are to rest our animals and our slaves on the Sabbath in order to recall the freedom given us (not, as we might expect, the reverse) long ago. We are to empathize with the poor and the stranger because *we* were strangers in the land of Egypt. We are to proclaim God's absolute and unshared Kingship, because once we knew what it meant to serve a human king who claimed to be a god. We are to teach our children early and often about the bitterness of Egypt, even if we are teaching them in Woodbridge or Winnetka or Westwood. They too have a right to remember, and we ourselves can recall only by sharing our recollections with them. We remember also by wearing the *tallit* during the day and by recalling it at night, by putting on *tefillin*, "a sign on your hand and a remembering between your eyes, that His Torah will be in your mouth, how He brought you out of Egypt with a strong hand" (Ex. 13:9). The blessings for Sabbath and Holy Days always recall the emancipation we continually celebrate. Since every good day can be good only for free persons, every *yom tov* (festival) is a recollection of our going forth out of Egypt. Even the *Sukkah*, whose primary symbolism is of the wilderness and God's providential care, helps "your generations recall that I made the children of Israel live in huts when I brought them out of the land of Egypt" (Lev. 23:43).

Exodus was a time when God and Israel were, for once, very close. Then, even little children and insensitive adults saw more than great prophets would see later on. Whatever a camera's eye might or might not have photographed at the Nile or at the Red Sea, Jewish consciousness saw God's personal deliverance. Exodus was and is the name for how the Jewish people understood its redemption and understand it still. We were there. There is here. Then is now. God is always on the job. That is why royal years are counted from the time of the Exodus rather than creation. Exodus is when history really began. We cannot trust our memories to let us remember or forget. By sign and symbol, by holiday and daily prayer, by teaching others and by caring for others, we *make* ourselves remember we were slaves and that we can be free.

We are also required to remember Sinai:

"Watch yourself carefully so that you do not ever forget what things your eyes saw, lest they leave your consciousness for the rest of your life. Make them known to your children and theirs: that day when you stood before Him, your God, at Horeb . . . " (Deut. 4:9).

Egypt was where God was seen acting. Sinai (Horeb) was, and is, where He was seen to speak. God is not imprisoned in silence; He is more able than we to say what is on His mind, and at least once, preeminently, He did. Revelation is God's unmediated self-disclosure. We "heard" it and so must now hear. We "saw" it and now can forever see. Sinai is not only an experience; it is also, for the rest of our lives, a task.

We are witness to Sinai by carefully studying the Torah because God's world is overdetermined. He did not say one thing in one way, but much more than we can ever figure out. His Torah is a beckoning, to which all our life must be response. One who chooses to forget is a sinner. So one who forgets God is in danger of being forgotten through endless time. But for us who choose to reflect unceasingly on God's communication, it is in remembering that we feel ourselves recalled.

We are also to remember the Golden Calf:

"Remember, do not forget, how you enraged Him, your God, in the wilderness . . ." (Deut. 9:7).

There were many times our people betrayed God "from the time you left Egypt until you came to this place." But the symbolic event remains the building of the Calf of God at the very moment that Moses was bringing His commandments down from heaven to earth. Frightened, leaderless, and provocative, our people deserted its invisible Redeemer and bowed down to one their own hands had made, as if it had led them out of Egypt and could speak. It is not pleasant for us to remember the Calf. As Freud discovered, one readily forgets what is unpleasant. Judaism insists, however, that one can make oneself remember by doing something and not trusting the unconscious graciously to surrender its own.

Not only the disobedient generation addressed in Deuteronomy must recall its sin, but all of us. It is not only one rebellion we are obligated to remember, but all the times we deserted God in His hour of need, or ran for cover at the very time He was showering us with revelation. We must deal with our shame before both our ancestors and our descendants, since we have not always been faithful to the task of transmitting the tradition. We must deal with guilt before God against Whom alone we finally have sinned. We must choose turning, the perpetual self-transcendence required of each Jew, who is never allowed to be what he was but must always turn into someone else whom he could be.

We deal with shame and guilt in the context of God's forgiving love. Surely we have built calves of gold and pride and race. We have worshiped and still worship gods of metal or consolation or reward. But the true God will accept our true repentance if each day we recall what we have done. Just as Exodus makes every day an instant Passover, so the Calf brings Atonement back every day. There is a time for guilt; we must remember hard what we have done, say it out, and then be reconciled.

I know a woman of forty-five who was alone in the room with her twin brother when he fell from a window to his death at the age of six. She cannot now recall how he fell or what she did. She cannot remember whether she pushed him or teased him or tried to rescue him from falling or stayed still. She cannot recollect her feelings at the time: guilt or fear or even joy. She cannot deal with her own anguish or remorse because, except for what others tell her happened, she remembers nothing at all.

"So I turned and came down the mountain, the mountain burning with fire, the two tables of the covenant in my two hands. And I saw how you had failed Him, your God, by making for yourselves a molten god . . ." (Deut. 9:15–16).

We are also commanded to remember the sin and punishment of Miriam:

"Remember what He, your God, did to Miriam on your way out of Egypt" (Deut. 24:9).

What God in fact did was to punish Miriam, Moses' sister and an important leader in her own right, with leprosy, for calumniating her brother. This is not exactly one of the highlights of the biblical narrative; it is scarcely the most profound or the most edifying incident in the Torah. Still, our teachers insist it must be recalled every day in order to remind us how dreadful is the sin of slander. Miriam spoke ill of her brother directly to his face, not in public or behind his back. She was a princess and a prophet, and yet even she was made leprous. How much the more will one who slanders in public, behind someone's back, be punished, if he has no such status to balance his sin. Moses forgave his sister, but God could not. So we too must be exceedingly careful about what we say of others. Calumny is a kind of murder, and much illness is a result of verbal assault on other people. The Kabbalah says that the great blessing in the Eighteen Benedictions, *Modim* ("We thank Thee . . .") is there to remind us of the true purpose of human speech. We are able to speak of God and must therefore not use our gift against man. The evil tongue is a paradigmatic sin; remembering Princess Miriam, we learn to curb our own inclination.

We are also to remember the Sabbath:

"Remember the Sabbath day, to make it holy" (Ex. 20:8).

One version of the Ten Words (Ten Commandments) tells us to *observe* the Sabbath, the other to *remember* it. Both were spoken simultaneously, miraculously, according to an old tradition. The rabbis understand that we are to do the Sabbath one day but prepare for it six. We are to perform its obligatory tasks and restrictions one day but understand their meaning all seven. With *Kiddush* on Friday night and *Havdalah* on Saturday night to give the special day an aesthetic framework, the task of recollection is a grateful one. The Talmudic sage Shammai, who is usually portrayed as irascible and intemperate, would spend all six weekdays shopping for his Sabbath delicacies, and we too are obliged to look out all week for the best food to fill our Sabbath table. Remembering always takes time and effort, but getting ready for Sabbath is a kind of foretaste of the pleasure the day will bring.

Days of the week are counted toward the Sabbath at the end: for example, today is the fourth day of the week in which, on the Sabbath, we shall read the portion of the Torah that begins, "You are Standing." Every time I write the date, I am getting ready for the Sabbath to come. Our preparation for Sabbath is continual and strenuous so that the Sabbath may be relaxed and open. We do our hard work for six days in order that the seventh may be different and good. Even if we cannot "finish all our work" in six, we act as if it were behind us when we move into Sabbath time. The Sabbath is a legal yet messianic limit to the busy-ness of the week, a play after labor, a rest after toil, a being after doing—and one that must be built for in advance. By living toward Sabbath, we change the character of the whole week. Its high point is not accomplishment but surcease; the greatest day is not the one on which most is done but one on which nothing may be "done." The week moves not toward more and more creating but toward Him who made it all before we came. In the commandment to remember the Sabbath, we recall ourselves to whom we really are. The Sabbath self is the one we are slowly becoming and will someday, somewhere, wholly be.

We are commanded to remember Amalek, the enemy of the Jew:

"Remember what Amalek did to you on your way out of Egypt, how he ambushed you and struck your feeble rear when you were exhausted, and feared not God" (Deut. 25:17–18).

Amalek has his special day: the Sabbath before Purim, that carnival of triumph over anti-Semitism. But the Torah also commands us to remember Amalek all the time. Anti-Semitism is not an optional memory. We are required to recall, coolly and in context, gratuitous violence against Jews, whose sign is Amalek. We are to fight smugness, a false transcendence of our historical fate. On the one hand, we are to "blot out the memory of Amalek," that is, to make perpetual war against those who hate us for no cause, to destroy their works, to give them no victories. But we are also bidden to remember our past so that we are not doomed to repeat it mindlessly. Not every people was Amalek nor every prime minister Haman nor every king Pharaoh; but some were, and we are not allowed to forget them ever. Amalek, no less than Sinai or Exodus, is the name for what happened to us, and we Jews are part of all that we have been.

Still, unlike most of the obligatory memories, no blessing is said upon recalling the name of Amalek. For we are obliged to destroy his every grace in the world, and the destruction even of the wicked cannot be an occasion to bless. Amalek, Hitler are not all; they are not even the ultimate significance of our people's history. But they are there, and we are not permitted to forget.

II

Judaism did not invent memory. Meticulous recollection is already in the Sumerian King List of four thousand years ago. The Chinese remember almost equally long, if also almost equally improbably. But Judaism does unique things with memory. It does not gaze back to some mythic time when "kingship descended from Heaven." It does not enshrine racial superiority nor national victories. Judaism remembers, instead, what God has done for our people, gratuitously, mercifully, and what therefore we owe in return.

Uniquely Jewish is the notion of memory as will. Memory is not seen as something that befalls a passive consciousness. It is something purposefully appropriated in awe and love by a Jewish person. As Johannes Pedersen, the great Scandinavian theologian of the Bible, says, "The Israelite . . . cannot at all imagine memory, unless at the same time an effort on the totality and its direction of will is taken for granted." Judaism is not an inert victim of its past; it confronts its past with all we are, to turn our present around until we will to change our will. No matter how normally chauvinist we would be, our past reminds us that we are among the victims and not allowed to count ourselves among the mighty of the world. No matter how evasive we are, our past puts before us a perpetual confrontation with God. We cannot surrender to the given; we are inevitably called upon to exercise our will.

Memory is not, to us, once and for all. What was, is again, and will be, not in some mechanical way as Nietzsche preached. For us there is no eternal return to a sacred moment but rather the updating of those moments again and again. Martin Buber says, "What happened once happens now and always." We cannot, even if we would, put our past safely behind us. It keeps cropping up ahead of us on the road. Sinai means not only that the Torah was given once but also that it is to be received every day. The Calf was dismantled once upon a time, but it was not forgotten; we build it again and again, and again take it apart.

My own personal identity is inextricably connected with my past. In Hebrew my name is Aaron Jacob the son of Moses the son of Aaron the son of Benjamin and so on, in principle back to the very creation of the family of mankind. I am someone whose name is on a time line which is not merely linear but also strikingly recurrent. My son, therefore, is Benjamin the son of Aaron Jacob the son of Moses the son of Aaron the son of Benjamin, and his son and daughter, God willing, continue infinitely the recurring list of names.

Franz Rosenzweig puts this in a dramatic way: "The fact of our everlastingness renders all the phases of our history simultaneous."

For him, Moses is not only a perpetual recurrence and challenge but our literal contemporary. I do not repeat, reformulate, and react to the Calf, the Exodus, the Creation: I am they. History, in the sense of challenge and response to environment, is a *goyische* experience, according to Rosenzweig. Jews remain what they always were, not only faithful continuators of their ancestors but replicas. Nothing happens to Jews; we simply remain with God in His timeless, eternal now.

Most of us cannot accept so extreme a formulation of our historic self-understanding. We insist on the plasticity, within definite boundaries to be sure, of Jewish fate. We claim as much freedom as any gentile, or at least almost as much. But even we often have the sensation of history breathing down our back, of the ineluctable grasp that our ancestors have upon us. One of the reasons young Jews sometimes rebel against being Jewish is this very constraint, the knowledge that our script is already written in the drama of mankind, and that our only liberty is in how we read our lines. Nearly all of my name is already framed at my birth; the "Aaron Jacob" I call myself is only a small part of who I am. The other names that are part of my own, stretching back to the beginning, define me whether I like it or not. Perhaps I am not simultaneous with that other Aaron who lived in the nineteenth century nor with the brother of Moses, but they are vividly present in my life, and I am not always sure who they are and who am I.

For Judaism, memory is not only will and recapitulation. It is also faith. Rabbi Abraham Joshua Heschel said, "To have faith is to remember. Jewish faith is a recollection of that which happened to Israel in the past." Christian holy days are, inevitably, mere commemorations of the birth and death of Jesus. Jewish holidays, equally inevitably, recall in faith the life story of our people, particularly the special times of Exodus and Sinai. We cannot feel God's presence all the time, some of us hardly ever. But we can feel that our ancestors felt Him near, and we can be loyal to their perceptions and to their commitments. Loyalty to what seems no longer present, sometimes brings back the absent and makes it live again.

A Jew need not affirm a creed so long as he does not dismiss a past. Our calendar is thus our only catechism. It makes us remember by regular celebration. It helps us revivify by regular performance. I may not feel free, but I can do a *Seder* in order to role-play a free person, and that itself can set me free. I may not feel devout, but I can blow the *Shofar*, and God only knows what that might come to mean to me. I may not feel compassionate, but I can act out God's benefactions until I start acting like Him, whatever I feel or don't.

Countess Levy-Valensi, a contemporary French philosopher, insists that by remembering we are also remembered. "In our historical experience is the articulation of the future, a redemptive temporality which orients mortal man toward eternal life." For the Jew, nothing can be more terrible than to be forgotten, to have the long list of names finally stop, the long list of memories finally fall into oblivion. We do not ask for paradise but only for something that will live on, some name, some self. And this is, indeed, promised us if, and only if, we ourselves remember. Our past orients us toward an eternal present. What we do with what has befallen us and our forefathers determines how much self we will ever have to be remembered.

In the final analysis, memory is therefore revelation. Plato once taught a slave to "remember" mathematics because, he insisted, all truth is available to man's creative recollection. Judaism teaches all us slaves to remember not only our mathematics but also our emancipation. God remembers us and will let us remember our own destiny. As Paul Minear puts it: "The experience of revelation crystallizes a new self-knowledge; this self-knowledge revises and revitalizes memory. . . . Self-knowledge requires recovering lost memory."

The task of Judaism is to recover what we have forgotten. We come to know ourselves by remembering who we once were. God reveals Himself in the spaces between our forgetfulness. He shows us how to know ourselves for what we are by recovering sacred texts etched on our own unconsciousness. Remembering alone has the power to bind us to His eternal memory. We say *Kaddish*, *Yizkor*, Sh'ma also for ourselves.

In our recollection is our life.

[*Tradition*, Fall 1975]

THEOLOGY

THE TALMUD expressly says that "the Sh'ma may be recited in any language at all" (Ber. 13a), but in every congregation I have ever heard of, including the most antithetical to the Hebrew language, it is always recited in Hebrew. Why?

The Sh'ma, a difficult verse (to say the least), is followed in our worship, according to rabbinic precedent, by an even more difficult one, the *Baruch Shem*, the meaning of which is distressingly obscure. Besides, one is directed to say the latter in silence, because otherwise one would betray a mystery. Why?

The *Rambam* (Maimonides) insists that God's unity is utterly unlike any singleness we can know. God is not one in the way that any individual or any set in our experience is one. Thus it is almost as correct to say that God is not one (as we know unity) as it is to assert that God is one. So why is the Sh'ma, apparently an assertion of God's unity, so important?

Heshel Tsoref, a Sabbatean heretic described by Gershom Scholem in his book *On the Kabbalah and Its Symbolism*, wrote three thousand pages on the significance of the Sh'ma. Why?

The only answer I can give to these, and to many similarly puzzling questions, is that the Sh'ma far outstrips our ability to understand the Sh'ma. It is, precisely and importantly, a cipher. There is much we do not know about God, and one of the things we do not know is exactly what it means to say that She is one. We are willing to give up our very lives for an idea whose denotation we cannot state. We are profoundly certain that God is one, but we cannot explain what we mean when we say that She is. We are all committed to ethical monotheism, but we are uncertain of what that implies or entails.

God is greater than all our theologies. The Sh'ma reminds us that we do not know what we often claim to know. The truth is that we do not know the truth about God.

What do we know? We know what we are commanded to do. We know what the mysterious half-unknown God wants us, unmysteriously, to do. We take upon ourselves the yoke of God's kingship which, like all sovereignty, and even more, is impenetrable, in order to take upon ourselves the yoke of the commandments. Out of the mystery, as Leo Baeck always said, emerges always and only the commandment.

The Sh'ma is a *pasuk* (verse), or rather several paragraphs, from the Torah. The Torah is the Jew's only path to God. We could not know God through any natural theology. The heavens declare divine glory only to those who know how to look beyond quarks and black holes and big bangs. Scripture alone authorizes theology and induces to prayer. Only what God tells us about God is available to us and that, of course, only to the extent that we can appropriate it.

The Talmud reminds us that the Four Letter Name comes one word earlier in the Sh'ma (which human beings recite) than in the *K'dushah*, an essentially angelic assertion. The Sh'ma is for human beings who do not "know" but who, alone of all creation, can "hear" and perform God's will. It is not an assertion of what the Greeks came to call "monotheism"; it is a Law to be performed in faithfulness and in love. There is no God but God, and we are called to be God's prophets. Hear, O Israel—because you are Israel—what God wants you to hear and do what God wants you to do.

And what is that? It is to love God with all we have and are. It is to believe the improbable, that the rain will fall and that peace will come if only we hear what God tells us. It is not going about after our own eyes and our own hearts but conforming to Divine direction. It is to stop whoring and to start performing. It is to act like Jews who may not know much about God but who have a terrifyingly clear idea of what Jews must do—in Gaza and in Glencoe, in synagogue and in business, in prayer and in sex, in hearing and in doing according to what we hear.

God is one. God is unique. God tells us Torah. God demands obedience. God is more than our idea of God. God is our agenda. God is not an idol. God is not silent.

The rest is commentary. Go and learn.

[*Ehad: The Many Meanings of God Is One,* Sh'ma booklet, 1988]

"LOVE YOUR NEIGHBOR as yourself" (Lev. 19:18) is one of the *gufei Torah* (Torah principles) that uniquely distinguish the nineteenth chapter of the book of Leviticus. Rabbi Akiba called it the "embracing idea of the Torah," and even Jesus distinguished it as one of the two "great commandments." All of us sense, somehow, that this verse is crucial, even uniquely crucial, to our task as Jews, but we are not quite sure what to do about it.

The rabbis are relentlessly unsentimental about the details of this law of love. It means that a condemned criminal must be executed as painlessly as possible. It means that a man should not make love with his wife in the daytime, at least if she is particularly ugly. It means people should never get married until and unless they have met face to face.

Rashbam says: man cannot really be expected to love his neighbor as himself. Even Rabbi Akiba rules that "your life takes precedence over your friend's." The Torah means, rather, that we should wish our fellow the same good that we wish ourselves. That may be the reason for the dative in Hebrew: "love *for* your neighbor," not "love *of* your neighbor."

But while love is a feeling ("this text refers to love in the heart," say the commentators), it is not only a feeling. It is not just spontaneous, sentimental, emotional. It is measured, obligatory, deontological. It is not about the quantity of our feeling but about the quality of our behavior. Rambam tells us that we cannot expect to care as much about someone else as about our own selves, but that we can and must act toward that other in the same character that we act toward our own lives. The commandment directs us to move continually outward with our feelings and with our actions. Others should more and more become like ourselves in our own imagination and in our own life.

There is a debate as to whether the "other" must be Jewish. HaMeiri, the Malbim, and many other authorities insist that the commandment applies, at least in principle, to all human beings. The Malbim says of humanity, "We are all members of one another, and therefore the heart must love the limbs and the limbs must love the heart." Israel may be the very heart of humankind, but it must care about the whole body. Nor is the commandment of love restricted to "believers." Love is ultimately, absolutely binding upon everyone who lives. It is divine metaphysics in its human face. It is steadfast, wholehearted, consistent, humane. It is neither a merely ethical obligation nor one that is only a "royal decree." Love is the place where the human and the divine intersect.

The test of love is love of the stranger. We Jews were strangers in the land of Egypt. We should know the heart of the stranger, therefore we must love the stranger as ourselves. The stranger, the alien, the poor person, the truly other is the mask of God. It is easy to love ourselves; it is not too hard to love those closest to us. But whoever is or ever could be "next" is entitled to our care. In the end, the stranger becomes our neighbor. God is estranged from no one of us. We Jews must try, too, to embrace all God's children in the encompassing privilege and duty of love.

[KAM Isaiah Israel Bulletin, April 24, 1985]

IN HIS famous book *The Idea of the Holy*, the great German Protestant scholar of religion Rudolph Otto claims that the holy is the other, the "numinous," the different, the spectacularly supernatural. How then is it that we Jews are commanded to be *K'doshim* (holy) ourselves? If holiness is precisely what God is and we are not, then how can we be expected to become holy too?

The imitation of God—more precisely, for Jews, the imitation of God's actions (which are all we really can know of God Herself)—is the supreme task for a Jew. We have no doctrine like that of the trinity, for example, which claims to offer information about the inner life of the godhead. We have no personal, immediate, direct union with deity, as mystics of all other faiths claim to have. But we do claim to know clearly enough some of what God does and what we must also learn to do: keep Shabbat, respect parents, live justly and fairly, even love our neighbor as ourselves. Not easy, of course, but not quite impossible either.

The Holiness chapter, Leviticus 19, is, I believe, the most crucial in the whole Torah. It combines what is usually thought of as ritual (Shabbat, sacrifice, the laws against idolatry) with the supremely ethical (just weights, not taking advantage of the blind nor cursing the deaf—even when they cannot hear what we are saying). It trains us not only to be humane but to be holy, like God. It tells us that the only way to become a *mensch* is to imitate God. It links the ethical moment to transcendent sources and eternal implications. Holiness is much harder than morality but also more plausible and, strangely but really, more accessible.

My neighbor whom I must love (even if I don't like) is the one with whom my life is connected: the nearest and not always dearest, the very one who sometimes makes me very, very angry. But, according to our rabbis, "neighbor" finally includes almost everyone: a prisoner about to be executed, an ugly fiancée, the poor among the gentiles. It is not easy to feel close to these strangers, but it is possible to treat them with a calm and persistent, even a sacred, love. It is possible to be someone like God, Who cannot really fancy all of us, with our sins and our peculiarities, but Who loves us with a radiance and a warmth that shines upon us all. That's what we Jews call holiness!

[KAM Isaiah Israel Bulletin, May 7, 1986]

THERE IS NO JUDAISM BUT ORTHODOXY—BUT ALL JEWS ARE REALLY REFORM

FOR WELL OVER a hundred years, we have been trying to find a theological alternative to Orthodox Judaism; I do not believe we have succeeded.

If Judaism is Torah—that is, if it is a response to God through obedience to His law—then Judaism must be "Orthodox" or nothing. If, on the other hand, we are free to pick and choose among traditional Jewish obligations, then we are, in principle at least, superior to the Torah. If the Torah is not, in a decisive sense, the world of God, who needs it?

Subtle and thoughtful scholars have proposed alternatives to a complete, blind acceptance of Torah. They have tried to distinguish between a core of Judaism, an essence that is immutable, and details that are historically bound and must be modified over time. But, after all, God is in the details, isn't He/She? If you're playing baseball, you can't throw a forward pass on the grounds that the details of the game change over time. You can, it's true, invoke the designated hitter and the infield fly rule to show that a few particulars have in fact changed slightly in our own memory of the game—but baseball is still baseball.

Martin Buber claimed that Torah is not law but the place where God and the Jew meet, and that each of us must hear when and where we are addressed in that Torah. He did not propose anarchy or mere subjective whim; in fact he was much more attuned to that traditional *halakhah* than is sometimes assumed. But he left our problem essentially unsolved: You may feel addressed by the commandment of *kashrut*, I, by the law of welcoming strangers; you by Deuteronomy, I by Mishnah. Who decides between us? Who brings us together as a community? Who is, then, the Revealer, and who the mere object of revelation?

Franz Rosenzweig refined our understanding of liberalism and the law by accepting in principle the whole of traditional *halakhah* but living only that portion of it that he could conscientiously perform. He would answer for those details of the law that he could not himself enact by pleading "not yet." I have described this view in recent years as "walking along Jew Street picking up all the packages of *mitzvot* that one can handle and leaving those that are, for the time, still too heavy." This view has the advantage of not identifying the whole tradition with that portion of the tradition that we find personally congenial, and yet leaving us not feeling guilty about that portion of it that we simply cannot live with in our time and place. And, as long as we have not eliminated parts of the *halakhah* from the Jewish agenda just because we find them too difficult or remote, there may come a time when we, or our descendants, will recover those portions.

The problem with Rosenzweig's view (and my version of it) is that most of us are too prone to rationalization, too comfortable with delay. "Not yet" can easily become "never." "Too heavy" is only too heavy for those of us who do not sufficiently exercise our Jewish muscles. If we really meant it, couldn't we here and now do more Judaism?

The truth is that we just do not believe in the Torah as it is. Eugene Borowitz, semiofficial theologian of Reform Judaism, and himself rather observant and deeply respectful of tradition, insists that autonomy is absolutely essential to the modern Jew. Moderns will not be bound by any rules that they cannot assent to out of their own free choice, and they cannot even imagine surrendering their decision-making to any rabbinic text or to any rabbinic body. Seymour Siegel, in his authoritative book on Conservative Judaism, limits the *halakhah* to those of its elements that are strictly within the boundaries of contemporary ethical standards and even contemporary taste. Borowitz and Siegel are truthful, and their reservations we all in fact share. But if freedom comes before obedience, are we who agree with them, who exercise our freedom, still authentic Jews?

Paul of Tarsus (Saint Paul) believed the Torah was inevitably too difficult for human beings to perform. It would not save the Jews because they could not obey it. They needed a readier source of salvation, or they would all be doomed to die in sin. Modern Jews agree, more than they think, with Paul. We do not accept Jesus as our personal savior, but we no longer believe that the Torah is immutable, complete, and salvific. So we are not Christians, but the question remains: Are any of us still Jews?

"Any of us" includes also those who think they are Orthodox believers but who trim the Torah, whether unconsciously or by design. The real agenda of present-day Orthodoxy in Israel or in America is primarily Shabbat and *kashrut*. Not much is said there or here about war and peace or about gossip and slander or about relations with non-Jews or with our own children. The observant only observe some of the Torah; they hear about only some of the Torah in most of their schools and synagogues. They only *want* to hear about some of the Torah; that way they can assume that they are "Torah-true" Jews.

When a group of the most observant Jews at Yale Hillel wanted to introduce a *mechitzah*—a partition between the men's and women's sections—into the service, they could think only of "Reform" reasons for doing so: It is a very old custom; it is beautiful and inspirational; more people will come to the service if we have a *mechitzah*; it is not so hard to do or so very remote from our present life. None of them gave the real reason, the only possible reason, in my view, for needing a *mechitzah*: God ordered us to have one. They really didn't or couldn't believe He did, so they came up with improbable arguments for an essentially lost cause. In the end, though they may have wanted a *mechitzah*, they did not *need* it.

Even at the highest reaches of Orthodox thinking, there is a deep division of opinion as to whether the *halakhah* is broad enough to direct all our lives, whether there is or is not an ethical demand that is above and beyond our legal norm. Some Orthodox scholars admit (or boast) that the really profound issues of our time (women, war, justice) are not halakhic issues at all, and that one can offer only personal advice or subjective opinion on these deeply divisive questions. But if the *halakhah* is not about deep concerns, then what is left of it? Is the *halakhah* to tell us what brand of tuna we can eat, how to pray (or, at least, what words to pray), but not to lead us through our own lives and our own history? Then it abandons us precisely when we need it most.

Some Orthodox Jews are confused. All of them (and all of us) are sinners. That is not the problem. The problem is that not one of them any longer believes with perfect faith in the Torah of Moses, none of them is committed to its total demand on our lives. It is not simply that any one of them can always find someone with a more strict view of the law than his or her own, but that no coherent notion of observance is anywhere to be found. Orthodox Jews are simply not what they think they are. Their failure, as ours, is unavoidable; they are radical dissenters, even if they do not acknowledge their own dissent.

If I am right, we are all—liberal Jews with easy consciences about jettisoning most of the Torah and Orthodox Jews who pretend they do it all but don't even want to know what all of it might be—in the same boat. Secularists and covenant theologians, neotraditionalists and humanists alike—we are all suffering the same loss of faith or loss of nerve. We will sink or sail together. We will live or die as a people together. In that, at least, there is a half-consolation.

If we can admit our terrifying disloyalties and our punishing confusions, there is hope. The Torah is more than we say it is. God is more sovereign than we have permitted Him/Her to be in our lives. The world we see is not all there is. Freedom is only true when it is disciplined and chastened. We *can* be Jews, though perhaps not at the same time also modern men and women. We can be saved, though not only by our own devices. Reform today is not as liberal as it pretends to be; Orthodoxy today is far less than authentic tradition requires; we are all less than our ancestors once were. But we are not lost. All our sacred past may yet be found; it awaits us always. And as we may find that past, so we may find ourselves.

[*Moment*, September 1983]

PART THREE

Mitzvot

SAMUEL DRESNER reminded me of a wonderful anecdote from Abraham Heschel. We asked Heschel about a noted American Jewish thinker whose work he rather disparaged. He told us this tale: There once was a woman who came to her rebbe with a complaint: my husband doesn't know how to play cards. Well, said the rabbi, that isn't so bad. No Jew has to know how to play cards. You don't understand, said the woman, he doesn't know how to play cards—but he plays.

Judaism is, among other decisive things, about competence. It is about getting the matter right: the right number of candles on Hanukkah night, the accurate story of the Exodus, all the melody and all the text. "An ignoramus cannot be pious," says our Mishnah Pirkei Avot, which no other religion would quite claim. To be a Jew is not so much to believe something or to feel something as to know. Most of us don't really know how to play cards—but we play anyway. No wonder we lose so often, no wonder we are often teetering on the verge of bankruptcy.

Knowing isn't everything; it is, profoundly, the only thing.

[KAM Isaiah Israel Bulletin, January 16, 1985]

SHABBAT AND FESTIVALS

THE OLD Reform law was strict about ethical matters: business dealings, marital loyalty, telling a lie. But it was also very concerned with certain so-called "ritual" matters: *matzah* on *Pesach*, fasting on Yom Kippur, doing something regular on Shabbat, even reciting the *motzi* before meals. It is just not true that Reform Jews were ritual anarchists or ethical freethinkers. Their duties, though fewer than those of the Orthodox, were upheld as matters of life and death for Judaism.

In recent decades Reform has vastly increased the scope of its religious practice. Fifty years ago Reform Jews knew nothing about *Havdalah* and little about *kashrut*. Today the list of Jewish options is much larger, and that can only be seen as a gain for Reform. How, otherwise, could we know what we personally should or should not do?

But there is also a loss. What was once (at least for some Reform Jews) a small but strict code has become a wide array of acceptable alternatives. The new freedom and the range are impressive, but we have lost something crucial in the area of discipline. Judaism is, I believe, not just choice; it is duty. Judaism is not ceremonial, free-floating, subjective. It is law and obligation, and it is objectively binding. Shabbat is not our own invention but one of the Ten Commandments; it is not a nice idea but what God wants us to do.

Can Reform Jews once again accept Shabbat as a God-given duty? Well, some of them used to, and they didn't think doing so abridged their freedom to be themselves. Shabbat was, perhaps, not well served by a Friday night service with its center in a long, theoretical sermon. We have now moved toward Shabbat dinners,

49

music, sharing, and communal study of sacred texts. These are much better ways to observe the Sabbath, but they are not yet *halakhah*. To them I would add not smoking, not driving an automobile except to services, not reading our mail, and, perhaps, not answering the telephone. In these matters, *halakhah* merges with deep psychological needs: in order to find ourselves in a technological world we must abandon some technology and rediscover our premodern selves. We must choose to be commanded again, remembering that God, not human desire, is at the center of Shabbat.

The "work" that is forbidden by Jewish law on the Sabbath is not measured in the expenditure of energy. It takes real effort to pray, to study, to walk to synagogue. They are "rest" but not restful. Forbidden "work" is acquisition, aggrandizement, altering the world. On Shabbat we are obliged to be, to reflect, to love and make love, to eat, to enjoy. We may not be able to observe all the commandments connected with Shabbat (I, for one, can't), but we are not free wholly to abstain.

We Reform Jews must learn much more about the Sabbath as theology and as law. Nothing Jewish is irrelevant or impossible in advance. When we learn more, we may learn about a Shabbat that is both harder and easier than the one we have. It is not in Heaven; it is not beyond the sea. Shabbat is in our mouths and in our hearts. It is part of the divine agenda but also wholly human and humane. Shabbat is a taste of eternity. Without Shabbat we may be lost. In its rediscovery we may yet be found.

[*Reform Judaism*, Fall 1983]

OUR JEWISH CALENDAR, as Franz Rosenzweig once said, is our catechism. A Jew may be defined as one who tries to live by the cycle of Sabbaths and Holy Days that make up the Jewish year. Most of us are part of that pattern, at least during the Jewish month of Tishri, which stretches from Rosh Hashanah till just past *Simhat*

Torah, and which begins next week. Most of us feel both moved and commanded by the Holy Days that follow one another relentlessly from the Day of Memorial to Rejoicing in Torah, from the Day of Judgment to the night and morning of dancing with the scrolls. It is a wonderful month. So is Nisan, when most of us begin with *Seder* and go on till *Yizkor*, sensing for at least a week the pulse of Jewish time.

But in between? Does our normal week lead up to Shabbat, or is the Sabbath just a day of rest and recuperation for the really important weekdays of our work? Do we even know when *Shavuot* or *Tisha B'av* comes? Do we celebrate Halloween with our kids even if it conflicts with our Sabbath dinner? Which is more important to us, Thanksgiving or *Yom Tov*? The World Series or *Oneg Shabbat*? The Gregorian calendar or the Torah's sequence of seasons lived with God?

I wish you and yours not only a year of joy and peace but a year of many Sabbaths and many holidays. I wish for all of us that we learn how to live in sacred time, attentive to the moods and messages of all the varied days of the year. And may our children come to know how they are inserted as Jews into universal human history via the graceful, happy life of festal holiness.

L'Shanah Tovah Tikateyvu.

[KAM Isaiah Israel Bulletin, September 23, 1992]

THE HOLIDAYS are very late this year, about as late as they ever come in the Gregorian calendar. So *Sukkot*, the harvest holiday, will be celebrated only a month or so before Thanksgiving, its American offspring. *Sukkot* is always somewhat anomalous anyway in a northern country where sleeping and eating in the barely covered hut is something less than comfortable. This year it will be even more difficult to pretend that the *Sukkah* is our home for a week, when even our well-protected houses are invaded by the cold. This year it will be even harder to make like Israeli farmers bringing in the autumnal sheaves.

But that is the point of the whole festival: life is itself an anomaly. We all live barely sheltered against the cold which, at last, will invade all our bones. The *Sukkah* of God's providence is over us always, but it cannot keep us from the rain or the frost. We are pilgrims, strangers in a strange land as were our fathers, and not even the warmth of the holiday, the gentle kindness of its symbols, or the love of our loved ones can protect us against the world around the booth. This year, more than most, we shall feel the chill as we say our prayers in the *Sukkah*.

It is very late this year to be a Jew, to be alive.

May you rejoice in your festival, together with the whole house of Israel, our brothers.

[Congregation Solel *Pathfinder*, October 14, 1970]

HANUKKAH IS about conflict, all right! It is not conflict between Syrian and Jew, but between Jew and Jew, between Jew and himself, which is decisive. It was not so hard to win over conquering armies, but it was almost impossible to defeat the Hellenization those armies brought. Priests apostatized, kings and princes surrendered, ordinary folk thronged to the gymnasia and to the pagan cults. Not one Jew was unaffected by the lure of Greek culture in all its ripe Middle Eastern decadence.

We learn from a careful study of Professor Erwin Goodenough's many-volumed research that Jewish tombs were decorated with gnostic symbols before the Christian Era and increasingly after the destruction of the Temple. Synagogues around the Mediterranean were models of pagan religious style: it is still hard to see what was Jewish and what was not. Saul Lieberman has demonstrated that the Talmud itself is full of Hellenisms: Greek rhetoric, Greek thinking, leading Hellenistic persons and themes. But what some Jews substituted for Judaism in Maccabean times, the Talmudic sages wove into the very Jewish fabric several generations later. The question was not whether or not to Hellenize, but rather how to be at once Greek and Jew. That is still our problem. Most of us spend more time in the gymnasium than in the *Bet Midrash*. Our children study five or ten times more science than they do Jewish texts. Most of us really think that Plato's *Republic* is a great book and *First Samuel* a primitive one. Gnosticism is, finally, the secret American creed, and Jewish notions like the resurrection of the dead or practices like complete Shabbat rest seem as impossible to us as they did to the early Hellenizers. The State of Israel tries more and more to adopt the language and values of its worst rejectionist enemies. None of us is safe from the blandishments and rewards of paganism. The Hanukkah victory is still to be won.

[KAM Isaiah Israel Bulletin, December 16, 1981]

PESAH IS: not eating *hametz*, having a *Seder*, remembering the Exodus, eating *matzah*, saying *Hallel* psalms, worshiping and refraining from work at the beginning and end of the holiday. That is pretty much the traditional approach to this holiday.

Pesah is also: thinking about freedom, giving *tzedakah* to the needy, joining with others in the redemption of our community, hoping to bring the messianic time. That is pretty much the liberal approach to the same holiday. Liberals are often quite casual about the laws of leaven; traditionalists often pay little attention to the philosophy behind the festival and its radical political implications. Either *Pesah* becomes all social action or all ritual, but for many Jews not both at once.

I hope we have no such problem. In our congregation, social responsibility has had a long and powerful history. It has become a kind of ritual obligation, deeply ingrained in our vision of Judaism.

But we are also keenly concerned with the dos and don'ts of Jewish observance. We do eat *matzah* and have a *Seder* and for a week we eat somewhat differently and come to holiday services. For us, Judaism is observing all kinds of commandments, and we are not much concerned if some people call them ethical and some people call them ritual. *Pesah* is a good symbol of the indissoluble nature of Jewish responsibility. Everything is owed to God. Everything means we must love our neighbor as ourselves. We cannot get out of Egypt alone, nor can anyone else bring us our freedom and our dignity as Jews.

Pesah is Liberation forever.

[KAM Isaiah Israel Bulletin, March 30, 1983]

REDISCOVERING THE OBLIGATION OF WELCOMING GUESTS

ABOUT A hundred years ago, a European rabbi named Israel Lipkin Salanter believed that certain central commands of Judaism were falling into disuse. In Vilna or in Kovno, in Paris where he wandered or in Koenigsberg where he died, there were many Jews who scrupulously attended to keeping *kashrut* and the Sabbath, to holy days and *t'fillin*, to family purity and to prayer. But these very same Jews, Rabbi Israel noted to his sorrow, were not very careful about the law against slander or usury; they were often inhospitable, and they were often exploitative or dishonest in their business. They cared a good deal about the purity of their kitchens but apparently not much about the purity of their hearts.

Rabbi Israel, of course, was a fanatic. He could not keep a job. He fell into long periods of deep depression. He wandered around Europe feeling at home nowhere and under the gun everywhere. Once he was asked to preach a funeral oration and his eulogy consisted only of the citation: "For man knows not his time; we are like fish taken in an evil net, like birds caught in a snare" (Eccles. 9:12). Entranced, distracted, he kept repeating the verse and then precipitously ordered the body removed. All his life he was the victim of punishing self-doubt and of an inordinate sense of guilt. He was a strange man but, I believe, important to us for what we need.

In our time there are no longer so many Jews whose *kashrut* and Sabbath observance are impeccable. Not so many who celebrate every festival and observe every fast. Not so many whose families are pure in a ritual sense or whose hearts are pure in an ethical sense. But there are many who are trying to recover their Jewish heritage, many who want to become what they feel they are. Jewish identity entails for many of us a process of rediscovering.

But in this sense we are not so far from the traditional Jews. Rediscovery of the Law unites traditional and nontraditional Jews in a common task. For traditional Jews the task is to perceive, as did Salanter, that some central laws have come to be treated as dead letters and must be revived. For nontraditional Jews the task is to learn what the Law is. For both kinds of Jew, rediscovery of the Law involves perceiving the way in which the Law subtly combines the ethical and the ritual—how it ritualizes the ethical and ethicizes the ritual, how the two domains mutually condition and facilitate one another. Rediscovery of the Law means recovery of the absolute unity of study and practice. There is no study without practice and no practice without study. On the one hand, Jewish tradition gives substance to the principle—first formulated for Western thought in a theoretical way by Aristotle—that the good person is one *habituated* to good, who learns to do good precisely by doing it repeatedly. On the other hand, Jewish tradition has always maintained what modern theoreticians of education are now beginning to formulate: that careful study of ethical texts and problems leads to *sensitivity* in performance of ethical obligation. Performance of law that is *mere* habit or unquestioning obedience to authority is not truly ethical behavior. One must become sensitized to the principle, or hierarchy of principles, operating behind the practice. Jewish law and tradition offer us strategies of ethical sensitivity.

One begins where one is. There is no wrong *mitzvah* in which to begin to be taught the meaning of duty and joy. As Leo Baeck said, out of the mystery of the Godhead there emerges for the Jew only and always the commandment. Every task can be holy; every truth must become a task. Judaism has a choreography of obedience that recommends itself to the neophyte as to the adept. It includes repeated performance, graceful performance, attention to inner nuances, and joy in the performance. A commandment must be performed carefully and not sloppily ("God is in the details"), with intention not merely to check off an obligation but to check out the Source. Unless we are Paulians, Karaites, or extreme humanistic Reformers, Judaism remains for us something we must *do* and not merely believe or pretend to believe. The commandment is the key that unlocks the Castle.

I shall here discuss, in the spirit of Rabbi Salanter, one key *mitzvah* that is hardly popular today. I came to study it by chance myself, when I was invited to help teach a seminar in hospitality at Yale Divinity School. I studied the article on *hachnasat orchim* (welcoming guests) in the great Hebrew *Talmudic Encyclopedia* and the (largely rabbinic) sources to which it sent me. Overwhelmed by the moral power of the commandment and by what seemed to me its wide-ranging theological implications, I was struck mostly by the simple facts regarding what it means for a Jew to be hospitable. Hospitality is not merely a response to conscience; it is a life-style. It is not merely something polite that nice people do occasionally as their hearts prompt them; it is what God requires every day. It is not a trivial courtesy but, in the highest sense, an act of *g'milut chasadim* (bestowal of lovingkindness), an expression of loyalty to fellow human beings.

Jews are commanded to open their homes to visitors, particularly the poor and the learned. Jews are not to convert their houses into fortresses protecting the nuclear family from invasion, but to sensitize their children to other people by inviting visitors regularly into their homes. The house is to be not a refuge but a bridge—if the analogy can be imagined, a kind of spiritually self-aware hotel. At the *Seder* on Passover eve we fling open our doors to extend the invitation: "All who are hungry, come and eat!"—but the invitation is actually operative throughout the year. Students were fed and housed in private homes on a regular basis; notables lined up at the synagogue door virtually to force visitors to the synagogue to become their guests for the Sabbath. A family that failed to garner a visitor experienced a sense of defeat. Some homes even had a flagpole for raising a banner that signified an invitation, public and dramatic, to all who needed a meal. All homes were to have four doors so that the visitor could enter from any direction. And in no case was the host to regard a guest—or the guest to regard himself—as imposing himself. The guest was always to be regarded as bestowing a sacred opportunity.

A passage on page 10b of the Talmudic tractate *Berakhot* ("Blessings") explicates the story in II Kings 4 about the woman of Shunam who, like Abraham our father, was a paradigm of hospitality. She had a guest room on her roof—with a bed, table, chair, and lamp— to which Elijah would come regularly as a guest. It was her best room, and she welcomed the prophet there long before she recognized that he was a holy man—a fact which she finally did recognize before her husband, since, as the Talmudic explication puts it, "Women understand guests better than men do." Why is this? One rabbi offers the explanation that she inspected the prophet's sheets and found that they were never contaminated by nocturnal emission; another, that she noticed that her guest attracted no flies. But might we not also say that her superior understanding of guests stemmed from the fact that women live in someone else's world?

The commandment of hospitality supersedes other very important laws. One is not permitted to go to the study house if he has no guest at home, but must remain at home till one comes. We are taught to make a place for a Sabbath guest even if we must violate the strict law of the Sabbath—by, for example, moving something in order to make his bed. Receiving strangers is an emergency situation which suspends many ordinary obligations.

Imagination must be employed in recruiting guests. We should live near the crossroads or the center of town where guests can find us, and not in distant suburbs where no one can find us except those to whom we extend an invitation and directions. The synagogue can be used as a temporary hospice, but a sincere host will try to live near the communal buildings to make it easy for guests to find his home.

The principal obligation is to organize one's home to make visitors welcome. Abraham is the symbol par excellence of the Jewish host. He not only welcomed the three anonymous visitors (Gen. 12:3) but was prepared for them. Swiftly mobilizing his wife, servants, and hangers-on, Abraham made sure the guests were fed, washed, and refreshed within the shortest possible time. All this was possible because his guests were anticipated.

The task of welcoming begins outside one's home: one escorts guests inside, offers them good food and water immediately, since they are always assumed to be hungry and thirsty. The host must welcome in person, even if he has a thousand servants. It is the direct presence of the host that is required, not merely what he or she can provide. The host must himself cut the loaf of bread and offer his visitors portions. He must give the departing guest provisions for the way, since "escorting is even more important than welcome."

None of this depends upon the mood of the host family. There is no time when the guest should be unwelcome, except when illness or the like makes the home dangerous. Guests should be welcomed cheerfully no matter how downcast or beset with troubles the host may be. One should not tell his guests his own problems but should listen to their recountings of experiences patiently and sympathetically. One should not worry if one's food or lodging is modest, but on the other hand, the guest should have the best food and bed available. The host must never watch the guest eat or keep account of how much the guest costs. The quality of the guest is not the point; while scholars are especially fortunate guests, even the ignorant must be gratefully welcomed. And the poor person is the preeminent guest. A guest invited for ulterior motives—say, one from whom the host expects a job or other favor—is no guest at all. If he thinks he is a recipient of real hospitality, the host is guilty of deceiving him.

The laws of hospitality signify a notion of human life that is profound and compassionate. "All men are poor when they are en route." We are all strangers and sojourners, as were our fathers; we are all travelers on the way, and we need one another to make our journey tolerable. No one is ever really at home, even at home. Conversely no one is *only* a guest, since it is his fellow traveler's house he shares. Who knows better than a Jew what it means to be an alien? Who should care more, then, for the stranger in his midst?

In some Eastern religions, the human being is identified with nature, *Tat T'vam Asi*: You are the World! There is no discontinuity between the world of things and the world of man. According to this doctrine, we are all part of the All. So we can never really be alienated or alone. But Judaism sees the world as not quite so hospitable to us and to our needs. We are exiled from the Holy Place; this time is not yet the Holy Time. No worldly place is therefore truly home. Even God, according to the Kabbalists, is in exile. He too is a Stranger who needs a welcoming family.

How we treat visitors determines what we ourselves become. If our children are taught to welcome the other person when he happens by, they will be sensitive to the presence of the Other. If, however, we teach them that privacy is more important than hospitality, that it is better to protect our homes and our possessions than to share them, then that lesson will have its impact too. If we think of ourselves as masters in our own homes, we shall never bow the head nor bend the knee to anyone who might be Master of us all. Unless we welcome all strangers, unaware, we shall miss the angelic guest who never comes announced.

Thus the ethical commandment is of the highest religious importance. Judaism does not merely teach us to be good; it asks us to be holy. Hospitality partakes of God's holiness; He has let us live a time in His world, so we can do no less to our own visitors and friends. Imitating the Divine Host, who is also a Guest, we learn to care for our neighbors as ourselves. In the *mitzvah* of welcoming strangers, we see the beckoning hand of a God who wants us to try to be Jews.

[*Moment*, May/June 1975—the magazine's first issue]

THE PROHIBITION OF SHAMING OTHERS

MANY IMPORTANT commandments have been abandoned by almost all Jews, including those who consider themselves observant. One of these laws, I believe, is the prohibition against shaming another in public. The rabbis say: "Whoever shames his fellow-person in public has no share in the world to come. He is one of those who will go down to Gehinnom and never come up again." On the other hand, it is clearly written in the Holiness chapter (Lev. 19): "You must sharply reprove your neighbor and not bear sin because of him." There was and is a clear responsibility to take a stand against sin, but as Rashi interprets the verse, never by shaming the sinner, or else one would, indeed, take on sin because of him. One is obliged to reprove even a child or a slave, and also one's husband or wife, but reproof must not be made by shame.

"Shaming" is vividly described in the Hebrew phrase as "whitening the face." Under accusation in public, one's blood leaves one's cheeks. One almost, as it were, dies of embarrassment, indicating that the sin of shaming is like murder. Murder, in fact, can find atonement if the murderer is truly sorry. But I may shame my neighbor without even knowing what I have done, in which case I will never repent for my sin. We are commanded rather to let ourselves be destroyed than to embarrass any other person in public.

Tamar, who had the goods on her father-in-law Judah after he visited her sexually (Gen. 38:25), never named him as the offender but only indicated what pledge he left with her, so that he could identify himself without being made ashamed. Joseph cleared the room before he disclosed himself to his brothers (Gen. 45:1) so that they might not be put to shame in the presence of the Egyptian court. For many generations, Jews have taken pains not to embarrass even a guilty person, much less one simply inferior in station or in power.

We are commanded not to give offense by words, by deeds, by epithets, even by hints. We are not to insult the stupid who would not even know they were being put down, nor our intimates, with whom we sometimes tend to think anything goes. Freud, in his wonderful joke book, tells of two men who behaved toward each other with scrupulous courtesy until each realized the other was a Jew, at which time they both put their feet on the furniture and dropped cigar ashes on the floor.

We are not allowed to recall someone's past offenses, blemished ancestry, or personal weaknesses. If someone owes us money, we must not go near him in public, lest our very presence put him to shame. If we are well dressed and affluent, we should avoid poor neighborhoods and needy people. If we are collecting for a cause, we must be certain in advance that anyone we approach is able to contribute. When we recite the verse from the blessings after meals—"I have grown old without ever seeing a good person in need or his children begging bread" (Psalms 37:25)—we should lower our voices in case there is a hungry person at our table. The Maharam said, "One who shames those who sleep in the dust has also committed a grave sin." We are not allowed to embarrass even the dead.

There is a precise etiquette for Jewish study. A teacher must not ask a student questions he probably cannot answer, nor the student ask questions outside his teacher's field of competence. Neither should they be queried in the presence of critical colleagues, nor when they have something else on their minds, nor when they first enter the schoolroom. Blessings over study are said together in case someone doesn't know the text by heart. So too, the recitation of the ritual of first fruits ordained in the Torah (Deut. 26:1) is always assisted by someone else's prompting (even if one is fully competent to recite, "My father was a wandering Aramean . . .") because the next person might not be able to recite the formula without help.

We should not watch someone eat (or drink or do anything) incompetently. We should not ask our host for what we don't see, because he may be unable to provide it. Virgins go out to find husbands (on Yom Kippur, according to the Mishnah) in borrowed garments so as not to shame any poor young woman. Invidiousness is itself shame, so all our dead are to be buried alike, says tradition, and thus no Jew need be ashamed. Rabba said, "One is allowed to shame himself, even though it is against Jewish law to do oneself harm." But one must never "whiten the face" of any other woman or man.

I believe that much of our civilization is based directly on shame. Prisons destroy prisoners by treating them shamefully. The young are harassed by restrictions (like the marijuana laws) whose only purpose can be to keep them down. Students are very often subjected to inane procedures whose effect is precisely to make them feel inferior. Blacks are treated patronizingly or disrespectfully even by whites who do not feel prejudiced, and by a system that in-builds invidiousness. Many blacks are now returning to the South where feelings are more open, rather than submit to our genteel "murder" in the North.

Some Israeli actions in the past (and perhaps even now) were designed specifically to demean Arabs. The deep penetration into Egypt, the destruction of the Beirut airport, the denial that Palestinians even exist: all these are, I believe, violations of the Jewish tradition, and they have cost our people dearly. Far worse is the gentle invidiousness of Israeli occupation with its assumptions of Jewish superiority and its desperate need to seem both powerful and just in a situation that cannot ever be both. But it is not only Arabs who are ashamed. When protesters demonstrated against government policy in Jerusalem some years ago, all Golda Meir could say to them was, "You are not nice." And Mayor Kollek of Jerusalem ordered them off his grass.

In the modern world, knowledge itself has become invidious.

We use our minds to master the cosmos and to surpass our colleagues. We make fun of what is intractably mysterious and act as if all can be known. The best and brightest among us serve the worst in order to demean those less successful than both of them. Vietnam and Watergate are both, as much as anything else, the tales of those who wished to grow powerful by undermining the personhood of other men. Dissent provoked disparagement, and disparagement, in the end, death.

Even the Jewish community in America no longer knows how to debate issues without destroying people. We package our women as Federation Fashionplates, condescend to our young by segregating them in do-nothing youth groups, ignore our poor and our old, and castrate our intellectuals by making them crawl for *kovod*. Our good causes grow by way of professional invidiousness, and our best institutions become training grounds for making and breaking reputations. Courtesy, patience, respect for others pay no dividends, though obsequiousness and hypocrisy often do. While Jewish life goes through one crisis after another, some of our celebrities still achieve and hold office by denouncing their fellow Jews, and raise money by insulting those who cannot give. Small congregations, small bank accounts, small IQs are literally of no account. It is only the successful who merit our attention, and even they not much of our respect. Rabbis are subject to relentless congregational gossip and honorable lay leaders to suspicion and envy. The American cult of success has undermined what should be essentially collective and collaborative in Jewish communal experience.

Perhaps the new *havurah* and Jewish anti-institution signify more even than new goals and new persons. They may indicate that, at last, we American Jews are ashamed of causing shame.

[*Sh'ma*, September 20, 1974]

THE OBLIGATION OF ASKING FORGIVENESS

MUCH OF what happens on the High Holy Days is done by God. We place ourselves in a vulnerable, almost passive situation in order that he may work upon our hungry, chastened selves His miracle of forgiveness. What He does only He can do. He turns us the way only He can turn. How we are changed can only happen when He helps us become what we never were before.

But only we can do what we can do, too. God is powerful and loving, but He cannot work against our own will, and chooses not to work against our own freedom. He does what He does: refine, transmute, perfect. But we must do what only we can do: consider, repair, get ready, go. He can receive our passionate will for reparation, but even He cannot become us. So we are left to finish up the work of the old year ourselves while the new one comes to birth.

Basically our task is one of earning forgiveness from those we have wronged. "Yom Kippur atones for transgressions committed against God but not for transgressions between persons until and unless the transgressor has appeased his victim," says the Mishnah in a classical place. The Great White Fast Day has the power to wipe away (inadvertent or unnoticed!) sins against God, but if we have sinned against woman or man (and we have), we must go to that one to seek pardon. If we have stolen goods, we must first give back what we have taken. If we have angered another unjustly, we must come with humble words to repair our injury. In any case, we cannot even begin the process of turning to God and being turned by God unless we first come to our human enemies and make them our friends again.

But how do we know whom we have wronged? Perhaps we made a curt response to a friend's or student's question, and the hurt remains deep. Husbands and wives are uniquely placed to do one another wrong even while thinking they are only being honest or funny. Parents and children have one another's pride and power in their hands: a child despised even inadvertently is a child damaged, a parent rejected even unconsciously is a parent dishonored and sometimes destroyed. Of course we do not know precisely what even we have done; that is the whole point of the *Yamim Noraim*. It is sins *bishgaga*, in blindness or error, with which the Holy Season deals. Sins *b'zadon*, recklessly or willfully performed, require other therapies than change of heart and confession in words. But it is precisely small and damaging, almost invisible sins that keep us from starting the new year anew. The solution is to ask forgiveness from all those we might have wronged, first among our closest (family and friends), our coworkers, or those in positions that make them vulnerable to our power and thus our power to hurt.

We fathers might well ask our children to forgive our impatience at their slowness to grow up and their unwillingness to grow to be like us. We husbands might well ask our wives to forgive our stereotyping them as providers of our needs instead of sharers of our souls. We employers might well ask our employees to pardon our use of the paycheck and the carpeted office to make them servants of our egos and not partners in a common task. We Jews might recall that we have demeaned Arabs, keeping them second class even when they are citizens of what we proudly hail a Jewish state, and have demeaned our fellow Jews, perhaps because they were foolish enough to vote for Nixon or old-fashioned enough to vote for God. We Americans might ask the world's forgiveness not only for Vietnam but also for the callous way we have miniaturized and trivialized our civil religion and our two centuries of democracy. We men must ask women's pardon; we whites the forgiveness of blacks whom we push out of our buses and out of our consciences at the same time; we rich the pardon of the poor nations whose ecosystems we unthinkingly corrupt and whose energy we blithely dissipate.

The list grows long and perhaps so vaguely distant as to make our apologies mere form. But the list of sins in the Holy Day liturgy is also wide without being in any way abstract: "under compulsion or by our own choice . . . hardening our hearts . . . uttering with our lips . . . unchastity . . . deceit . . . in speech . . . against our neighbor, our teachers, our parents . . . with that evil inclination which God gave us for good . . . by denying, lying, scoffing, slander, eating, drinking, demanding interest, in haughtiness . . . the sin of casting off the yoke of God's commands, causeless hatred, confusion of mind, breach of faith, tale-bearing, mindlessness . . ."

Perhaps the purpose of all our contrition is to bring to consciousness our half-remembered sins. A general act of confession helps us visualize our personal situation in the midst of people whose lives we have sometimes embittered with our words and deeds. The presence of those close to us whom we have hurt and whose forgiveness we seek reminds us of others far away whose goods we have carried off and whose welfare we have subverted by how we live. The Presence of the One Who forgives inadvertent sinners drives us to ask the forgiveness of other people whom He also loves and whom we have treated unjustly.

Sins against persons can only provisionally be distinguished from sins against God Himself anyway. The *Birkei Yosef* says, "So long as a person has not appeased his/her friend, even that part of the transgression which is a transgression in his/her relations with God is not atoned for." God is the very One Who is present in all our human transactions, and it is He Who suffers when we subvert or undo our love of others of His children. The sins described in the *Al Het* prayer are almost all "ethical" in nature but, by that very fact, "religious" as well. God cares about blacks no less than about Shabbat, about slander no less than about prayer. That must be said to observant Jews who identify observance with piety. But the larger, less ritual-centered group of Jews must be reminded that in Judaism being good is no simple matter of deciding to be good. Ethics is an ever-receding goal. Sin infiltrates and corrupts the best of our intentions, and the best of us stands always in need of forgiveness, both human and divine. Our religion is a way of organizing, yes even ritualizing, our terrible need to turn.

So we must ask for our friends' forgiveness and go back again (at least three times) to seek it from them. They should let us be forgiven if they can; we summon others to stand with us in our plea if necessary, we hound them with our contrition till they let us free of what we have inadvertently though cruelly done. Because they need to be forgiven, they must forgive. Sin is everywhere and in everyone, but sin is what God forgives, if we forgive each other too.

It is not easy to ask forgiveness. I know, since I have been able to do it only a few times in my whole life. Seeking pardon means acknowledging how wrong we were, how much smaller than we thought we were. But giving forgiveness can be even harder. I still remember a man who almost twenty-five years ago lied about me to my family and friends, and though I am always polite to him, I have still not forgiven him for what he did. Part of me even hopes God will never forgive him either.

But if God will not forgive him, God will not forgive me. My "enemy" and I are in the same boat. My victim and I are in the same boat. In a certain sense, even God and I are in the same boat. There is only one boat. I will try, therefore, to ask the pardon of those I have wronged. I will this year try to pardon those more visible and more multitudinous (I hope!) who have wronged me. For, as the Kabbalists truly said, "The prayer of one who does not banish hatred on the Day of Atonement is never heard."

[*Moment*, September 1976]

THE MITZVAH OF SEX

THE COMMANDMENTS are not moral rules. They are religious obligations which emerge from all human situations in all of which, the Jew believes, God has an infinitely relevant stake. The *mitzvot* are addressed directly to the person or to the community in the real world. They do not so much tell him what to do as orient him to the significations of his living and to the horizons of his meta-ethical decision-making. They do not simply forbid or permit so much as they clarify, refocus, and chasten.

But the atmosphere of conventional Jewish piety, at least in our Christian *galut*, tends to be merely repressive. Those who know the Jewish sources best often present them, heretically in my view, as precisely moralistic and abstract. . . . Among more traditional guides, the language tends to be strict and off-putting for modern Jews, feeling their way toward sexual norms. The smell of Puritanism contaminates our most serious formulations of what we should not do as bodies or as men.

No one can pretend that the rabbinic texts are "with it" in any crudely postmodern sense. And no one can accuse the rabbis of *nibbul peh* (dirty mouths) or *p'ritsut* (obscenity, recklessness). Yet both the language and mood of the Talmud are clearly more relaxed about sexual matters than more recent Jewish teachers have permitted themselves to be. They speak an openness to the erotic which could decisively revise our present self-understanding in sexual matters.

Rab, as well as Rabbi Tarfon, both used to declare, "Who wants to marry me for today only?" when they visited a strange city (T.B. Yoma 18b; Yeb. 37b). They were not, surely, sexual athletes, but neither do they come on like most of us who have followed in their rabbinic calling.

It is perfectly true, as our anti-Christian polemics show more clearly than do our codes, that for rabbinic Judaism, sexual pleasure is a very great good. Talmudic piety generally emphasized the joys of the body much more frankly than we are accustomed to do. The same Rab whose need for sex is so openly described said, "Man will have to render account for all the pleasures he saw but refused to enjoy" (J.T. Kid. 11, 65). *Iggeret Hakodesh* makes clear that women as well as men have a right to sexual gratification: "It is proper to woo (one's partner) with kind and seductive words and other such methods so that they have a common intention toward God."

Even the Rambam, heavily influenced by Greek ascetism and widely attacked for his antipathy toward the body and its perversities, admits: "A man's wife is permitted him, so whatever a man wants to do with his wife he may do. He may have intercourse any time he wants, with any organ he wishes, in the customary way or not, as long as he does not waste his seed. Still, piety urges that a man not behave foolishly in sex, but make himself holy during intercourse, as we explained in the laws of knowledge. He should not violate the usage of the world since sex is really for the purpose of reproduction."

In a dazzling adumbration of sexuality, the narrator of Genesis moves from the *ezer k'negdo* (Gen. 2:18) to the doctrine of "one flesh" (Gen. 2:24). The first human commandment is not only to be fruitful but to be sexual for its own sake, since humanity is achieved by abandoning the polymorphous satisfactions of the maternal home and coming toward that other who is to be our sexual partner. God chooses us to bring together the flesh he has sundered, in order that we may be integrated with our own potential self. If Shabbat is the true climax in the creation of the world, sexuality is the true climax in the making of man. Commenting on Leviticus 18:20, the Ramban asserts that "sex has the triune purpose of procreation, detumescence, and excitation." And Ibn Ezra comments that not only procreation but relief and animal pleasure are implied in the laws of copulation. . . .

Among the Jewish mystics, human sex is both frankly described and rendered as a theosophic mystery. Man and wife are to be for each other, but they are also for God, and He enters directly into their physical sharing. The obligation to satisfy one's wife is unsentimentally *halakhic* (required in Jewish law). A man owes *onah*, regularly expected intercourse (see *inter alia*, the *Mekilta* to Exodus 21.10). Sex is commanded, "good" in a rigidly metaphysical sense, whatever an individual husband (or wife) might feel about it. It belongs not primarily to the realm of the psychological or even to the ethical, but to the religious. Proof of this is found in the traditional view of adultery. We learn in the *Pesikta Rabbati* (Chapter 24): "Rabbi Isaac said: In all other transgressions we find, for instance, a thief gains, while the victim of theft loses; a robber gets something, while his victim suffers a loss. In adultery, however, both sinners get something. Who loses, then? The third (God), the Holy One, be He blessed, loses, if one dare put it that way, since He destroys the elements." Braude interprets the last phrase to refer to those "elements" designed to establish the original paternity of the unborn child. In any case, there is a clear admission that adultery is not a pure loss humanly but only religiously, vis-à-vis God.

In practice this is certainly the case. One can imagine an instance where husband, wife, and interloper are all "winners," where all human relationships are apparently improved, where adultery was in fact therapeutic. We certainly know about cases in which all concerned believe one or both partners' adultery made viable their marriage which otherwise would have ended with great suffering to an entire family. But the rabbis do not admit this possibility, which belongs to the realm of the human-ethical, into the arena of metaphysically grounded obligation. Adultery is punished by death meted out by the court. It is forbidden for reasons that lie beyond the merely prudential. The adulterer, according to Job 24:15, "waits for dark, thinking 'no eye will see me,' puts a cover over his face." The adulterer buys happiness, for himself and/or others he loves, only by dissimulation, by becoming what he is not, by hiding his face from God's.

Indeed, on the tablets, "Do not commit adultery" is inscribed opposite "Have no other gods before my face." Anyone who is faithless in one is faithless in the other. Or (euphemistically) "if someone eats his own food while fantasying it to be his neighbor's, or drinks from his own cup while imagining his neighbor's, he violates the seventh commandment" (*Zohar: Sh'mot*, 90).

Idolatry and adultery are both confusions of identity. A man no longer knows who is his own wife or his own God. He literally disintegrates by generalizing his love in several directions at once. He has to imagine being someone he is not and loving someone else's love in order to have sex—or to worship. He is no longer "one flesh" with his own specific flesh. He has done wrong even if he has done "well." That which can emerge from an I-Thou relationship cannot ever emerge from an I-Thou-she/he conflation. No matter who "profits" from the new sexual experience or the new religious one, God loses. One wife, one God: these are not ethical norms, they are religious commands.

Sex is therefore a postmoral issue. It cannot be confronted either by a puritanical repressiveness which insists that conformity to hypocritical standards is the decent thing to do, or by the meta-ethical extrapolations from psychology of a Norman O. Brown who would conduce to high-minded, principled regression. It can only be dealt with in the broader context of the religious life.

Sex is not a problem to be solved but a life to be lived; it is illuminated not by moral strenuousness but by psychotheological experience. It is about God more than it is about man, and about man-and-woman with God more than it is about man with woman. It is about man as creation more than it is about man as sexual animal or man as Spirit. That is why, as Eugene Borowitz has demonstrated (in *Choosing a Sex Ethic*), our tradition leads sex inevitably toward marriage.

Not because sex is dirty, or even because it is clean, but because it is a *mitzvah* it therefore inclines toward the commanded ambiguities of marriage rather than to the ethical antinomies of unmarried love. If one were to ask only, "What is right?" he could never be answered nor know what to do. But if he asks, "What does God want of me?" he can know he must embrace *kiddushin*, the separateness and discipline of marriage. Ineluctably the religious person selects (or, rather, is chosen for) marriage. Not to avoid sin but to be available to holiness (and thus to adultery too). God is there only for one who seeks Him; true sexuality in all its rich problematic is only real for one who is unafraid to commit wrong but terrified at not acting at all, since only an act can instruct.

"Take wives and bear children and take wives for your sons and give your daughters to men" (Jer. 29:6). "One may be able to marry off his son, but his daughter? Can he insure she will marry? Let him give her a dowry, clothing, precious jewelry, so that men will jump at her" (T.B. Kid. 30b).

Rabbi Leo Jung has been right for decades in asserting that Jewish parents and the Jewish community must make it possible for the young to marry. Premarital sex and promiscuity are not, properly, religious issues. Indeed, premarital sex is itself marriage according to our teachers, provided the couple intends it (see *Talmudic Encyclopedia s.v. biyah*; Mishnah *Kiddushin*, beginning). Only in marriage do the meta-ethical issues emerge; marriage is, accordingly, a commandment not only for the couple but for the community (Maimonides: Forbidden Intercourse 21.25f.; T.B. Yeb. 62b).

To encourage early marriage, our community will, however, have to come off its sanctimonious high horse. It will have to admit the legitimacy of all kinds of marriage "ceremonies," even the most unceremonious. It will have to stop being more Catholic than the Catholics about divorce. It will have to frame its thinking about sex in authentic Jewish categories of obedience and freedom, not quasi-Christian/Hellenic ones of decorum and propriety. It will have to surrender its American capitalist notions of acquisition as precondition for marriage, which, in appearance at least, some of our teachers seem unfortunately to have endorsed in advance (Deut. 20:7 ff., T.B. Sotah 44a). There can be no greater *mitzvah*, if one agrees with R. Tanhum ben Hanilai (T.B. Yeb. 62b), because in marriage, and only in marriage, can one find joy, blessing, good; and if one agrees with those "in Israel" who amplified further, only in marriage are Torah, protection, peace, and even life.

In all his Jewish sensuality, commitment and freedom, the author of *Ecclesiastes* instructs us: "Enjoy life with the woman you love." It is good Torah, but, like all Torah, easier said than done.

[*Sh'ma*, October 8, 1971]

PART FOUR

Judaism as Social Activism

A THEOLOGY OF ACTIVISM

I BELIEVE that Judaism mandates a quite specific political ethic which is binding upon all Jews. I include among our political obligations the amelioration of inequality, offering sanctuary to those fleeing oppression and tyranny, and a perpetual struggle for peace, even at some risk to our own security and safety. The rabbis insist that *"Elohim m'vakesh et hanirdaf"*: God always prefers the underdog, not only when the oppressor is evil and the oppressed good, but even when the oppressor has good reasons and the one he pursues is an entirely evil person.

There are specific entailments of this view that I do not propose to ignore. We are not permitted to make war against the government and people of Nicaragua. Jews must support the rights of the victims in South Africa, in the Soviet Union—*and* in the United States, *l'havdil*. Jews must endorse a freeze on nuclear weapons, a rapprochement between the nuclear powers, and an ultimate disarmament that will make war far less lethal, if not actually impossible. I believe that Jews must support the legitimate right of Palestinian self-determination, with no illusions about the meaning of that right: a Palestinian state beside Israel—though not, of course, instead of Israel. I believe that these "left-liberal" political goals are precisely mandated by Judaism as I understand it, and that no Jew is free to abstain from them.

The Jewish community must often work for these goals with other religious and secular Americans. I know that the synagogue is not created to enact the program of the American Civil Liberties Union, for which one of my sons works, nor of the Democratic Socialists of America, to which my other son belongs, nor of those

76

Middle East peace groups to which I have given much of my life. The synagogue is a metapolitical institution, designed to implicate us in ethical tasks but never pretending that it is a (merely?) political instrumentality.

I know, also, that these issues are complicated and sometimes intractable. I know that sometimes we on the left have done more harm than good by trying to do good (Ethiopia? American hunger and welfare projects? Unconditional détente with totalitarians?), and that even when we do good, it will not be good enough. I am also aware that our own personal lives are not so orderly or so ethical that we can be imperiously dogmatic about the largest and most persistent issues of humanity. In addition, other groups, like the Catholic church, have recently assumed a leadership that the Jewish community used to occupy, and it might well be their turn to take chances by offering themselves to the next American revolution.

It is also true that Jews in politics are especially vulnerable and that the Jewish community in America remains interstitial, successful but not safe, powerless even amid its smugness and its wealth. These United States are *galut*, exile, indeed, and it would be folly to claim that America's welfare depends primarily upon us Jews. Jews in the Republic of South Africa also feel deeply threatened, and while it seems clear to me that they are dangerously wrong in supporting an insupportable government, we must realize that when we oppose that government, we oppose what they think of as their own safety and well-being. In Israel, too, when we come out foursquare for a Palestinian state, we must acknowledge that a majority of Israeli Jews will be against us. Do we have the right or, as we assert, the duty to work for their good against their own will? In any case, they surely have the right to act in their own self-interest—and, it seems perfectly clear to me, the Palestinians also have that right. A black government in South Africa, an Arafat-led Palestinian state, might or might not be good for the Jews. I am in favor of such a state purely on Jewish grounds, but I have no illusions that it would be unproblematic or entirely pure.

Philosophers tell us about "incommensurability." That doctrine seems to mean that some issues cannot ever be settled because no standard exists that can be shared by opposing sides. If one side thinks abortion is murder and the other speaks only of a woman's right over her own body, there is no way for them to compromise their differences of opinion. . . .

We must live in a time of ambivalence. We vacillate between idealism and cynicism. We feel the incommensurability of all human judgment, not because we are humble but rather because we are afraid. Dogmatists rally their troops and dogmatic unbelievers, theirs too. But "the best lack all conviction," and the Jewish ethical elite is hedged in by self-doubt and by inhibition. Kahane and the "crazies" know exactly what they want. They are coherent and to many convincing, though they are also demonic and dangerous. But the rest of us are unsure and impotent, for good reason and for no reason at all. Our faith is not faithful, our doubts grow, proliferate, and encompass everything that we have dreamed to do.

Yet clearly the positive commandment of Judaism is to begin to act again and again, in the face of all doubt and with due consideration of all that negative experience can teach. Our rabbis taught that "These and these are the words of the living God," meaning not that Hillel and Shammai were equally true and equally false, nor that we cannot know whether the school of Rabbi Akiba or that of Rabbi Ishmael was right. We vote to decide how to act; we mediate the incommensurable. Rather, what this doctrine asserts is that truth is found only when the two opposites coexist, the majority and the minority, the right and the left, I and you.

God is above all our systems and all our political gestures. We need each other's dissent and each other's critique. We need to listen to the other where she is. Distance and relation together, in Buber's phrase, alone can make us free. Avoiding recklessness without trepidation, on the one hand, and febrile constraint, on the other, unafraid to fail, but eager not to hurt, nonviolent, yet sometimes self-sacrificing, political to the end but with a politics under God and under God's judgment, we have to try to do what we are commanded to do.

God will complete our imperfections. She will not forgive our self-defensive cowardice or our fear of failure. I believe that the program outlined in the first paragraphs of this article is both intellectually defensible and ethically necessary. I know that it requires and will receive your criticism. I am proud of the causes I have supported for forty years, but not of the "success" that has followed and eluded all those causes. I believe that God really does love the oppressed, but I know that my own identification with them is factitious, even absurd. I fear that God is not on my side, but I hope against hope that I may sometimes be on God's. Jewish politics is asymptotic. We move always closer toward the Kingdom and work for its fulfillment, but only the Messiah will finally make our dream of a good world come true.

[*Sh'ma*, February 20, 1987]

CIVIL RIGHTS

FAR MORE IMPORTANT to America, I think, than most of the "issues" that fill our daily press is the wave of sit-in strikes that began in Alabama. They show that progress must be made, in the final analysis, by people who care. Negro freedom will be fully won, in the end, by colored men. In a time when the political parties look more and more alike and the private man feels unable either to make progress or to prevent it, a few teenagers show us that action can still be both responsible and effective. I take pride in their religious courage and in their human achievement. I hope our children grow up like them.

But I am envious too. I wish we could be there now where history is really being made. I wish that six or eight of us could take up signs and walk in front of the Woolworth's store in Highland Park and say: We too demand that you let colored people eat with us. Not just six people, but six speaking, walking, asking in the name of Solel. What that might mean to the college kids in Montgomery! What that could show about our concern for man and for our feelings about America! What a Passover we could have!

I suppose there is no way for Solel to picket Woolworth's, or, in other words, to take any really serious social position. I suppose that we are condemned to convincing each other of things we already believe. I suppose we will end like all the others, wistful and banal. But if we had cared, what we might have done!

The Congregational church, surveying rather pessimistically the future of the church in American life, says this month: "This is the great challenge facing the churches in the next quarter-century—to meet the revolution of rising expectations with a commensurate revolution of rising responsibility."

I shall have to write the Congregationalists to say that Solel will pass this revolution.

[Congregation Solel *Pathfinder*, April 5, 1960]

I SAW HEROES at the great civil rights march in Selma, Alabama, last week, though I was not one. I saw freedom embattled and triumphant, though it was only a freedom *from* something and not yet a freedom *for*. I saw God in Selma, Alabama, too, but no more Himself than elsewhere in His world. I saw hope emerging from hopelessness, yet I am still not wholly reassured.

Men in Selma are still men. America is focused and ennobled there, but it is still America and not the Garden. The Negro is more daring and more strong in Selma than in Chicago, but he is still only a human being. Solel people were tried and trustworthy in Selma, but our congregation will have to go a long way to be worthy of their trust. Judaism spoke in Selma, but ever so softly and with insufficient clarity. . . .

We shall need a *Seder* this year too.

[Congregation Solel *Pathfinder*, April 7, 1965]

I KNOW HOW the black militants feel; I too am bitter about those who now use Martin Luther King's death only to mock his life. The Jewish community goes around with long faces, but our hospitals have been fighting for five years against the union King gave his life in Memphis to help. Our congregation has come up with a little money and food—but when King spoke from our pulpit we had many complaints and a few resignations. The mayor of Chicago is respectful to his memory now—but he was King's implacable and remorseless foe during the Chicago campaign. The president makes sincere speeches to honor his memory—but only after ruthlessly using and then discarding him while he was alive. Congress is sad—but it blocked the civil rights bill and opposed the Poor People's Campaign and predicted that any attempt to get more for the ghettos would unleash a dangerous backlash.

We are all sorry that he is dead (really sorry, I think, for ourselves, now that there is no buffer between us and violence), but where were we when he was alive?

Attacks on Dr. King are continuing after his death, too. Because he was courageous, they say he was reckless. Because the black American is not yet out of Egypt, they say he was a failure. Because Dr. King was a real Christian, they call him an Uncle Tom. His pacifism was cowardice; his idealism, wooly-headedness; his self-sacrifice, masochism. The bravery of a marine killer goes unquestioned, but the martyrdom of a man of peace is made to look suspicious.

When he died, the very first white reaction was to seal off the black ghettos; the first black reaction was to steal TV sets. Militant blacks are using his death to prove that Whitey can't ever be trusted; white men of power are using it to put down any possible successors in black leadership. The Christian church forgets that King called it his greatest disappointment; the synagogue forgets that it has studiously ignored his pleas since a Birmingham rabbi lectured him while he was in jail.

He preached nonviolent revolution; we almost all believe in violent counterrevolution—using the full power of the state to put down the complaints of the suffering, the cries of the Negroes, the recalcitrance of dissenters. King's life and death were among poor black men in America; our hopes still ride with the rich, the white, and the powerful.

Yet in the end, if there is a God (and if not, how could there ever have been a Martin Luther King?), he will win, not we. From his grave, like his master of Nazareth, he will move men for a thousand years. From his silent pulpit, he will speak more eloquently than the multitudes of comforting and comfortable preachers in all the silent denominations. Before he died, Dr. King saw our foreign policy begin to swing around; he felt the Poor People's Campaign building; he was vouchsafed a personal vision of God's redemptive love. He died without fear, without bitterness, without defeat.

It is too late for us to go with him to Birmingham or Selma or Washington or Cicero. It is too late for us to hear his prophetic voice (except on videotape). It is too late for us to tell him that he was right all along—that we, in our lives and in our sayings, have been dreadfully, dangerously wrong.

But it is never too late to turn to God. It is never too late for a Poor People's Campaign or a black revolution or the American dream. It is never too late for peace or for justice or for compassion. The old days of black-and-white-together may be gone, but the task of the white man is unfinished.

In ten short years, Martin Luther King completed his work. We have hardly begun our own.

[Congregation Solel *Pathfinder*, April 24, 1968]

THE NEGRO REVOLUTION AND JEWISH THEOLOGY

AT THE CONVENTION of the Central Conference of American Rabbis last June, a telegram was read from Martin Luther King appealing to the Reform rabbis to leave their meeting and come to St. Augustine to join with him in a creative witness to the struggle for equal treatment there. The officers and social-action chairmen of the Conference did not respond. Of the entire assembly, only some sixteen rabbis made the difficult journey south. The rest—the overwhelming majority—stayed on in Atlantic City. So did I.

I must ask myself what the meaning of my refusal to answer Dr. King's call was, a refusal shared by nearly all my colleagues on this and nearly every other occasion. On the face of it, my record is as good as anyone's: I have not only signed but initiated petitions for equal housing. I went on the Washington march in the summer of 1963 and another time visited my senator, Everett Dirksen, who informed me that clergymen had powerfully influenced his decision to support civil rights legislation. I have preached on the theme of racial justice *ad nauseam* (that is, to the point of my own nausea; my congregation much prefers hearing about Negroes to hearing about themselves). I have picketed a Jewish hospital together with Negro workers asking for union recognition, though many angry board members of the hospital were on my own synagogue board. I have raised as much money for SNCC and NAACP and ACT as anyone I know, and though those organizations have never put me on their decision-making committee (perhaps they don't have one), CORE did once throw me a birthday party. If there is a black Jew any-where, I am he. And yet I didn't go to St. Augustine.

The most obvious possible reason is that I was scared. It is per-fectly true that I am afraid of violence and even more of jail. My friends who have come back from Jackson and St. Augustine and Birmingham didn't look well, at least for a while. Even a short stay in a Southern jail produces in most of my kind an hysteria which often culminates in either mania or depression. But I do not think it was jail I feared. I have risked more than jail for causes I supported much less strongly than the one in question. I am no hero, but I have done my duty even when it looked to cost more than this one did.

The real reason for my refusal, one shared by nearly all my col-leagues and, in my opinion, paradigmatic of the whole Jewish com-munity, is a deeper one. It is more than the sum of my personal inadequacies. It is wider than the total anxiety of the community. It is not something we do when our worst natures take over; it is an act (or an unwillingness to act) that comes from our whole existence. When I said "no," it was a purer and more profound saying than any "yes" which I had more superficially produced before. When I said no, I meant it. No—I do not really wish to work with you! I do not wish to swim with you! I do not wish to go to jail with you! I do not wish to eat your food or be one of you!

As an American rabbi, I am inevitably and incurably bourgeois. I live off men who live off workingmen's work: entrepreneurs, ad men, promoters, small manufacturers, salesmen, tax experts whose function in American society is only to grease the wheels of capital-ism—that very capitalism whose profits are squeezed from machines destined to displace the Negro as America's muscle. The American Jew is the most marginal and therefore the most loyal of capitalists. He lives on the fringes of the large corporation, doing its bidding on request, defending its policies which keep him in the waiting room but rarely give him the executive key. And because he is not quite in and not quite out, he defends most passionately American free enterprise, the good life of *Life* magazine and the TV commercials (which he writes, partly because he so desperately needs to believe them), and the lily-white suburb. The American Jew lives by his superiority to and distance from the American Negro and the American poor. And I live off him. Both of us are terribly frightened by the new American revolution. Like most revolutions in the past, this one is likely to do the Jew no "good."

But what of those more courageous Jewish congregations that have held fast in an integrating community? Are they not the proof that I am unusual or wrong? They at least stand in place amid a rising and threatening tide of lower-class delinquency all around them. They do not move, some few do not move away, and for this they deserve all honor. But the integrating congregations, too, are islands. Gingerly they court a few upper-middle-class Negro professionals. Carefully they produce community organizations that will defend their interests (the cautious, University of Chicago–sponsored South East Chicago Commission, not the Woodlawn Organization, disciples of radical organizer Saul Alinksy; the Urban League, not ACT), interests that are sharply distinguished from the needs of the Negro masses. In a braver, more subtle way than my own congregation of ex-integrationists, they too are saying no. In league with the white universities and the white power structure, the urban synagogue absolutely refuses to share the militant Negro cause.

I have said we refuse because it will cost us too much to say yes. But will it not cost all white America a great deal too? How can we concede to power-hungry young demagogues of the unwashed blacks the right to make our decisions? How can we support hospital strikes, stall-ins that will clog the highways, meetings that denounce the mayor, fund-raising enterprises whose funds are never accounted for, young radicals who court death in the South provocatively and sometimes, we suspect, unnecessarily? How can a convinced bourgeois ever support an authentic revolution?

If he does what he believes he should, he cannot. He will find "good" reasons not to. He will approve of integration but oppose every possible step toward it. He will support nonviolence (which secures his own skin) but never participate in direct action. He will praise the dead Medgar Evers but not the living Rustins and Farmers. He will listen to the sermons of Martin Luther King and cherish their homiletical skill, but he will not do what they ask him to do. The bourgeois Jew will hold art fairs for civil rights organizations and not demand to know where the money goes, because he does not really care. It is the show, the pseudo-action of support that counts for us, not the deeper negation it masks. Our minds and our hearts and our fearful flesh agree that the Negro should be made to behave in a way protective of our own imperiled American success. That is to say, he should remain our slave.

It is very pleasant to be someone's master, to lecture Dr. King as a Birmingham rabbi did, to play cat-and-mouse with the revolutionaries as the best of us do. It is very stimulating to sing the freedom songs and march in the freedom marches as I have done, and then retire to a suburban study to read Heidegger and *Midrash*; it is reassuring to do what I want to do and be able to believe it is the right thing I am doing. It is much easier to write about not going to St. Augustine than to go.

And so we have the enormous literature of Jewish affirmation-negation: the useless personal recall of Norman Podhoretz, the pretentious inanities of official rabbinic pronouncement, the pathetic false starts of the congregational social-action committees, the second thoughts of Philip Roth and Will Herberg, the reservations, the posturings, the agonizing, and the lies. With all our philosophic and literary talent, our American Jewish literature is utterly banal on the revolution. It cannot learn to say what it cannot believe, and so it wallows in poignant irrelevance.

What we cannot believe is that God is a revolutionary. So long as we act by our lights we shall act poorly, because our insights are really self-interest and our convictions mere rationalizations. Marx meant *us* when he said we do what makes us rich, and believe what lets us do. Freud meant *us* when he said that words do not express so much as suppress, that only acts can dissipate ambivalence. Our whole hope for wholeness is to find an Archimedean point, a place of relation in which we do not merely express our private wish but are revealed and commanded and empowered.

Liberal Judaism quite early distinguished sharply the prophetic teaching of social justice from the more profoundly prophetic poetry of encounter. We liberals have tried to believe for a hundred years that there is no (personal) God and (Deutero-) Isaiah is His prophet.

But our theological convictions have come home to roost. A God Who is my own best nature is not God enough. My own best nature does not care much about the Negro or the poor. A God Who is Idea or Process or mere tradition is a God out of things, an ahistoric deity Who could not care less about Americans in revolution, simply because He *cannot* care. We have built our action programs on the shifting sands of humanist caprice, and it is no wonder now that they come rumbling down about our shoulders.

Thus Reform rabbinic pronouncements look just like statements from the ADA, and Judaism is merely the enactment of Democratic party platforms of some years back. Our Reform movement divides between the various theological neotraditionalists, on the one hand (Isaac Wise, Kohler, Cohon, Silver), who are silent in controversy and vote Republican, and the flaming liberals (Stephen Wise, Horace Wolf, Israel), on the other, who eschew "mysticism" and want to get about the important business of making religious action come true. Both sides are finally disappointed: the old-fashioned theologians who produce no disciples because they could not connect their word with their God, and the liberals who have only the same old political liberalism to sell, because they know no Teaching God to teach them something new. The same thing happens in Conservative and even in Orthodox circles: on the one hand, disciples of traditional theologies who cannot speak to the cruces of their time, and, on the other, the perpetually up-to-date who cannot convince because they merely enunciate and never discover, because their words speak louder than their acts.

The radical isolation of God from man, the loss of *mitzvah*, the refusal to see our own time as God's *kerygma* (proclamation), has castrated us and left us powerless to act. What one sees in the Negro revolution is men not trying to get what they want (Dr. King and even Dick Gregory have more to gain elsewhere; even the very poor have still their lives to lose) but seeking what they have been made to know is wanted on high. The revolt of the underprivileged against us who are overprivileged is not simply a war for redress; it is also incipient revelation.

We Jews are ambivalent because in our heart of hearts we think we are free. The Negro even at his worst is simple and emancipated because he has discovered that no man but only God rules. Nonviolent direct action is an affirmation of the Kingship of God, that He alone is Power, but that we are yet commanded to act. Judaism has become violent nonaction, a principled inactivity which, profiting from the exploitation of other men, is therefore built on violence and force. The Negro defies police power and fierce human opposition to obey his God; we are loyal to our white communities and seek better police protection while by every act and by every refusal we defy God. Thus is revealed how we have lost that sense of commandment by which alone (and not easily, in any case) a man or a people can transcend themselves and learn to fulfill other men's need before and even in opposition to their own. Only out of the excruciating dialogue of prayer and confession and hearing can a man or a people learn to obey God and link their world to Him.

I believe that most of us know this much. We know that the obedience to commandment is the only path to encounter with God. And *therefore* we withhold. We refuse, as a community, the sacraments of prayer and devotion. We refuse the central command to study sacred texts. We refuse to segregate ourselves as a holy community or to integrate ourselves with the great unhappy multitude of men. We refuse to support with our money whatever most certainly signifies the sacred. We systematically diminish the synagogue, the rabbi, the custodians of tradition, and those who seek a new way to mediate revelation. And we do these things, uniquely in all Jewish history, not because we are atheists but *davke* because we are anxious believers.

If God were dead, as the philosophers feared (or hoped; it may come to the same thing), we should not need to run so fast from Him. If we were full-hearted *epikorsim* (heretics), we could even do right and not fear that He was behind it all. We could dispense with the secularized synagogue, phony religious education, and our naive and ritualistic social-action programs. But we know, somehow, that God is not dead, nor does He sleep. We know that He is present in all His ancient and terrible wrath, and therefore we seek to evade him with our refusals.

The charisma of "We Shall Overcome," the martyrdom of the Reverend Bruce Klunder (the Unitarian minister killed in the South), the preaching and work of Presbyterian leader Carson Blake and the neo-Orthodox King have no present analogues in the Jewish community and are likely to have none. Our only prophets are novelists whose pens scratch gall, or poets of another time who have lost God, or rabbis fiercely loyal to their calling but forgetful of Who it is that called them. Even our most alienated Jews know that in the great American rallies and private agonies, we Jews are strangers. We no longer know how to pray for forgiveness and hence cannot work with poignancy or effect. All our touted institutionalized wisdom remains abstract. All we good men trying to be better are not good enough for times that demand heroes and not simply decent folk.

At a public meeting, the representative of the American Jewish community in one of the largest of Southern cities rehearsed last year the failings of the Negro freedom movements: they were confused, incompetent, ill-advised, dangerous. I asked him what the leaders of that movement thought of us. He admitted candidly that there had been no communication between them and us for a long time. We have nowhere a liaison with Utopia. When the Messiah comes, he will not find the Jews ready, because we have no committee charged with discovering the Man of the Millennium. What is more to the point, we do not want to know where the revolution moves and by Whom, for we guess by a racial intuition (or just plain common sense) that where thousands are gathered in His name, He too is there.

To meet God is to face annihilation and rebuke. It is to be cast into the dust and hurled to the sky and again cast down. It costs a lot of money. It hurts. It undercuts all the comfortable and conformist housing that we use to cover us against the rain. It lashes us with a wind of awful, rushing force. It sends us back to the Bible no longer critical and cool but whimpering for a word of consolation. It sends us back to the synagogue not for Bar Mitzvahs and self-congratulation but for atonement and instruction. It sends us back to our own loved ones surprised that they have not been swept away by the vengeance of a just God.

What we fear from Martin Luther King, what I feared to find in St. Augustine, is not only a hard job but a hard Taskmaster. My liberal theology had protected me against surprise or rebuke. The God of my father and my grandfather had learned to be polite. Chastened, He did not ask for much nor, to be sure, promise more. He was decorous and decent. He was a True Liberal.

But that God could not help me or mine when we walked in a shadowy land. He was only a name. He was only an Idea. The true God Who found me in my personal despair and Whom I have ever since evaded with more ingenuity than success is the same God Who finds our black brothers in their American Egypt and has promised to set them free.

I owe this God something. A tithe of my money; a tenth part of the total budget of my congregational and communal funds. A building one-tenth as fine as our own building built by us for us. A tenth of the time I would rather spend playing or reading or basking in the affluence that mistakenly He had given me. Concern. Concern for one poor man, one Negro, for all poor men, for all the hidden disadvantaged.

But I must not pay *aggadically*, out of the goodness of my crooked heart or the shame of my acquisitive community. Rather: *halakhically*, legally, as a constituent requirement for membership in the community, as dues financial and moral for the privilege of being a Jew. Of every ten words I write or speak or publish, one must be for those not of my skin or condition. Formally, unimpassioned, bound. Unsentimentally, relentlessly, I must pay.

I pay God by repaying not what I think I owe nor by doing what I should like to do, but by responding to His prophets, the emancipators, and to His friends, the poor. I am no Christian saint required to kiss their wounds or delight in their dirtiness. But I am a Jew condemned to do their will, to find at their side the task I share with Him.

The evangelistic program of the Christian church may be faulted when it is self-seeking or manipulative. But essentially it reflects the true rabbinic strategy of winning a world for God. In modern Judaism this can only take the form of service political and personal and not conversionism. The Jewish community must become a pressure group for higher taxation (which would, more seriously than is now contemplated in Washington, moderate the economic gaps), for mental health (which is the most tragic problem of the poor), for civil rights. What is needed is not mere pronouncement, which is everywhere felt to be labial and unimpassioned, but direct action under the rule of Torah. This kind of involvement will frighten many Jews away. If it is authentic and rigorous and not merely bourgeois do-goodism, it will make all of us anxious. But it is also capable of purifying, partly by diminishing in number, the mixed multitude that constitutes our Jewish polity today. And who knows what allies, human and superhuman, we might thus acquire?

The time for refusal is over. Judaism teaches that we achieve theological insight not by Greek speculation nor yet by mystic ecstasy, but only by living Law. Our goal is not impossible self-realization. Our aim is not coldly ethical. What we seek, and in seeking begin to achieve, is the meeting with Him Who has chosen us from among all nations to suffer and to witness.

[*Judaism*, Fall 1964]

I BELIEVE that what I wrote in *Judaism* in 1964 is still true now, thirty years later. But I have learned a good deal in the eighties, especially by serving on the transition team and ethics committee of Chicago's Mayor Harold Washington. His was the great era in Chicago politics for Jewish-black collaboration. Washington needed Jewish voters and Jewish skills. We needed his brilliant understanding of black talent and his ability to keep demagogues in the black community at bay.

Harold Washington was a remarkable man, absolutely free of any kind of prejudice or bias. He was proudly black and as proudly a leader of all the people. He combined the talents of reformer and boss, of intellectual and showman; he was for black pride and for coalition politics. His death was a disaster from which we have yet to recover. But something changed once and for all during his administration. Equal opportunity, if not equality of result, is permanent and irrevocable. The police department and the civil service will never again be lily-white; the city of Chicago will never again belong to any group but only to all.

In the real world, Jews and blacks inevitably have differing agendas but also, at their best, not dissimilar motivations. When blacks follow the model of Martin Luther King's activist nonviolence, and when Jews stop trying to protect their newly won wealth and white-skin privilege, they have common work to share. It is the task of making America more equal, more like the ideals that we have all professed and all betrayed. . . . To some extent Jewish and black desires are contradictory. But there is an overriding need for a more equal America, a more caring community for all of us. That is the mandate of our several religions, if not the drive of our private desires.

Jews and blacks may be natural antagonists; we are, however, supernatural allies in the Kingdom of God. Perhaps only there, in the end, we surrender our prejudices and our particularities in service of a universal good. Jews will not find that surrender easy. . . . Only messianic politics can be worthy of our four thousand years of prophetic and rabbinic search for justice.

It is time to demythologize the black-Jewish dialogue, to stop pretending that we have exactly the same proximate goals or strategies. What we do have is a desperate need for one America instead of a nation divided into rich and poor, black and white. What we can hope to achieve is a slow surrender of what we want to keep for ourselves in favor of what we know God wants for all human children. True leadership of each of our separate communities will not play on our fears or on our pride but will, like King and Heschel, like Moses and Akiba, call us to a higher and more truly self-denying task. As the great contemporary Jewish philosopher Emmanuel Levinas puts it: we are all hostage for one another, we are all at the disposal of one another, we are all protectors of each other's fate.

God may yet fail; we may yet fail God. We may continue to sunder America and our world. Or we may turn in repentance, for that is what it will take, and at last bow to the will of a God who has made us all to be one and may yet make us whole.

[Speech to a Conference on Blacks and Jews
in the 1960s Civil Rights Movement, at Dillard University
in New Orleans, April 1994]

VIETNAM

DURING THE recent controversy about Vietnam at Solel, I found the unwillingness to discuss the issues by far the most depressing and pervasive fact. Men of goodwill can disagree; I found many who would not even discuss their revulsion against discussion. Having considered this very strong hostility to airing the issues, I think it takes eight major forms:

1. *We may discuss domestic but not foreign policy.* This dangerous distinction ignores the completely interrelated character of the two. What happens in Vietnam *is* domestic policy, and not only because Americans are killed or less money will be available for antipollution programs. Domestic issues are almost all part of the great consensus, anyway, and if there are any moral problems for Americans they are much more likely to relate to foreign policy.

2. *Issues may properly be discussed by "political" but not by religious groups; we are not gathered together to discuss controversial subjects; for us to take a stand on any political issue would be to break down the wall of separation between church and state.* What in God's name *are* we gathered to do? Has it nothing to do with life and death, with war and peace, with good and evil? Our concern is not really unwelcome to, even when it is critical of, the administration. Our whole democracy is based on the widest possible discussion of *all* issues, and our religion is a religion of political action. The separation of church and state means only that the government must not establish or favor any church or all churches, not that churches should not contribute to political decision-making. If they do not (as in Nazi Germany or Red China), they betray their Founder. Religious groups, of course, have no special insights unless their convictions are themselves illu-

minating, but neither can they be dismissed as less competent than the army veterans, the intellectuals, or the TV producers. They (we) may turn out to be correct rather more than occasionally.

3. *We may criticize Republicans but not Democrats.* This sounds silly once you say it, but I know that many of our members who loved what we said about Goldwater are angry because the same thing now has to be said about the Democratic Goldwater (LBJ). But religion must be nonpartisan (not nonpolitical); we have no right to trust anyone just because we voted for him. For the Jewish community and its religious spokesmen to remain safely in the pocket of the Democratic party would be, in my opinion, a disaster.

4. *We may discuss controversial issues, but not on the Sabbath.* I too would rather meditate and pull myself together on the Sabbath, but can we insulate God's day from God's world?

5. *It is all right for rabbis to say things about moral issues, but not laymen.* I should like to believe that rabbis are uniquely in touch with the truth, but alas, Judaism will not let me. We are all just Jews, with only the power that God gives us to see the right, and we must try to help each other see it.

6. *It is all right to discuss issues but not to make any statement of conviction or conclusion.* How could people know before discussion that it could not produce a conclusion? Of course it might not; probably we would find it too difficult to come out with a useful and still popular position. But we can't know that for sure until we try. Our congregation spent a year forging a Statement of Principles. How can we know for sure that our principles do not apply in Vietnam?

7. *Experts may decide, but not laymen.* The experts decided the Bay of Pigs and Dominican Republic fiascos. The experts now seem divided (Kennan versus Rusk); they are always divided. Nor may we cop out of our democratic responsibilities by pretending that the hard moral questions are only scientific and technical. That is what Eichmann said.

8. *Gentiles may have an opinion, but not Jews.* This, the most deep-seated and irrational but also the most pervasive of objections, leaves me almost (but not quite) speechless. Let the Unitarians, the

Presbyterians, the Congregationalists, let them all have peace programs and discussions of foreign policy, but not the Jews. Let the
Council of Churches and the Catholic Bishops say whatever they
want to say—but not the UAHC. Let the Friends and the ADA and
the Yale professor and the senator from Oregon say as much as they
please—but not the rabbis or the congregations. This objection is
straight out of the ghetto. In America, need we say it, Jews are citizens. Solel is an American Jewish community. It has the right to discuss anything. It is limited only by its competence to make
decisions. And it serves a God Who is not pleased with silence.

[Congregation Solel *Pathfinder*, March 16, 1966]

THE DAY you get this *Pathfinder* we shall, God willing, be in Washington. We shall speak in our several voices the Congregation's
prayer for peace in Vietnam. We shall listen, respond, and connect
to our state's and our country's leaders. We shall do what we can do
to end the fighting and the death.

But we need what you at home can do, too. You should write to
your president and senators, now. You should support those who are
facing a tough reelection campaign on a platform you helped build.
You should cooperate with organizations that express in purely political terms the significant convictions you share. You should send a
check to the Solel Discretionary Fund to pay for those going to
Washington who couldn't go otherwise. You should pray that we,
your friends and comrades, speak with dignity, persuasiveness, and
compassion. You should pray that we do not make fools of ourselves.

But there is a thing worse than making a fool of oneself. It is to
make a tool of oneself, an instrument that does evil without wanting
to. Uncertainty about the future is inevitable, but apathy is a sin.
Not knowing exactly how to stop the war is universal, but not trying
to do something about it is a grave transgression. Confusion about

first steps and next steps is difficult to avoid, but not saying what one thinks to be true is cowardice and atheism.

We who speak for peace in Vietnam may well be mistaken. We are surely less than perfectly equipped to solve all the complex issues involved. But we are doing what we believe God asks us to do, and you must do that too.

[Congregation Solel *Pathfinder*, November 29, 1967]

Members of Solel flew to Washington for the day to lobby members of Congress and the administration on Vietnam.

MY GRANDMOTHER used to scour all the daily papers looking for Jewish names. Sometimes she came upon names of gangsters, sometimes of Nobel laureates. She was overjoyed when she found a Jew who had done something praiseworthy; she was horrified when she found a Jewish name connected with crime or sin. And then there were again and again the Jewish victims: Six Jews (and forty non-Jews) killed in an earthquake! Three Jews (and twenty-four others) die in plane crash! It was not that she was insensitive to gentile suffering; she was a very compassionate woman. A merciful daughter of the merciful. But her Jews belonged to her. Their death (their sin, their accomplishment, their story) was always hers.

That is why my mind keeps returning to you, Sandy Lee Scheuer, dead of bullets from the guns of the Ohio National Guard at the age of twenty. To you, Sandy Lee Scheuer of Youngstown, Ohio, student at Kent State University, shot to death by draft-dodgers in American uniforms in Kent, Ohio. I was not absolutely sure you were Jewish, Sandy, but your well-groomed picture reminds me of all the Jewish girls I used to love, and I suppose your name gives it away.

When the Weathermen [early 1970s violent white revolutionaries] were roaming the streets of Chicago breaking windows and screaming their insane love for Ho Chi Minh, a black friend of mine asked me why I was not in the streets with them. "But," I explained, "I don't agree with them, not with their goals (a Red dictatorship to replace a Red, White, and Blue one), not with their tactics (premature, haphazard, reckless violence is surely counterrevolution). Why should I be in the streets with those kids?"

"To be with them," said my black friend. "When our kids go out, win or lose, right or wrong, we go out with them, to see that the police won't push them around. To see they stay safe. We don't have to support them, just to stand around and keep our eyes open. Where were you protective Jewish parents when your own kids were getting smashed on the head in Chicago last summer or this fall? Don't you care about their lives?"

Where were we in Kent, Ohio, or New Haven, Connecticut, or at all the hundred campuses and cities where our kids (*our* kids, grandmother) were standing alone and frightened and (as we know now) in terrible danger. Where was the Jewish presence at Washington or Selma or Woodstock—a few "radical" cells, a noncongregational rabbi, an occasional bureaucrat from one of the Jewish civil rights agencies—who else? Who else standing between our kids and the guns, between our kids and the American troops, between Sandy Lee Scheuer (and, God help us, Jerry Rubin too) and death.

It is, of course, true, that if the great, empty congregations and the dying, endlessly self-protecting organizations have nothing to say about Cambodia and Kent State, they have nothing to say. It is true that such silent and self-serving congregations, such irrelevant "Jewish" organizations will lose all our youth. It is much more important that they will deserve to lose them. They (we, grandmother, we) were not there, in any sense, when they shot Sandy Scheuer of Youngstown, Ohio. We waited around to read her obituary in the morning paper.

Much of the explanation of our long silence has to do with our fears for Israel. We have been afraid to make President Nixon the least bit angry for fear he would withdraw his faltering support for Israel and leave our brothers alone to their fates. We have been afraid to denounce the Cambodian invasion for fear it would make an Egyptian invasion or a fatal atrocity more likely. We were concerned to protect the Daliahs and Yigals, and we forgot about our Marks and Sandys. We bound ourselves so tightly and so unthinkingly to our perception of the Israeli cause that we have no *koah* (energy) left for our own Jewish kids fighting the draft, standing up to the guns and finally bleeding in the streets—alone.

And what use is our cowardly acquiescence to Israel? Is a wider American war in the Far East really likely to free American help for the Near East? Because we have stood silently by the blood of our own children, does Spiro Agnew love the Eastern Jewish establishment or the Jewish networks any the more? Because we have not stormed the Pentagon or surrounded the president in our rage, is anyone thereby convinced that we are good Americans? Has Julius Hoffman canceled out the Yippies and the SDS—or are we not as far from being safe or powerful as we ever were?

An Israel that can only survive if American Jews support the illicit, bloody adventurism of their own country cannot survive at all. American Jews who separate themselves from their own blood children in order to look more respectable or to become more powerful will end up neither respectable nor powerful. By any standard, our priorities require that we connect with the agony and travail of our American and American-Jewish young. That means draft counseling and sanctuary, it means physical and moral presence at the scenes of their rebellion. It means coming to understand, if not always to share, their concerns and their asseverations. It means understanding why they are troubled that Israel's friends are so often on the right in America, and why they are eager to extricate ourselves and our fellow Jews from the kiss of death proffered by Billy Graham and the warmongers and the Southern congressmen. It means weeping for Sandy Scheuer, killed at Kent State University, as well as for the Jews who die defending the homeland in a war they do not want.

Any hope of avoiding polarization has been finally shattered by the news from Cambodia and Kent. It will no longer be possible for us to be cool or neutral or patient. Our old liberalism is dead in a country that demands its sons kill and die in the new Far Eastern crusade. American Jews will now have to make decisions we have too long postponed and too readily forgone. We will have to take sides at last: with Sandy Lee Scheuer or with the men in American uniforms who shot her dead.

[Congregation Solel *Pathfinder*, May 13, 1970]

THE CITIES

IT WAS AFTER DARK and the gates of Branford College were closed and locked, but I had a key and I was to open the gate to prepare for the Sabbath evening service in the Memorial Room at the base of Harkness Tower. I fumbled with my keys—the house key, and the second house key which makes sure that the house is safe in case the first lock is picked, and the car key, and the trunk key, and the key to my office, and several other keys, and finally I found the right key and put it into the lock, and a man came and stood beside me.

He was not as young as a student should look and not as old as a professor feels. And he was not as white as someone who I thought could walk around this newly apprehensive campus without arousing suspicion. "Will you let me in with your key?" he said. And a hundred notions passed through my head—of rape, of murder, of burglary, of danger to the college (a forbidden act to let someone in without examining his credentials)—and, on the other hand, the shame of judging someone I didn't know, or excluding someone because of his age or his color or his size.

So I fumbled with my keys some more, and finally a student from Branford College came along and said, "C'mon in, Joe," and let us all in.

We are frightened here at Yale, and we are right to be frightened. We are afraid of the stranger and sometimes of one who is no stranger at all. We are afraid of being attacked. We are afraid of being afraid. . . .

The Hebrew Bible is perfectly clear on the point that one need not throw oneself open to the violent stranger in the night; that rather one may do literally anything against the one who comes to assault one's body. And it should be clear to all of us that there is nothing irreligious in defense of one's person, that there is nothing religious about being vulnerable, that there is nothing good about being weak and nothing evil about being protective.

We at Yale live in the inner city surrounded by slums and confusion, by poverty and crime, and there are no islands in this city where we live. The dream of the ivory tower and the safe refuge are gone. But the problem is not surrendering those illusions. They were never good illusions. They were always dangerous illusions. The problem is what one does, having given up the illusion. Is panic the proper reaction to danger? Is terror? Or planning? . . .

Some of us went to the administration a few years ago to speak about Yale's true task in this community, to talk about health care, to talk about helping schools and helping people, and we were told, "The University must keep a low profile." What is called low profile in New Haven is called in Washington "benign neglect." If you don't think about them, they won't be angry. They won't notice that they are poor and you are not so poor. They won't notice that their education is bad and yours is superb. They won't notice that they live crowded in slums and that you who think you are crowded live in expansion and safety.

But they noticed, and they came, and they come, looking, watching, and sometimes stealing and hurting. As if it were possible to live on the border of two worlds without contact. As if it were possible to lock out all those who are darker or poorer or different from us. The Bible also knows about that. The very same chapter that permits self-defense against aggression also says: "Wherever there is an orphan or a widow you must not take advantage of them. If you take advantage of them, they will cry to me and I will listen to them and my anger will burn against you and I will kill you with the sword and your wives will become widows and your children will become orphans." It is the law of the Scripture and also of the world that oppression brings retribution, that benign neglect brings bitterness and panic in its wake. . . .

We cannot be invulnerable surrounded by vulnerability. Our role is in the city and not away from it. Whatever that means for you, for me it means running for office in New Haven's Seventh Ward, which includes everything from Chapel Street to the Hill— all kinds of people. I, who had global ambitions, now find myself running for Democratic chairman of the Seventh Ward. It is not exactly what my mother had in mind for me. But it says to me that their world and my world are the same world, as they are the same ward, and if I cannot represent them I cannot be represented. So I must go to them and ask for their vote. . . .

The religious person is the one who wants what he believes and who risks for what he seeks—not needlessly, not foolishly, not vainly, not dramatically, but who is willing to go where there is some danger for what is valuable. And so I walk a few blocks to New Haven streets that I have never seen, to a neighborhood less familiar to me than Nairobi or Paris, and I knock on a door, and a black man opens it and looks at me suspiciously, and yet he is friendly, and he says: "Come in and tell me why I should vote for you."

Why should he, indeed?

[*Yale Alumni Magazine*, April 1976]

MONEY

I ONCE MADE the controversial statement that to Judaism nothing is more sacred than money. I was accused of rank materialism, confirming all the old canards about what Jews prize most highly. But I still believe I was right.

Of course, the point is not having money, or making it for that matter, but using it for the perfection of human beings, for relieving pain and suffering. I worry about how money is raised and spent in the two countries I care about most.

In the United States the rich have grown significantly richer and the poor significantly poorer in the last decade. Taxes are used for defense against an enemy that no longer exists, to pay back victims of the criminals in the Savings and Loan debacle, and for other such questionable purposes, but not sufficiently to educate our children or to provide health care for Americans the way many other governments do. . . . I don't like our expensive little wars in Grenada, Panama, or Iraq. I don't like how our country deals with our money.

Nor do I like it that Israel spends a million and a half dollars a year to protect Arik Sharon's house in the Arab quarter of the Old City of Jerusalem. There are lots of shekels for young Jewish colonizers to be bribed to move to the occupied West Bank, but not enough for Ethiopian or Russian immigrants to live decently, even in welfare hotels. That can't be the best use of Israeli (or American) funds.

A person or a nation can be judged by what he or she or it does with his or her or its resources. Generosity counts, prudence doesn't hurt. The great Hasidic master Nahman of Bratslav said we should worry about the needs of our own soul and of the other person's body; most of us do just the opposite, and that makes all the difference.

[KAM Isaiah Israel Bulletin, October 23, 1991]

PART FIVE

Teaching

EDUCATING

I AM what is laughingly called an educator, but I have plenty of reservations about school. I was delighted to see that some of our high school and junior high school kids were willing to cut school to come to our *Sukkot* services. I am delighted when kids cut school to go on peace walks, to attend teach-ins, to do any one of a hundred different things.

When we were kids back in the 1930s we cut school for lots of goofy reasons: Milton Berle at the Chicago Theater (he would call out, "How many from Senn? How many from Hyde Park?"), Frederick Stock at Orchestra Hall, warm June days at Montrose Beach, and all the Jewish holidays (the Conservative congregations were jammed, and the Reform kids sometimes came too). I think all these were (and are) more important than school.

We live in a suburban community that puts classes above learning, teams above sports, credits above maturation, and everything above religion. The high school has become a kind of sanctified prison where kids serve time; the only way it could be different would be if kids were willing to give it up for something better sometimes. One learns by reading not by sitting, by taking part not by serving time, by education not by school. The kids who grind the hardest, are most "conscientious" (which is to say, most hung up), know the least. They can't write, they can't think, they can't feel. While, mysteriously, those of us who went to Milton Berle and *Sukkot* services somehow learned what school was trying to teach too.

My critics will remind me that cutting school doesn't get a kid into college (that federal penitentiary of the mind). They might be wrong, but to be honest, they might be right too. I am no expert in getting people into Harvard, only into heaven. And for that *Sukkot* and Selma are more effective than Boredom 175. There is lots of learning in heaven, we are told, but not much school.

[Congregation Solel *Pathfinder*, November 3, 1965]

IF I AM remembered in a hundred years it probably won't be for my good looks or my several hundred more or less forgettable writings. It won't even be for heading the first American Jewish group for peace in the Middle East, or for a hundred small, safe actions for justice. Nor for having the privilege of being a rabbi in several congregations whose reputation will outlive by centuries that of any of their more famous rabbis. If I am remembered it will be for helping to found Reform Judaism's first summer camp institute.

It was in 1948. Gene Borowitz and I had been ordained for about three weeks when we began impetuously to create the first study camp for Jewish high school students. We didn't know exactly what we were doing, since no one had done it before us, but we did invent a daily schedule of prayer, study, singing, eating, and sports, which is pretty much the way it is still done in all the many UAHC camps across the country. We met in Lake-of-the-Woods, Michigan, and a hundred wonderful kids came from just about everywhere. One of them is now president of the largest synagogue in the Chicago area. Three are rabbis. Many more are leaders in the Jewish United Fund, academies, sisterhoods, and Jewish action groups. Several, to be sure, have converted to some other religion. At least one is dead.

Wherever something good is going on, you will discover alumni of Union Institute (in Oconomowoc, Wisconsin), the long-lived successor to our first, short-term experiment. Olin-Sang-Ruby Union Institute is a place where our young people learn to do Jewish. There is no real substitute for our camp, though it is also no substitute for a school, a youth group, or a synagogue. Everything we do in our own congregation is done by some people who learned what to do and how to do it during a summer at Oconomowoc. Your child desperately needs our camp to stretch her Jewish muscles and to grow in wisdom and in knowledge. Besides that, and perhaps most important of all, it is fun to be Jewish at camp.

Where would American music be without Interlochen, or American executives without Aspen? That's where we would be without OSRUI. Come on in, campers, the water's fine.

[KAM Isaiah Israel Bulletin, January 13, 1982]

DEAR KAY,

I write you a public and not a private letter for two reasons. One is that I can say things this way that were just too hard for me to say last Sunday. The other is that I am a rabbi and therefore I must respond not only to your magnificent challenge but to the needs of many others. This is true, even though I have been thinking all week only about you.

It is hard to be fifteen, isn't it? And yet, how we really envy you! It is hard to guess the breadth and splendor of the world, its tragedy and glory, without being able to fill its empty spaces with experience. And yet how pure you are! How unsullied your blind love is, and how strong your anger! I am ashamed that such innocence can never again be mine.

What was it you said? That you do not wish to be Confirmed because you cannot promise where your lifetime loyalties will lie. That the ethics and the law of Judaism seem to you somehow a betrayal of the divine goodness that is all you want. That we, your parents and your friends and your community, do not share enough of your vision or support your hope. That there is a burning passion for goodness in you which no mere religious institution can obtain!

You cannot guess how banal all your notions are. They have all been said before. All of them. The Prophets hated Jewish self-deception more than you do. The Hasidim also sought to strike right to the heart of goodness where God lives. The Reformers, like you, wanted to share the truth of brotherhood with everyone in the world.

But for us these are just notions, mere ideas. For us they are truths only remembered, or, what is the same thing, forgotten. For you they are still contemporary and, indeed, you've found them out yourself. How simple you are, Kay, how right!

I cannot argue you back to the highway on which the rest of us are going somewhere. I cannot claim you with slogans or recall you with love. I fear for the lonely choice you have made, and I regret that I have no words to hold you back. And yet I thank my God, who is not quite your God, perhaps because you are purer and more lost in dreams, that one like you is still possible.

You are embarking on a long road which I could never risk. You are leaving more of our world than you know. But in your pain and lonely trust we are all blessed. How remarkable that you could still create yourself among us all.

Go toward peace, Kay, for peace is not your present. Go whatever way you must. We shall love you even if you never can come home.

[Congregation Solel *Pathfinder*, May 2, 1961]

DEAR JON,

This is the first time I've ever Confirmed a son of my own; so if I'm a little nervous, forgive me. You've been pretty good about not riding your dad all year, and I'm truly grateful.

I would like to tell you everything I feel about your Confirmation, but I won't, or I can't. It combines pride, fear, hope, love, and joy. I do not know what you will make of yourself in the end as a Jew or as a man, but I cannot imagine not being proud of you.

You know that many of your coreligionists, your fellow Jews, were murdered for doing what you will do this *Shavuot*. You have spoken yourself of the agony of your brothers in the Soviet Union even now. So I cannot pretend that being a Jew is only fun and games; you wouldn't believe me.

You have felt *Shoah*, *Tisha B'av*, some kinds of polite anti-Semitism, many unspoken kinds of fear. But you have also seen Israel, Solel, *Pesach*, and, in your own ways, the God of Israel too. I do not think you are afraid to be a Jew.

Your world will be very different from mine. You have already seen more and learned more than I did when I was a dozen years older. You have been thrown into more scientific knowledge and more human failure, more know-how and less know-why, more triumph and more despair than any earlier time has ever witnessed. You yourself were born in the midst of a war and, unless your world is changed beyond recognition, you will die in a war. I do not envy you.

But I pray for you. I hope you will be brave enough to be yourself and humble enough to know you are not All. I hope you will be intelligent enough to accomplish all you can, and humble enough to know how little any of us ever accomplishes. I hope you will be strong enough to try to be a Jewish man, and humble enough to need to and to want to. I hope you will do better than I did—but not too much better.

Congratulations, and God bless you and all your classmates, now and in the years to come.

DAD

[Congregation Solel *Pathfinder*, May 31, 1967]

TEACHING THE BIBLE TODAY

IN 1927 Franz Rosenzweig wrote a letter to Jacob Rosenheim, leader of separatist Orthodox Judaism (*Agudat Yisrael*), in which he set forth his views of the Bible. Two years earlier he and his coworker, Martin Buber, had begun their translation of Scripture, and he was vigorously conscious that they were trying to do something unprecedented and of surpassing difficulty. He wanted to assure Rosenheim that, while his views had nothing in common with the neo-Orthodoxy of his time, they yet were "faithful" in every real sense of the word.

Buber and Rosenzweig constantly walked the "narrow ridge," accepting neither a liberalism that regarded the Bible as a document for human history of particular interest to Jews but revelatory in no way distinct from any other great literature, nor an Orthodoxy that made the Torah so utterly different that it became almost a sacred irrelevance. Thus Rosenzweig writes to Rosenheim that for him belief in the holiness of the Torah has nothing to do with the question of its origin, presumed or authentic. For the Bible to be sacred it need not have come to us in any special way. Rosenzweig believes in *Torah min Hashamayim* (Divinely revealed Torah) while suspending any question of *Torah l'Moshe miSinai* (Torah revealed at Sinai). In the final analysis, the two questions have nothing to do with each other; the crucial question is: What do we have? The secondary one is: How did we get it?

Franz Rosenzweig reads the Torah as we have it, as one great document, bracketing any question of how the canon came to be what it is. Not the "original" authors, inaccessible and mysterious as they must remain, but the redactor (the editor of last resort, whoever and whenever he was) is, for us, the mediator of the Word. Using biblical criticism's scientific terminology, Rosenzweig calls him "R," but that signifies not (only) Redactor but Rabbenu, our master Teacher. The Bible is finally one book, and translation or interpretations turn on reading it in its own powerful context. Fifty years later Brevard Childs of the Yale Divinity School, in his commentary on Exodus, has begun to use this technique for the postmodern Christian reader. He too sees the Bible precisely in its "canonical" form, behind which we often cannot penetrate and never need to go. Documentary notions of the Bible being composed of numerous separate texts are in great doubt now, but even in Rosenzweig's lifetime the work of Benno Jacob and Umberto Cassuto had begun to rock the Jewish scholarly world, at least, and render nugatory some of the nineteenth-century German Christian biblical scholar Julius Wellhausen's hypotheses on the origins of Hebrew faith. Still, Rosenzweig took no sides in the scholarly debates. He had another task: to recover the depth and power of the "Torah now in our hands," as Maimonides called it.

Accordingly the Bible must be read dialectically: written word against oral tradition; what we have against what Jews have understood it to mean during all the various centuries of our study of Scripture. Our Bible is indeed, as Jakob Petuchowski insists, the Bible of the Synagogue. We have no other Bible and we never did. The *p'shat* (straightforward meaning) always came freighted with interpretation. Eisegesis (reading one's own ideas into the text) is the inevitable other side of the gold coin of exegesis (interpretation out of the text itself) that some claim alone is genuine. The Jew reads his Bible as a Jew; he cannot and should not pretend that he is innocent of any prehistory. He does not come to it newborn but instructed and chastened by generations of earlier readers, commentators, and "learners" like himself. He will not permit the old Prophetic voices to be wholly swallowed up in later rabbinic modalities, but neither can he falsely pretend that biblical voices have no echo, no ambiance, no horizon.

Scholarship, *Wissenschaft*, is not the enemy of commitment. Even Leopold von Ranke, the first, most critical of historians, was a believer. On the contrary, we cannot empathize with our biblical predecessors until and unless we also meet them faithfully. God as well as history speaks through a learning that knows its own limits and shares those insights that only commitment can lend to learning. We do not wish to go back to any prescientific way of looking at biblical texts. We want, rather, to be beyond *Wissenschaft*, to sublate *Wissenschaft* so that we may know more than any formal knowledge teaches. We have no quarrel with the scientific study of Judaism as long as it knows that Judaism is much more than what it studies. We have no quarrel with traditional believers as long as they do not identify their own beliefs with the history of Israel's faith.

The Bible, of course, is a book. When we read it, as we must, like any other book, we learn that it is also strangely unlike any other book. The word of man is also precisely the Word of God, and only it is. As Buber later wrote in his *Eclipse of God*, "Human substance is melted by the spiritual fire which visits it, and there now breaks forth from it a word, a statement which is human in its meaning and form, human conception and human speech, and yet witnesses to Him Who stimulated it and to His will. We are revealed to ourselves, and cannot express it otherwise than as something revealed."

A traditional Jew can only confront the Bible honestly by foregoing his own preconceptions, by nakedly opening himself to the wholly unexpected. He must not force Scripture to affirm what he already holds, merely to authenticate his present conviction. He must not be guilty of pious anachronism or dogmatic presupposition. A liberal Jew, any modern, critical person, must, however, forgo his doubts, suspend his disbeliefs and hold himself open to the infinitely self-renewing power of the word. Neither task is easy. Both are just barely possible.

Teaching Bible to university students (and to other adults) is both necessary and possible. Necessary because they do not know the book, possible because it can be learned. At Yale the American

Studies Department found that their students' knowledge of Scripture was inadequate for the study of American literature, and instituted remedial sections to prepare students to approach their own literary history, one that consistently refers to biblical themes. The Department of Religious Studies, confronted with enormous new enrollments in their courses on the Bible, discovered that most of the students (like many in Yale Divinity School as well) simply had never read most books of the Bible and were registered to do what they might have done long before in religious schools but somehow never did. Jewish students, of all varieties and denominations, betray sketchy acquaintance with biblical texts, even if they happen to know somewhat more about Jewish holidays and Israeli history, or even if they can make out the Hebrew language. Some have heard the Torah read (not, usually, carefully translated, and almost never interpreted and discussed) during the Sabbath service, but they have rarely even turned the pages of most of the rest of the *Tanach*. Hence a study of Scripture is necessary.

It is also possible. Unlike the vast Talmudic literature, for example, it is of manageable length. A good semester course can cover a major book (like Deuteronomy) or a small one (Song of Songs) with additional comparative materials of many kinds. For those who cannot read Hebrew there are now excellent English translations as well as important ones in other modern languages. A weekly informal course can complete the two Books of Samuel in a year or the Five Books of Moses in about three. Everyone senses that biblical material is absolutely basic; they soon learn it is also striking in its concern with living issues. It is as available in some respects to the neophyte as to the Talmudist, to the student of comparative literature as to the theologian. It is ancient and elusive and profound, but it is also straightforward and quintessential. No text could possibly be more than that.

The real question is not whether but *how* to teach the Bible to modern university students and to other adults today. First of all, I believe, we must teach them *p'shat* (essential meaning) and not *d'rash* (interpretation). *P'shat* does not quite mean the plain sense or simple meaning of the text, as several recent studies have proved. It is a far more flexible and rich methodology than that. Still, there is a difference between reading what is there and using what is there for what is not. There is an irremovable distinction between going out to meet the Bible (to be sure, with all we have to bring) and forcing the text into our own, necessarily narrower categories. Teaching Bible means disclosure, confrontation, even careful extrapolation; it should not mean sermonics, manipulation, or historicism. However much we want to use the text to prove something (even something true), the text must remain more sacred than anything we ever could prove. The simple meaning of Scripture is, of course, not so simple, but it is far more precise and instructive than any interpretation, even and especially our own.

The preferred method of learning is discussion and not lecture. When I work over Jewish texts with students in an open discussion, I feel myself back not only at the University of Chicago Great Books seminars where, sixteen years old, I painfully worked through the *Republic* and *Paradise Lost* with gifted teachers who could both listen and respond, but also back in a most traditional *Bet Midrash* where any Jewish scholar proved his learning not by displaying it in a fine discourse but by leading his students carefully into the intricacies and depths of the sacred word. Jewish learning is not hearing someone talk about a book; it is studying a book under expert teachers who are also themselves "students of the wise." Rabbi Solomon Goldman once said to me that Jews do not read books, they only study them. If a book is not worth studying, he said, it is not even worth perusing. But study classically means study *b'havruta* (with a learning partner, aloud), in a community, with a leader. The words may be read alone or together, but meanings can be disclosed only to a community of learners.

The leader's role is, therefore, delicate. He or she cannot and should not pretend to know less than he does, though, of course, not more either. He is *primus inter pares* (first among equals), not master of all he surveys. He or she must, as Maimonides tells us in *Hilchot Talmud Torah*, sit equally with his students and not above them, perhaps preferably in a circle of chairs. He may neither dominate nor absent himself; he must listen just as carefully as he speaks. He must steer the discussion's tone between levity and overseriousness. The Bible is important, but our own views are somewhat less than final.

It also follows that group size is crucial. Three people are too few, fifty too many. Within those limits, various numbers are possible. While I prefer a group of fifteen (that is the number set for Yale College seminars by the administration), I have found that five or thirty are both feasible. The room must be big enough to hold the participants but not too big so that it intimidates them. The same could be said for the teacher. His or her task is not self-presentation nor pontificating. It is precisely *explication de texte*. The group teaches each other, and the teacher is the teacher of them all who is taught by them all. Ideally the student remembers less about the teacher than about the text; a good teacher is translucent to what he is teaching, and this is never more true than with biblical material. Many years ago a fine teacher introduced me to the Book of Exodus. I remember much about him, more about what he said about the book, but most about the book itself; I have often merged the teacher into the book.

The leader is present more to raise questions than to provide answers. The text is, itself, a kind of answer, though one that, like all profound answers, raises ever new questions. The Bible is a mystery to be confronted, not a problem to be solved. Over and over again, in teaching Bible commentary, my teacher, Abraham Joshua Heschel, would ask: "What is Rashi's problem?" What is the question that gives rise to the interpreter's "answer," and what questions are raised by that answer itself? Questions should proceed from the relatively minor to the most general and profound. We might begin the study of the Flood with a trivial question about why the raven preceded the dove, since it did not in the earlier comparative Near Eastern material. Then, or another time, we might think about the deeper problem of a good person in a bad generation. Finally we must sometime talk about the meaning of the world-covenant and the promise of unending human history.

In thinking about the Creation story, we might begin with the special formulation of the creation of mankind which differs subtly from those that frame the earlier of God's creations. God does not (cannot?) produce a person, like a world, by fiat. Perhaps the fact that God cannot bring himself to call human creation "good" (although the sixth day as a whole is "very good") shows a certain ambivalence about His final creature. He would have good reason for that. Nehama Leibowitz is often brilliant at raising small questions that open out to vast concerns. My only objection to her method is that it leaves the questions only partly open, and "solves" problems that are too mysterious for solution.

Questions that are posed should not be left vague or completely open-ended, but they must not be seen as gimmicks or entering wedges for a preconceived solution. The truth is that we do not know the truth: the Bible asks unanswerable questions, and we must not claim more than to have posed them carefully and looked hard for explanations. The end of each session should not leave the class with a sense of closure, however much they might enjoy the sense of having solved a venerable riddle. Their mood should rather be one of being driven back to the text to look again at what seemed at first to be an answer but turned out to be a deeper and harder question. It is good for us Jews to have to read the Five Books over and over again, year after year. The mere act of repetition says that the meanings elude us as we go out to grasp them. A class should reflect something of that infinite longing which is beyond both failure and success.

The kinds of questions posed should not, in most settings, be only scientific or aesthetic. It is a help to know source criticism, which divides the text into distinct documents and strata, if only to discover that it too is no answer but a series of insoluble puzzles; still, criticism is not our final task. Nor are we to see the beauties of the Bible as literature unless, as seems to me increasingly the case, literature itself is swallowed up in a much larger category. If I am forced to give a name to the kind of questions I think are posed by Scripture, it would have to be "existential," but that word too says considerably less than I mean.

The Bible is not only a book about what happened. It is also about what happens; not only what was, but what we are; not only about ancestors but also, since what happened to them is "a sign" to us, about ourselves. The themes of family, law, power, lust, faith and faithlessness, nationalism and war, suffering and death are the great themes not only of world literature but of human life. Thus our questions must not be of the kind: In Scripture, who is said to have lived the longest life? Rather: How can a holy land be promised and how rightfully taken by force? No one is more subtle in this kind of ethical-personal query than the French savant Emmanuel Levinas, who goes to the heart of Scripture and rabbinic texts not with the equipment and concerns of the specialist but with a philosopher's questioning passion and a Jew's conviction that there is more in the Bible than is dreamt of in any person's philosophy. The Bible is not so much a book as a world, and our study of it must be not the study of literary forms only, but of life. Technical questions can often lead beyond themselves: our task is not to find out only what is said but also what is meant. We are not critics of the Bible but its co-conspirators. . . .

I am, we are, the skein out of which Scripture is continually woven. I do not read Wellhausen or Cassuto to find out where they are wrong, not even where they are "right," but to read the Bible over their shoulders with my own eyes. It is a great accomplishment to be a biblical scholar, a still greater one to be the addressee of the biblical message. And that each of us can be.

Our method of study must be dialectical, not apodictic. The text is always, as Heschel says about all God-statements, an understatement. It is always more than we say it is, never less. So we must use the Socratic method more honorably than Plato did, not to prove what we already really know but to sharpen our sensibilities in order to know and feel more. The text eludes our pursuit, so we must redouble our pace. It is beyond our reach, so we reach ever higher. We can never specify it in some final fashion, only point to it and use it to point to where it points. Everyone can read the Bible except one who thinks he already has.

It is very useful to use the Bible to interpret itself. There are in it apparent contradictions. I believe there are also real contradictions. Good! Use the contradictions dialectically: what is the truth in each? how does one limit or refute the other? why are both necessary? Some truth, not the least important, can only be stated paradoxically; much can only be understood by a method of query and response and query. Solutions stifle, but deep questions drive inevitably deeper into our souls. A good Bible class is very confusing, though not obfuscating. A good teacher teaches the Bible's wisdom and his or her own ignorance.

The class will therefore be filled with controversy. It will not conform. There will be no consensus. Each view of each student, especially the teacher-student, will be resolutely attacked. Nothing will be admitted without debate. We must each be humble enough to see our own pet ideas demolished, and proud enough to war against other people's interpretations. The class will sound more like a bazaar or a courtroom than like a Quaker meeting. Class members will be on their toes, not on their best behavior, because we honor Scripture best by taking it seriously enough to argue about it, not for the sake of argument but for the sake of Scripture. Something important is at stake. We are not debating fine points of scholarship, except as those show us that we are the subject of our own debate. The adversary proceeding is crucial to our innocence or guilt, as in a courtroom. It is essential to our method that anyone may speak and no one may be ignored. But no view is final, and no agreement is sought. Each debate ends in a Talmudic *teiku* (unresolved question): inconclusive, unfinished, ongoing.

Tradition is a more valuable tool than mere innovativeness. A good word from an old interpreter often helps us more than an ingenious speculation by our contemporary. No interpretation or interpreter is privileged, not Rashi, not Buber, not the teacher of our class. We are all in it together, the dead as well as the living, the medieval as well as the postmodern. Times rejoin each other. Nothing seems more old-fashioned than the day before yesterday. Nothing is more radical than naked tradition. No scholar but has his day, no idea exists whose time will never come around. We are not in the business of thinking up a new thought, certainly not of deconstructing the old one, so much as in discovering our past, imagining the present, and remembering what many before us have already forgotten.

Apologetics has its place, but not in the kind of biblical study here envisioned. Our present task is not to defend the Bible against its detractors ("primitive, bloody, tasteless") or its people against their enemies ("Why did Abraham lie, Moses kill, the Israelites commit genocide, the Prophets exaggerate, Ezra legislate ethnocentrism?"). We must assume that the Bible can withstand relentless criticism. It does not need any of our ineffectual apologies. We owe the text honesty, which means confronting jarring as well as comfortable passages. I have personally found far more significance in passages that offend me than in those that soothe, though the latter also have their time and place.

The Bible is not the Boy Scout Manual. It is not above the fray; it *is* the fray. It does not condescend to our moral dilemmas; it makes them dramatically vivid and often heartbreaking. Its God is not Olympian and will not conform to our image of Him. Its Torah does not mandate the ethics of John Stuart Mill or John Rawls. Its central characters are always ambivalent and sometimes doomed. Its holiness is a holiness of expectation, not one of accomplished fact. We should not try to smooth out its wrinkles nor hide its warts. We need not judge it in order for it to judge us.

A Bible class should not be manipulated but opened wide up. Data must be fully and precisely put. It is important how many times and where a specific Hebrew word is used. It is important what is said and left unsaid, who is described by whom, how the Commandments in Exodus differ from those in Deuteronomy. Biblical material is as precise as a sonnet, more careful than a mathematical formula. Accuracy in interpretation is essential. We must be attentive to detail if we are to encompass signification. The Bible is not a book for speed readers. Revelation cannot be skimmed. Erich Auerbach, the Holocaust refugee author of *Mimesis*, has taught us that, unlike a much more explicit Greek literature, the Hebrew writer alludes and refers, speaks in silence, subtly. No one can teach the *Tanach* who does not believe God is in the details, especially in the most boring ones.

We teach carefully but never completely. We teach parts of the Book, never all of it. We grasp some of its meaning, never the whole of it. What we are currently studying is not all there is; things may seem lopsided if we forget there is more—and different—wisdom elsewhere in the Book. We need not assume previous knowledge to begin to teach the Scripture, but we must emphasize that learning some of it may be not only incomplete but also misleading. A little revelation is a very dangerous thing.

"Turn it and turn it, for everything is in it" (*Pirkei Avot*). Everything! More than we expect. More than we want. More than we can understand. More than we can teach. More than appears on the surface. More than moves in the depths. More, perhaps, than anything human beings have ever, unaided, themselves produced.

[In *Go and Study: Essays in Honor of Alfred Jospe*
(B'nai B'rith Hillel Foundations, 1980)]

THE UNIVERSITY

JEWISH EXPERIENCE is vividly present at Yale. I mean the *Sukkah* on the Old Campus, the eating club where some fifty students eat kosher food twice a day, the Brooklyn accents and the weekly contacts with Israel, the old-new faces and the grand old concerns. I mean the fifty or sixty people who study the biblical portion of the week with me, and the many others who learn Hebrew or Yiddish or Hasidism in our Hillel classes each week.

I mean the dozens of religious studies majors who are led through the intricacies of our tradition by master scholars who are still more rabbinical than they would desire or admit. I mean the sheer percentage of Jewish admissions—which looks like one-third—in what was once the bastion of quota-protected anti-Semitism, or at least was thought to be by most American Jews who thought about Yale at all.

Something has profoundly changed—something affirmative, something new, something that has parallels in all the great American universities but scarcely anywhere with a more flagrant pride. Jews are at Yale, and many of them are very Jewish Jews.

But this, of course, is not the whole story. Half the kids who come to see me are inquiring about a prospective marriage to a non-Jew and are more or less surprised that I cannot endorse their nuptial plans. For all the hundreds of people studying Judaism or praying in one of our three Sabbath services each week, far more couldn't care less. Though Yom Kippur fills the Law School auditorium beyond its legal capacity, most Jews at Yale pass their four years untouched by any smidgen of Judaism and don't miss it at all. While many non-Jewish kids are constantly talking about becoming

Jews, Jewish students are still experimenting with some Eastern faith or home-brewed cult, though fewer, I think, than a few years ago, largely because fewer are experimenting with anything at all.

The Jewish student at Yale seems, on balance, to be balanced and secure of place. Why then does he also seem so often to be gloomy and repressed? Why does one see so little touching or kissing or laughing? So little political or even personal concern for the cheated of the world? Why are the kosher meals filled with talk about exams and papers, the Sabbath *oneg* (party) so grim, or at least so refined? Why was even *Simhat Torah*, when by traditional demand we drink and dance with the scrolls, why was even that day so decorous and serene? Is this phenomenon simply the wholesale incorporation of the Wasp ethos, a typically Jewish attempt to become more *goyish* than the gentiles in whose midst we live?

But no one could be more *goyish* than a Protestant at Yale: the Yale style of speaking but avoiding, of living side by side without living together, the ineffable cool—all these constitute the mythic hallmark of the Wasp ascendant. Nor is it all negative. The Yale student is invariably polite, intelligent, considerate, and, like the gentleman he is, will not inflict pain by consciously doing something cruel. But student and faculty are hard to meet, hard to find on the street even, hard to pin down or pick up, hard to hate, hard to love.

Everyone at Yale, and Jews no less than most, everyone is very busy. Busy reading, busy in labs, busy keeping a fellowship grant or publishing another book, busy doing better than others or at least not less well, busy surviving the intellectual obstacle course. I see casualties every day in my office, and I would guess a lot of people quietly hurt at Yale. The faculty seems to the students by and large capable and fair, but also remote and ultimately, crucially inaccessible. . . .

The American Jewish community has not supported the Hillel program at Yale (or most anywhere) very generously. Where a Protestant community of almost equal size has eight or ten chaplains, I am the only rabbi at Yale. Where the smaller Catholic congregation has a superb chapel and many fine meeting facilities, I work out of a basement room in the Yale Station post office, and out of a large old house which was quickly decaying until my wife and I moved in, and which remains heavily mortgaged to the University.

No one can believe that we do not mail letters to our students because we cannot afford the postage, but that happens to be true. No one believes that our annual budget is only fifteen dollars per student, but even that is probably an exaggeration. The fabled Jewish generosity extends to many needs in many parts of the world, but by the time the money gets to Yale it looks niggardly indeed. And so our students feel neglected or abandoned by a Jewish community which, they know, can afford million-dollar synagogues and elaborate overseas programs but doesn't seem to think their needs are crucial for the future of American Judaism.

My life has been complicated and enriched by the presence of many exciting colleagues and especially by William Sloane Coffin, Jr., a man more considerable by far than his legend. Many Jewish students, many students with many shades of opinion, look to Coffin for what they do not easily find elsewhere: an example. It is not only his indelible preaching (unlike anything I have heard since I was ten years old and listened enraptured to Stephen Wise), his warm charisma, his guts. What makes Coffin so important to so many students is that *Yale has not changed him*. It has instructed him, given him a bully pulpit, sometimes lionized him, sometimes harassed him, but has never succeeded in making him someone else. It is fear of being changed against one's will that seems to me the hardest burden of Yale. Coffin is an example for those who struggle against the tide.

Not everyone, of course, is changed, undone, betrayed by self or school. A student about to finish his doctoral program came to tell me he had painfully saved several hundred dollars against any emergency while he was in school. Now that he was about to finish, he did not need the bank account any longer. Would I recommend a small, struggling philanthropy to which he could give the cash? He wanted to thank God in that traditional way for permitting him to finish Yale. Suppressing the desire to name Yale Hillel his beneficiary, I steered him to a fund for aged rabbis. And thanked God myself, at least for now, that my lot has been cast. . . .

[*Yale Alumni Magazine*, November 1973]

"FIND A LIFEBOAT": THE INSECURITY OF INTELLECTUAL LIFE TODAY

I HAVE a stronger and stronger sense that, in the more than forty years since I was an undergraduate here at the University of Chicago, something has gone wrong.

A few examples:

My friends in the civil rights movement, my black friends who were isolated embattled radicals in the early sixties, are now the establishment in many places. For example, in Washington, D.C., the mayor, the city council, the power structure are exactly the same people who twenty-five years ago were in the civil rights movement. And nothing is better in Washington than it was. That's very frightening, I think. That everything we did, which I would not undo, and of which I remain proud, was—in a technical sense—inconsequential.

Of course, you can point to victories of voting, and so on; maybe a little less discrimination in housing, but I have the feeling—perhaps you do too—that to grow up in the Taylor Homes today is as bad as anything ever was for a black person in Chicago. With a black mayor whom I will again vote for, and with all the successes we have had, something didn't work. The question is whether it couldn't work, or it could have worked but we didn't do it right, or what?

There was also in the intellectual area a certain confidence which is gone. I remember when I was taught the "new biblical the-

128

ology," it struck me—and it still does by the way—as revolutionary in importance that Karl Barth, on the one hand, and Martin Buber, on the other, and Von Rad were consolidating a truth that nobody would ever be able to deny. People could build on it, people could refine it. In an introduction to a book, I wrote: "We are all disciples of Buber, and we will be for a thousand years." That confidence in the giants—and they were giants—Niebuhr and Tillich I heard at this university, and Hannah Arendt—the work of those giants has collapsed. There is not a stone left upon another stone.

In my mind they haven't fallen. In what I hold to be self-evident, my teachers still live. But I can't convince anybody of that. There is nobody who believes with the confidence that I did, and to some extent still do, because the evidence is unsatisfactory. . . .

The man I admired most in the civil rights movement in Washington, Ivanhoe Donaldson, a brilliant young black, is in jail for embezzlement. Of course, every movement has its crooks. Zionism had its crooks. The civil rights movement had its crooks. The peace movement had its crooks. And the University has its crooks. But it seems to me rather symbolic that "the best and the brightest" didn't just make mistakes but were mistaken. That's the question I want to put to you.

I was never an expert in science, but I imagined that science was in some sense true and important, and powerful. Now my friends in nuclear physics or MB&B (molecular biology & biochemistry) talk like mystifiers. Their theology is more exorbitant than mine. And the last thing in the world they talk about is truth. They have no pretense. They have models and they have paradigms and they have quarks and they have black holes, but they don't have anything that's true, because it turns out that science is not about truth. Maybe it's about falsification, but it isn't about truth. It's about a certain kind of aesthetic enterprise. While I find that refreshing, it's also disconcerting.

Social science is in a shambles. How would you like your child to grow up to be an economist? God! Better the kid should be a Wall Street lawyer, right? A rabbi, anything but an economist! They cannot agree on anything. And where they do, under the influence particularly of this University, they are certainly mistaken, and probably dangerous. Social science shrinks into trivialities. I think of the ambition of the social scientists of this University in the forties, the wide-ranging sociology which did, in fact, mark an epoch in the history of sociology. You know the work they did studying the city, and so on. Who does that anymore? Where do you find anyone who reads that anymore?

Others of us in the humanities read the Great Books, not because they were beautiful but because they were true, because if we read Shakespeare and Goethe and Homer and the Bible they would teach us essential, personal truths. Does anybody read that way anymore? Does anybody think that by reading a book—any book—you change your life? If I understand deconstruction at all, it is simply the demythologizing of precisely that—there is no book, there is no text. All it is is an opportunity for projection, but not for transformation. The notion that a great book—that there *is* a great book, a canon—is itself ludicrous. Even if there were a great book that you could read and become a great person—which is what our ambition was—that ambition would be regarded as mythical, extravagant, and probably insane.

Psychoanalysis. My friends and I were of the conviction that Freud was onto a very profound truth which would, on the one hand, change the nature of human nature and, on the other hand, produce successful persons who had discovered themselves in psychoanalytic therapy. Who believes that anymore? Certainly not the psychoanalysts. Some of the patients still believe it, but the analysts certainly don't. I was invited to speak this year—the first rabbi ever—to the American Psychiatric Association, whose members were nonpsychoanalysts. But the Psychoanalytic Association was meeting simultaneously, or just before. They attended the same meetings, although they do largely very different things. The agenda is now set by the nonpsychoanalytic psychiatrist, even for psychoanalysts: the agenda of drugs, behavioral modification, community therapy, deinstitutionalization. The psychoanalysts, in their own little group, don't know what to say to each other anymore. They are now—for the first time, I believe—jumping into the much larger group of psychiatrists who know what they're doing, because what they're doing is plumbing. This notion of an elite, sensitive awareness of ambiguity, of repression, of the Freudian categories, is lost forever. Psychoanalysis is no longer conceived of as a way of truth but as a patient's sacrificial surrender of illusions. It is not a way toward something great but a descent from a high mountain perpetually shrouded in cloud.

Literature. I mentioned the deconstructionist movement. Having spent eight and a half years at Yale, much of it with Harold Bloom and Geoffrey Hartman, I learned from them that literature is about criticism. In other words, the great enterprise of reading means to take in each other's washing, and that's all. It becomes a finicky, doctrinaire, highly effete cult of ingenuity. And that supplants what some of us believed we would have in the reading of great books.

Philosophy. I suppose that when I started studying philosophy, it was the end of an era; what came afterward was analytic philosophy, which itself has now dissipated or fragmented into a thousand pieces. But I did study Wittgenstein, who still seems to me a classically important philosopher, and who said, "The purpose of philosophy is to teach you to pass from a piece of disguised nonsense to something that is patent nonsense." Where do you go from there? He was certainly the greatest philosopher of the twentieth century. The purpose of philosophy is to unmask the pretense of nonsense, which leaves it nonsensical, except that you know it. And that's the advantage.

Okay, religion. I would say that the time in which I grew up, religiously, was a time in which neo-Orthodoxy in all of the great traditions was very powerful. It was the time of Barth, Tillich, and Niebuhr, of Buber and Rosenzweig. They had just died or were still alive. Even in the Catholic church I studied Gilson, Maritain— names that I guess are hardly known anymore—and we thought we had achieved, or were in the process of achieving, a postliberal revolution. We were not fundamentalists; we were not literalists. But we were in touch with a profound revision of the liberal tradition, which revision would return us to classical sources and the classical modality. And it did.

Now you look at the new *Encyclopedia of Religion*, which came out of this University this month, and see where religion is currently. I don't want to exaggerate, but it seems a kind of minor aspect of anthropology. In some ways it is more ecumenical: not just Christianity, but now Judaism, Islam, Buddhism, and the Hindu traditions, the native American traditions, and the primitive traditions are very much in evidence as they were not for many years. There are important articles on Kabbalah and peyote cults and Australia, and almost nothing about the Bible, almost nothing about theology. Because that's not where it's at anymore. The neo-Orthodox tradition fell apart, if that's the word to use. When the great article by Krister Stendhal in *The Interpreter's Bible* was revised in the supplement by James Barr, he said, "Nothing will supplant Stendahl."

Neo-Orthodoxy supplanted liberalism. Liberalism supplanted Orthodoxy. After neo-Orthodoxy comes nothing. Nothing unitary, nothing convincing, nothing powerful—anthropology, a little about this and a little about that. It's very learned; I don't mean to disparage that. But the center of gravity in the Divinity School right now is either Wendy O'Flaherty's brilliant excurses into another world, or David Tracy's dismantling of the Christian tradition. That follows a generation of reconstruction, which follows a generation of liberalism, which itself had a kind of gospel, a very powerful gospel. Shirley Jackson Case, Henry Nelson Weiman are names that none of you would know. But Henry Nelson Weiman (also my teacher) believed in something. Now it is not about believing in something; it is about unmasking something. It is about dreams, lies, and other truths, to use Wendy O'Flaherty's categories. It's about unconscious process, not the making conscious of unconscious process but the entering into it, which is an abandonment of the possibility of truth.

Even a plain acquisitiveness doesn't seem to have its kick anymore. That's a change. If I'm right, it's a different kind of change from the changes of the past. It's a change so traumatic that one is glad not to have to live into the twenty-first century because one cannot imagine a consequence. Look at the presidents we've had in your lifetime, a series of impossible presidents, one after the other. How did that happen?

I won't say that in my childhood there were great presidents. Calvin Coolidge was president when I was born—not exactly a great light. We had our nonentities. But Roosevelt was not a nonentity. He may have been venal but not a nonentity. Wilson was certainly not a nonentity.

And now look at the Supreme Court. It's not just that in my judgment Rehnquist is wrong or that Sandra Day O'Connor is mistaken. It's that they are inconsequential. They literally don't know what they're doing anymore. Some of the great conservatives whom I disagree with and who may have held us back nevertheless knew what they stood for. And the liberals. Holmes, Brandeis, Cardozo certainly knew where they were. Can you say where Sandra Day O'Connor is? There's no one there, no standpoint on which she rests. The incoherence of the decisions is more frightening than the decisions.

That a court may be mistaken is one thing. We may all be mistaken. But you can't tell if they're mistaken. You don't know what they said about church and state. You don't know what they said about abortion, or why they said it. That's different from anything in the past. And I think decisive of the future.

I consider this a kind of vertigo. It seems to me that students are now tied into their technical work to avoid the dizziness of thinking about the world. I too am guilty of that. I also wrote for the *Encyclopedia of Religion*. That, one can do. You study the sources, you write them out, and you don't think about what it means, just what it says. That's very comfortable. It's what you do instead of wrestling with ideologies and philosophies.

Students are very competent, but the competence is in service of incompetence, of *non compos mentis* (mental nonfunctioning). The competence is in service of God knows what. You will revise the tables of the elements, but everybody knows they don't represent what I was taught they represent. Probably they represent construction of reality, not the discovery of truth.

I have no solution to all of this, but this is what I have to say about it. A paradox of learning is that one cannot begin nowhere but only somewhere. If God is reduced to my idea of God, truth to methodology, or compassion to critical thinking, then even critical thinking is impossible. And my idea of truth or God will be simply puerile.

Liberation from dogma occurs only when and if one accepts something that cannot be proved and uses it against what seems easy to prove but isn't so. A university can learn and teach only if it struggles for a certainty, just as a person can only sharpen her mind against the whetstone of ultimately unassimilable truth. Max Horkheimer says, "When an active individual of sound common sense perceives the sordid state of the world, desire to change it becomes the guiding principle by which he organizes given facts and shapes them into a theory. The methods and categories as well as the transformation of the theory can be understood only in connection with his taking of sides. This, in turn, discloses both his sound common sense and the character of the world."

Freedom is therefore, I believe, a term of art which has only a dialectical signification. One is only free under the yoke, as we put it, of the Commandments, the yoke that Jesus said was light. Only by commitment to the One who is not I, or we, and certainly not IT, is it possible to educe, to stand out, in some truthful way. It is only by entering emphatically some humanizing theological, philosophical system which we did not create, which preceded us and which will live after us, that we can hope to survive into eternity.

This is Emerson: "Devotion may easily be greater than the wretched pride which is guarding our own skirts. Be another: not thyself but a Platonist; not a soul but a Christian; not a naturalist but a Cartesian; not a poet but a Shakespeare." A recent *New York Times* piece was headed, "Where is Emerson When We Need Him Most?"

We need a community of struggle. No one can do this alone. We need a canon that we can criticize but not deconstruct, understand but not recreate. One that we can subserve without subservience. We need a heteronomous place to be free, an other by which we become an "I," a "thou"; and perhaps a God to worship.

Rabbi Nehunia, in the Chapters of the Fathers, says, "The person who accepts the yoke of Torah removes the yoke of government and conformity." If we come to study naked and uninstructed, we fall into utter dilemma. We suffer vertigo, disorientation. But if we come disciplined, convoked, not only are we safe from some outward fascist government but we may make our little world a less despairing place. We may be empowered to act humanely in human time, in life which is also a school.

Somebody said tonight this school is a strange mixture of arrogance and bottomless insecurity. It's a pretty good description of the intellectual life these days. Too much arrogance and too much insecurity. My judgment is not that the insecurity comes from the arrogance, but that the arrogance comes from the insecurity. To be secure means to enter a world that exists and cannot be withdrawn. Rav Kuk, first chief rabbi in Palestine, before it became Israel, said we must renew the old and sanctify the new. That means, I think, that the neo-Orthodox was not false; it was incomplete. It is to recover our religious past in as complete and authentic form as we can, without rendering it idolatrously overdetermined. It is to go back in order to go forward. It is to stand within the tradition in order to emerge as a self from that tradition. It is to prepare for a century that has little hope and no faith at all. Maybe we are in the first century, a metaphor that I love. Hiding in the catacombs. Writing the Mishnah. Witnessing the signs, the first signs perhaps, of the decline and fall of the Roman Empire. Or maybe we are a thousand years later, preparing a renaissance that none can foresee. In any case, we are at the end of the twentieth century. Some of you will be leaders in the twenty-first century. The wreckage is all around you. Find a lifeboat. And press on.

> [Excerpts from a speech delivered at the University of Chicago in 1986 as part of the Episcopal Chaplaincy's Last lecture series, later printed in *Religion and Intellectual Life*, Winter 1988]

PART SIX

Israel and the Middle East

PURSUING PEACE

THE UN APPEARANCE of Yasir Arafat, speaking to the General Assembly in 1974, did nothing to bring peace closer to the Middle East. His bombastic rhetoric, his gun-toting militance, and his generally unimpressive statesmanship were deeply unfortunate. That his reckless speech seems designed principally to protect his flank against leftist attack on Fatah, his faction of the PLO, makes it hardly more attractive. Nor was Israeli Ambassador Tekoah's response very useful either. He spent much of his precious time trying to prove that Palestine equals Jordan, an equation disproved by the murder of some three thousand Palestinians in one single month, "Black September" 1970, if by nothing else.

Still, Israel and the PLO will have to find some way of talking to each other, as writers like Boaz and Yovel have been saying in *Ha'aretz*, the leading Israeli daily, week after week. The two have common enemies like Palestinian hard-liner George Habash, King Hussein, and atomic holocaust. They have common needs since they represent contiguous, interpenetrating constituencies which suffer parallel discrimination. Does the PLO really represent the Palestinians? Imperfectly, of course, and incompletely at best, since no elections have been permitted on the West Bank or Gaza. But better, surely, than that Bantustan (artificial "homeland" under Apartheid) which some right-wing Israelis project as an acceptable alternative to King Hussein, after he failed utterly in his attempt to recover a land and people whose allegiance was never his in the first place. We may be sure that natural enemies of the PLO, like the Saudis and Sadat, would never have given them recognition if they did not believe that any alternative would be more bloody and more revolutionary yet. The PLO is not exactly the government-in-exile it pretends to be, but it is the one address to which Israel can and finally must send its proposals for the future. For years the government of Israel has said it would talk to anyone, anytime and anywhere. The persons are the PLO (and other Palestinians, but not the latter alone), the time is now. And the place could still be the UN which, for all its political partiality, is still mankind's indispensable forum.

But the PLO will have to make concessions to our side if it hopes for anything more welcome than our unyielding hostility. I believe we can support what is clearly their present goal: a second Arab state between Jerusalem and Amman, even if the Israeli government has long seen that as permanently unacceptable, as though a single superstate on both sides of the Jordan would somehow be inevitably more peaceable. We can support the goal of an independent Palestine if and when it serves Jewish interests in addition to the overriding common need for peace. Nor does the PLO necessarily have to renounce its long-held dream of a secular, "democratic" state embracing both populations. What it *must* renounce is the use of force in achieving that goal. Lots of other countries wish other countries would fold up (the United States and Cuba; the two Vietnams, Koreas, Germanys). What each may not do without just retaliation is attempt by violence to destroy the integrity of the other government, and that Israel must require of the PLO.

In addition, the principle of symmetry requires that whatever one country demands it must permit for the other: secure borders, treaties of friendship, no foreign garrisons, freedom of thought and action for its minorities, full religious freedom, no support for terrorist incursions of the other nation. There is a strong reason to believe both that the Palestinians would profit from agreement on such terms and that Israel would surrender only territory that the international community (and its own official policy) defines as someone else's in any case.

A symbol of détente could facilitate a face-to-face meeting between the two antagonists who talked only to each other's empty chairs at the UN. I suggest that if the PLO could achieve the release of some Jews presently incarcerated in Arab jails, and the Israeli government could surrender some Palestinians under "administrative detention," that would be a sign of goodwill. It would also accomplish the distinct achievement of relieving some Jewish and Palestinian suffering. Many more projects might emerge from true (or even something less than "true") meeting between the two sides. There are, of course, dangers in any such confrontation: dangers of hypocrisy, dangers of cooptation, dangers of reducing the will to survive. But there is no other alternative except war, which, I pray, remains unacceptable to anyone who loves his people. Even if, God forbid, war should finally come, Israel must have proved to all its people that it had left no stone unturned in its search for peace. The last, the heaviest, the most unyielding stone is the PLO. American Jews could, if they have the strength, help our brothers to raise it while there is still time.

[*Sh'ma*, December 13, 1974]

[AFTER THE Rabin-Arafat handshake and Declaration of Principles:] When Arafat went to the United Nations almost two decades ago, I wrote a piece for *Sh'ma* that advocated, almost exactly predicted, the PLO-Israeli concordat of this year. Of course, others would say that the pact could not have been sealed in 1974 while the Soviets were still powerful and disruptive, or when the PLO was rich and not, as now, beleaguered by Hamas extremists. But, it seems to me, acting on the policy we proposed would have saved many lives lost in the successful Yom Kippur War and in the failed Intifada—on both sides.

I do not feel like a prophet; prophecy has fallen to the lot of fools in our latter days. But I do feel like a premature antifascist. There were Americans who opposed Hitler too early and paid a price for it. I feel like those of us who opposed the madness and cruelty of Vietnam but found our hawkish opponents running the United States throughout the dreadful eighties. When Breira (an American Jewish support group for Israeli peace and security, and for a nonviolent Palestinian state on the West Bank and Gaza, in 1973–1977) proposed, almost twenty years ago, the same agreements that Rabin has now signed (including the inevitable peaceful Palestinian state that will be its final consequence), we were vilified, denounced, called self-haters, isolated, and, finally, eliminated from the Jewish scene. We were surely premature; we may have even been wrong, but we were not fools and we were not unfaithful Jews.

It was strange, accordingly, to see the very people that had strongly opposed our peace proposals sitting in the Rose Garden of the White House to watch its fruition while most of us were watching on television. Not jealous, we are pleased that in the end the Jewish community has suddenly come over to our views. It is the Lubavitcher Rebbe and Norman Podhoretz who are in the minority now. They have, as we had, a right to express their views. So, of course, do Israelis of all parties.

But the message is not theirs of "not one inch of our occupied territories" but of reconciliation and of peace. Clearly, at least it has always seemed so to us, a Jewish life, a Palestinian life is worth more than holding on to an unwilling and a bitter subject population. "Enough," said the tough old soldier, Yitzhak Rabin, at long last. And we of the small, lonely, often confused, but unyielding Jewish peace movement can only add at last, Amen.

[*Sh'ma*, October 15, 1993]

[AFTER THE Camp David agreements:] *Shalom* does not mean peace. *Shalom* means something like integrity, fullness, success, wholeness. It is much more than no fighting, though it always includes that too. *Shalom* is what we do not yet have, not in the Middle East and not anywhere else in the world I know about. What we have—and this we have everywhere and always—is the *possibility* of *shalom*, of turning the present into a future of justice and goodwill among persons.

Menachem Begin doesn't, however, move us toward *shalom* by insisting the Palestinians may never have their own state. "Never" never applies in international relations. Arafat doesn't move us toward *shalom* by threatening Sadat and others with physical retaliation. It is the PLO's violence and lack of political acumen that have isolated them from indispensable friends around the world. No one could feel good about making a murderer head of state, though lots of states are headed by (ex-) murderers.

Peace need not be based on inordinate trust in one's present or former enemy. It requires only the possibility that peoples sometimes work in their own self-interest. That is what Sadat did when he realized that if the Israelis could not be defeated in the Yom Kippur War despite their intelligence failures and their being victims of successful sudden aggression, they probably could not be defeated in war. That is what Begin realized when he finally came to the conclusion that if five major victories over all the Arab nations could not gain peace, fighting never could. That is what Carter realized when he saw the Soviets delaying and disrupting Middle East peace talks in Geneva and giving Syria more tanks than fought on both sides at Stalingrad or El Alamein.

Now it is time for other peoples to see what is and is not possible. A Palestinian state is still possible, beginning, as the Jewish state did, with limited autonomy under "imperialist" suzerainty. It is not possible to achieve it by killing more children at Ma'alot or more athletes at the Olympics. Syria can get back the Golan, but not by armed intervention, only by political compromise and by coming to terms with Israel's existence. King Hussein can be relevant again if he stops pretending he never took CIA money or that he has any real independence of U.S. policy. The Soviets can be important when they stop gunrunning and start working for social and economic instead of military gains in the area.

None of this is yet *shalom*. There are too many sheiks and kings and feudal rulers and politicized ayatollahs for this to be called the time and place of true peace. The Israeli *Likud* coalition is still too hard-line and manipulative to be bearers of conciliation throughout the whole area. But there are real changes and real possibilities. Something will never be the same again. An Arab state has said that Israel exists as of right, though not of course from Suez to Jordan as of right. Israel has admitted there are Palestinians and that they are not just a name for terrorist bands. The only possible conclusion is that they also have a right to a homeland precisely like and in peace with the Jewish state.

Abba Eban said at Yale not once but many times: A Palestinian state beside Israel, yes; instead of Israel, no. Maybe Begin cannot bring himself to agree, but Peace Now and many other Israelis already are clear about it.

An American hegemony can be neocolonialist. If so, as in Iran and soon in many parts of Latin America, it is doomed. But American self-interest does not require control of foreign populations. It needs only an environment for nonviolent political process. The Saudi princes have more to fear from their own people's revolt than from Israel or the United States. Libya's Khadaffi, like Ugandan dictator Idi Amin, is not the enemy only of America but of his own slaves and subjects. When Begin is removed from office, it will be by Israeli votes, not by a PLO bullet. America can nurture peace and gain from the nurturance without inflicting a Pax Americana upon unwilling populations. There is a great deal that still awaits responsible compromise. But the pattern is available. Sadat, Carter, Begin are not saints or ever were; they are only a faint but real symbol of a *shalom* that is still to come.

[*Sh'ma*, April 27, 1979]

"BREIRA" AND DISSENT IN AMERICAN JEWRY

In 1977 Breira, an American Jewish group of which Arnold Jacob Wolf was national chairperson and which supported reform of American Jewish communal life and peace and mutual recognition with the Palestinians, aroused harsh opposition and controversy. Rabbi Wolf was invited to speak about it to the national convention of Conservative rabbis.

SOME SAY we are naive because we do not realize that the Arabs are, after all, Nazis. I do not believe the Arabs are Nazis. I believe they are our enemies, in some cases implacable enemies about whom I have no illusions, but they do not believe in killing Jews just to kill Jews. They are trying to recover a land they think, I believe mistakenly, is wholly theirs. Therefore their war against all of us Jews is a war between two versions of ideology and national rights. Such a war can be mediated. But if we of Breira are wrong, if it is true that Arabs are Nazis, then understand very well that it is not simply we who are wrong—it is anyone who believes in the remotest possibility of peace. Israel is then condemned to war from generation to generation, a war which we could not survive, God help us.

The second criticism of our dissent is that we make it look like American Jewry is divided. Well, American Jewry *is* divided! It is divided, but not about the security of Israel. It is not divided about the essential, absolutely irrefutable rights of Israel to survive. Rather it is divided about territories, it is divided about peace talks, it is divided about priorities and elections. I do not think it looks bad for us to be divided on these matters. I think it would look strange and peculiar and dangerous to a typical non-Jew if we Jews agreed in every single particular.

We are accused, in the third place, of using public media for dissent. For many months we have sought to go not to public media but to Jewish media. They, however, have refused to publish our Breira platform, have refused to publish our programs for American Jewry, and have published only news of the few significant or insignificant meetings that some of Breira's members (*not* Breira) have had with Palestinians, including some PLO members. That, in the American Jewish community, represents all the news. The hard, week-by-week work of understanding ourselves and understanding Diaspora-Israel relations has never been accurately reported by a kept press which is not interested in the truth and which is rarely willing to reproduce it. That is why you have the impression that we care only about the PLO. The real nitty-gritty of our dissent, the real work that we have been doing for months, is simply unavailable to you.

In the fourth place, we are accused of placing the Diaspora above Israel, and that is also a false accusation. We were asked in the Israeli embassy a few months ago whether we in Breira believe in the centrality of Israel. Answering for myself and not for my organization, which can have many different spokespeople, I said that while I do not believe in the centrality of Israel, I do believe in the indispensability of Israel. Arthur Waskow answered, "Mr. Ambassador, you have the image of a wheel with spokes to the center; we have the image of a coin, with two sides." There cannot be an Israel without the Diaspora. There cannot be a Diaspora without Israel. We are each indispensable to the other. I consider ours to be a legitimate Zionist position. But I also consider the ambassador's a legitimate Zionist position. I would like to see an honorable debate among our several positions, because it may be that we are wrong. But I do not think that such dissent is illegitimate.

In the fifth place, we are accused of reducing contributions of people and money by asking Jews to consider the possibility that Israel is sometimes wrong. There is no evidence for this accusation.

For fifteen years I served in a congregation that heard not only from me, with my Breira-like position, but also from Uri Davis, the most extreme pacifist, leftist Israeli I ever met, from Fawzi Al-Asmar, who represented the hard Palestinian position before there was a PLO, and from Menachem Begin and a great many other left- and right-leaning dissenters. Our congregation was so notable in the Chicago community for its contribution to the United Jewish Appeal that I was placed on the national Rabbinic Advisory Committee of the UJA. That congregation, which had heard dissent about Israel since its inception, put its synagogue building on mortgage in order to contribute the money to the State of Israel. I do not know many congregations which did that, whether or not they ever heard from the other side. That same congregation has sent every Hebrew School graduate to a summer in Israel for a dozen years. To give another example, at Yale, where week after week all kinds of views are heard, students contributed after the Yom Kippur War at least as much per capita as any other Jewish student group in America.

Hearing the truth or truths seen from many sides, or even truth and falsehood, is the way not of reducing interest in and loyalty to Israel but a way of increasing it. Today our people are not so much questioning Israel as questioning the monolithic character of the American Jewish response to Israel. They are drifting away, as figures from UJA prove, but not because of Breira. We have recovered more young Jews, more "New Left" Jews, more angry Jews, more intellectual Jews than any organization in the recent history of the United States. The others are drifting away because some of us no longer look credible, because we do Israel the terrible disservice of pretending that it cannot sustain a critical analysis.

The last and most difficult accusation against us, one which I cannot refute, is that we are not risking our lives and therefore have no right to certain views. The last time a famous American Zionist accused me of that, I had no answer. But when I got home I reflected that his son was at Harvard and my son was on a Nachal (military/agricultural) *kibbutz*. If everyone could agree that hawks and doves, left and right, have no right to talk about anything in which Israel's risk is involved, I would assent to that moratorium, at least for myself. Perhaps Breira would too. But that time is not in the near future.

I do not agree that it is only we of the "left" who risk Israel. It is also those who resist any compassion, any compromise, any concern for those with whom Israel must ultimately come to terms. If there is risk to be taken, we are all at hazard.

Have we given Hitler a posthumous victory by equating Nazis and Palestinians? Have we projected our own guilt for the Holocaust and what we did or did not do upon our brothers in Israel? The real issue, it seems to me, is repressive, manipulative, professional control of Jewish organizations, not for Israel's safety but for naked self-interest. Breira is not the enemy of Israel but rather the enemy of repression and power-seeking.

Are we, in the end, one people? Rabbi Heschel said, "There is a price to be paid by the Jew; in order to be a man he has to be more than a man; in order to be a people, we have to be more than a people." What Israel needs desperately is our concern for its soul. What we need so desperately is an Israel that is unafraid to dissent with *itself.* We do not need Israel to be more *macho* than we or more Jewish than we or to win wars because we often lose. We need Israel to be a Zionist, Jewish state. This Zionism is not the "instant Zionism" of Norman Podhoretz, which cannot abide criticism, but the rich-textured Zionism in which some of us grew up, the Zionism of controversy even in the midst of despair, even in the midst of Holocaust, a Zionism which grew out of a world of dissent. Where are the successors of Haim Greenberg, Stephen Wise, Louis Marshall, and Abraham Heschel? If there is none, it is because there is no audience worthy of them, because we have contemned our heritage of dissent and nonconformity. *Ahavat Yisrael* (loving other Jews) means the willingness to share even those problems that cannot be solved, to respect fellow Jews in *Gush Emunim* (the Israeli settler movement), and even in the Jewish Defense League (whom I first defended against the Anti-Defamation League ten years ago). It means remembering what *halbanat panim* (the prohibition of publicly shaming others) is. And it means remembering that all Jews are brothers and sisters and must treat each other that way. . . .

I believe in dissent out of love, and in love that, as in any true family, comes only out of dissent. What is at stake here is democratic Jewish life in America and Israel, and, God willing, all over the world. What is at stake here is the real power of the Jewish religion to compel and constrain and refute but also to permit and expand and instruct. What is at stake here is the vitality and moral hygiene of *Klal Yisrael* (the Jewish people). If Israel fails, we die, but if we fail because we tried to be more McCarthyite than McCarthy, then Israel dies too. I believe that God will protect Israel, God will protect Israel with our help. But we must keep the Torah for Him, and we can do that only by treating each other with respect. . . .

[Speech to the annual convention of the
Rabbinical Assembly (Conservative), 1977]

A proposed resolution against dissenters was tabled after this talk and succeeding debate.

LOOKING AT ISRAEL

THE SOVIET UNION brought down an unarmed civilian plane which was apparently overflying some of its sensitive military installations, causing loss of life and international protest.

The Soviet Union regularly ships guns to Central America in order to bring civic disorder and revolution.

The Soviet Union is headed by a hard-line former terrorist and spy who has resolutely opposed all moves for reduction of tensions.

The Soviet Union has invaded neighboring nations, occupied and subdued them, annexing whole populations of different conviction and background.

The Soviet Union permits dissent and debate among elites, but no freedom for its occupied or second-class populations.

The Soviet Union has been repeatedly condemned by the international community but defends its actions by reminding the world that it is surrounded by much larger, hostile enemies who have refused to live with it in peace. In order to defend its right to exist, it has even quietly threatened the world with nuclear destruction.

Now go back and, in reading this piece, please substitute for "the Soviet Union," each time, the term "the State of Israel."

[KAM Isaiah Israel Bulletin, October 19, 1983]

The publication of this piece led to controversy and ferment at KAM Isaiah Israel; some were outraged at the comparison. Extensive public discussion, meetings, letters, and bulletin pieces on all sides followed.

ZIONIST DREAMS, ISRAELI REALITY

THE DOWNING of the Libyan airplane was not so much an international incident as a symbol of what Israel has begun to become. Not, despite her fanatical enemies, a conventional, power-mad bastion of imperialism, but rather a frightened and thus inevitably trigger-happy, besieged yet somehow also haughty, developing nation. Is this what a hundred years of Zionism has led to: more danger to Jews than in the *golah* itself, more recklessness and violence than in all of our long Diaspora history?

Zionism, as I understand it, meant and means primarily the end of subservience to other men's determination. It meant the fulfillment of God's promise (Lev. 26) to "break the bonds of your yoke and make you walk upright" (*kom'miyut*). Zionism promised and promises a new, organic authenticity, a Jewish life lived out of inner standards, in dialogue with Jewish sources, speaking the Hebrew language, without the circumlocutions and the evasions of all our fearful ghettos. Zionism opposed and opposes that comfortable liberalism that substitutes premature utopianism for patient Jewish messianism and which asks us to become part of the nations instead of a nation dwelling alone. Zionism opposed and opposes that Orthodox petrifaction that treated the *halakhah* as a fortress to be defended and not a life to be lived.

Zionism also opposed and opposes Christian denigration of Jews and Judaism, the brutal repression by those who were not entirely sure that their Messiah had come and had therefore to throttle us whose Messiah was always yet to come. Zionism refuted Pauline

Christianity for which hope meant always the distant otherworldliness of the *parousia* (Second Coming) and the irrelevant comfort of the *eschaaton* (End of Days). Zionism refuted Christian *agape* which, seeking to love the neighbor better than oneself, ended by requiring that he become oneself. Zionism attacked the *ecclesia*, the church triumphant, which demanded that all men become her children and that all men worship the man she called God. Zionism refuted Christian *pistis*, a faith in dogma, doctrine, and salvific paradigms, an individualistic belief in an incarnate God, without Law, without community, and without toleration.

Against Christian claims, Zionism reasserted perennial Jewish values: the holy understood as the secular under God; faith as faithfulness, Israel as the truly chosen people; the "way" of Torah as a disciplined, commanded life; history as the promises of God unfolding in the lives of men. Zionism looked back to traditional Jewish self-understanding, to the prophecy of Zechariah (Zech. 14:21) that even the pots and pans in the new Jerusalem would be "holy to *Adonai*," to rabbinic service of God through commandments and communal discipline. Revolutionary Zionists like Moses Hess and A. D. Gordon and Rav Kuk and Martin Buber superbly refracted these traditional Jewish norms until they shone forth with a profoundly innovative communitarianism in the *kibbutz* and a brave new Exodus from lands where Jews could no longer live or could not live like Jews. The conquest of the Land and the conquest of labor and the conquest of self-hating atavisms were all achievements of Zionism as the authentic and unique national movement of the Jewish people everywhere.

Much has been achieved: more pride and more scholarship, more unity and more stability than could have been predicted from the early history of European Zionism. Exiles have been gathered, including many who had forgotten that Jews are exiles, no matter how comfortable their lives. The Jewish state is a fact, ineluctable and glorious, but it is not and may never be the Zion desiderated by the movement or foreshadowed by the tradition.

There has been in Israel a steady retreat from socialist and religious egalitarianism. The *kibbutz* is isolated and diminished, and if it is the glory of our propaganda, it is also a vulnerable island in a sea of capitalist encroachment—and now knows it is. Where pre-Palestinian Zionism was open, the State of Israel has become triumphalist and often also expansionist. The mood of its people coincides all too nearly with the program of the Movement for a Greater Israel. Percentages of party representation remain the same as they were a half-century ago in the European Zionist Congresses, a stunning indicator of cooptation and congealed constituencies. Despite the fact that the population has become increasingly Middle Eastern and strikingly young, governance by coterie, even by *landsmanschaften* (connections of geographic origins in Europe), continues unmodified and unlamented. New groups and new ideas are harder to discover or to support than they ever were in the historical Zionist movement.

Israel colonizes the "administered" territories without regard to international law or to the rights of the indigenous Palestinian nationality. Israeli forces go deep into Egypt or Lebanon—sometimes to ferret out spies and terrorists, but often to carpet-bomb wholly innocent Arab neighbors. Few Israeli soldiers die now (thank God!), but, as in Vietnam, its pilots can rain death from skies which they and they alone control.

Zionism opposed Orthodox unilateralism, but in the Jewish state, Orthodoxy is empowered, entrenched, established, and corrupt. While deeply traditional Jews like Yeshayahu Leibowitz and Professor Urbach denounce clericalism in its Jewish, un-Jewish form, the Orthodox establishment continues its veto over free religious expression by Israeli Jews and blindly contributes to the militarism of many religious citizens.

Zionism spoke movingly of *kibush ha-avodah* (the dignity of work), but increasingly in the Jewish state hard work is done by Arab hirelings and by volunteer Americans who enjoy getting their hands dirty for a while—and this even in socialist *kibbutzim*. It did not take Ben Aharon to see ahead a Jewish Rhodesia with the end of the Zionist dream of dignity and self-realization through labor, a dream curiously enough now sweeping lands of affluence and pollution while a poorer Israel sets its sights on consumption and ridicules any ecological concern. Did Zionism mean to create an American-style supermarket on the Mediterranean built by Arab masons and carpenters?

The power and strategy of the military is both open and deeply threatening to the Zionist ideal. Generals are kings, and ex-generals run the country; they raise an Idi Amin in Uganda who then drives their own and other people out; they conscript children of the East to man their patrols and defend their swollen borders; they use up resources desperately needed for education and for housing and for health while refusing any move that might lead to détente with Arab nations; they recognize the Thieu regime in Vietnam on its very deathbed. The Russians are practically gone from an Egypt that offers to recognize Israel, but Israeli generals are still passively waiting for the phone to ring. The United Nations and the Friends and some of our best senators from the United States are painted as enemies of the Jews, thus inevitably alienating young Jews who still believe in peace and work for it, even in the Middle East.

Jabotinsky, the lifelong *bête noire* of the Zionist movement, is now posthumously rehabilitated to become a hero of the Jewish state with his name on a hundred street signs and his face on thousands of stamps. Violence, repudiated by the Zionist leadership, at least until Chaim Weizmann, is defended subtly by Eliezer Schweid and blatantly by *Gahal* [Begin's party, later called Likud], until the repression of whole populations in Gaza or the downing of a civilian aircraft is seen as defensible by all and glorious by some. Israel sends to America not her scholars or her farmers or her singers, but generals and strategists, as if the Six-day War were her finest hour and *Tsahal* (the Israeli Army) her greatest accomplishment.

The decline of the Dayan family symbolizes the swift decline of the Zionist idea. A classical *halutz* (pioneer) grandfather; a brilliant and self-assertive general for a son; a grandson and daughter who are jet-setters and Beautiful People. One need not wonder what Shmuel Dayan would say about his grandchildren's sophisticated decadence, but the view from present-day Israel of what the generations portend is far more obscure.

A downed plane is not itself a mark of anything; a single example provides nothing. But examples seem to converge and to indict. Israel may be the Jewish state; it is not now and perhaps can never be Zion, the Zion of Scripture or the Zion of the Movement, in Moses Hess's words, "the historic ideal of our people, none other than the reign of God on earth." But what Israel will become depends on other than the will of men, even men who call themselves Jews. "That which cometh into your minds shall not be at all. You say: we will be like other nations, like the families of other countries. As I live, says God, with fury poured out shall I rule over you."

[*Sh'ma*, March 30, 1973]

ISRAEL AS THE FALSE MESSIAH

IT IS TIME to review the permanently impressive arguments of the great anti-Zionist thinkers of the last century and the earlier part of our own. Their suspicions of a renewed Jewish politics were not, as in cruder, self-hating versions of anti-Zionism, motivated by an alternative European nationalism (though some of them have been so accused) but by a close reading of Jewish history and faith which could not come to terms with its reduction to or its equation with the petty neonationalisms of modern times. Writing before the Holocaust, or even after that disaster but consciously in spite of it, they insist that, on purely Jewish grounds, no state could be authentically or admissibly "Jewish."

Hermann Cohen, the greatest thinker of modern Judaism, believed that Israel, the chosen folk, was God's idea, an ideal community which proleptically modeled the future unity of humankind. This task for which it was chosen would, of course, involve suffering (Zionists made the error of wanting to be "happy"), but any alternative would surely involve something much worse: suffering without signification. Franz Rosenzweig considered Jews a transhistorical people, touched with the fire of God's revelation and permanently immune to the blandishments and perils of history. Better by far for us to remain in our metahistorical role than to attempt to ape merely historical peoples whose fate was, in any case, sealed. There is no safety in the struggle for power or security. Our only (partial) safety is, as always, in God. A version of this sharp rejection of the myth of Jewish statecraft is still found in Yeshayahu Leibowitz's book *Yahadut* and in his recent essay on "Idolatry" found in the volume *Contemporary Jewish Religious Thought* in which, though himself a loyal citizen of the State of Israel, he shows how the pretense to a normal historical Jewish existence leads to an inevitably antireligious outcome, that Israelis' only hope is to see the state as marginal or even antithetical to Jewish beliefs while accepting it as a proximate value, a mere tactic without any spiritual signification whatsoever.

Among the Orthodox, Samson Raphael Hirsch insisted on a Judaism remote from political ambition, and not only on the grounds of his presumed European egalitarianism. From the beginning of the Hasidic movement, there was a deep pietistic ambivalence, not only about messianic aspirations but about the place of *Eretz Yisrael* in Jewish consciousness. Stories about *tsaddikim* (rabbinic leaders) who made *aliyah* (to the Land of Israel) followed by immediate *yeridah* (emigration) and the insistence that God could be served anywhere, since He was everywhere without qualification, made any political need for the Holy Land suspect and finally trivial. The late Satmar Rebbe Joel Teitelbaum mounted a consistent and Jewishly profound critique of Zionist claims, denying especially the assertion that political sovereignty had anything to contribute to messianic possibilities (see his *Divrei Yoel* on the Torah).

In recent years an impressive literature has been created in Israel itself, a literature of disillusion, a revisionist history combined with a hermeneutics of suspicion. Simhah Flapan, in his last magisterial work, *The Birth of Israel*, unmasks claims that the Jewish state has been only an innocent victim of Middle Eastern politics and proves that Israel itself has been aggressive and threatening from its inception. Benjamin Beit-Halahmi documents the story of Israel's and Israelis' support for one corrupt regime after another, including the unspeakable Bokassa, the tyrant of the Central African Republic, as well as fascists of every stripe, in his book *The Israeli Connection*. I have discussed the dialectics of Zionist thinking in an essay in the Wolfe Kelman *Festschrift, Perspectives on Jews and Judaism* (Rabbinical Assembly, 1978).

In an interpretation of the rebellion of Korah and his band in his *Moses*, Mordecai Martin Buber explains precisely why the rebels were enemies of God. They claimed that the people Israel was holy in principle and that holiness is a datum, a fact, a present reality. That claim would have made their own desire for political supremacy valid. If each Jew was already holy, then anyone could be Moses and nothing more was required to validate the insurgents' claim to power. But the authentic biblical notion of holiness is, rather, that it is a task, an infinite commandment, which one must always strive to become. To claim holiness in the present historical moment is to prophesy falsely. So Korah must be not only refuted but destroyed.

I believe that Buber was unmasking the dangerous religious Zionism of Rav Kuk (chief rabbi of Palestine), whose mystical views on the holiness of the Jewish people are well known. For Rav Kuk, the land and the folk were, in literal fact, holy, and therefore even the atheistic *kibbutzim* and the ignorant builders of the state were unknowing agents of divine purpose. Buber feared, prophetically, that this triumphalist theology would lead to something very like expansionist *Gush Emunim*, a movement that puts naked Jewish interests ahead of all political realities and humane values, on the ground that Jews are uniquely chosen to survive and to control, as Rav Kuk's son, Rabbi Tzvi Yehuda Kuk, taught.

But it is not only Rav Kuk who comes in for our renewed inspection and suspicion. Abraham Joshua Heschel insisted correctly that Jewish faith was a spirituality of time and not of space. Still, after the Six-day War he wrote *Israel: An Echo of Eternity* (surely his weakest book), in which he attempted, unsuccessfully, to deny what his other work had demonstrated. Emil Fackenheim, once our most persuasive professional theologian, has become an extreme Israeli chauvinist, arguing that since powerlessness formerly endangered our people, our power is not to be subjected to any moral criticism or to standards that have long been considered as ethically Jewish. Richard Rubenstein has mounted a powerful defense, not only of intransigent Jewish politics but of the supremacy of a realistic neopagan religiosity over Jewish monotheism with its inevitably undermining and critical universalist morality. Elie Wiesel criticizes

Gorbachev and Reagan justly and with conviction but has nothing to say about Jewish crimes against humanity or about Israeli militarism in Lebanon and in Gaza, thus undermining his claim on other people's concern with regard to our people's just demands. Gershom Scholem, in a recent article on Judaism in *Contemporary Jewish Religious Thought*, asserts that there is, in fact, no single, specific Judaism which could serve as a standard for Jewish behavior, but only a generalized national creativity which variously throws up mysticism and rationalism, *devekut* (experiential clinging to God) and unbridled political Zionism, without any way to demonstrate that one is more authentic or more defensible than any other.

Jewish history is still open, Israel must be relentlessly demythologized, the Messiah has not yet come. The most we can claim for Zionism now is a small, ambiguous *tehiyah* (rebirth), not a cosmic *geulah* (Redemption). We must continually refine our political behavior in the crucible of Jewish self-criticism. We must try to live a post-Zionist, religiously responsible national life.

As I write these words in early 1988, the guns of Gaza are not silent. Jewish policemen and soldiers are shooting and beating relatively innocent Palestinians. American Jews are, in consequence, dreadfully confused. The best Israelis are ashamed. Perhaps, God forbid, the great anti-Zionists were right after all, and Israel itself is a sin against God. The "Canaanites"—the movement in Israel to break with the Diaspora Jewish past and identity—described by James Diamond in his important book *Homeland or Holy Land?*, were already conscious of deconstructing Judaism precisely in order to create a new kind of nation. In any case, what we need now more than self-vindication or even strictly objective reevaluation is simply *teshuvah* (spiritual return). We have all sinned in silent acquiescence. After forty years we all have need to begin again to be Jews—in the Diaspora and in the homeland too.

PART SEVEN

Judaism and Other Faiths

A JEWISH-JAPANESE ENCOUNTER: THE EMPEROR'S BROTHER, FRIEND OF THE JEWS

A HANUKKAH PARTY in the Allied forces' Tokyo Chapel Center [during the Occupation in the early 1950s] is pretty much like any other anywhere. The Jewish community invites the servicemen stationed in central Honshu, and the evening follows the program ordained of old by the Jewish Welfare Board. Still, there are regional distinctions. Although most of the GIs come from Flatbush or Omaha, here and there is a uniform of the UN Forces on "R&R" leave from Korea—a Turkish Jew, an Ethiopian Falasha, a Londoner. And the Tokyo Jewish community itself smacks more of Kiev or Berlin or Tientsin than of Brooklyn. It is made up of Jews of disparate backgrounds, united only, it seems, by past persecution and the English they speak now.

The last party was only fair. . . . The services were brief and impressive. But there was an undeniable shortage of women, the real point of the whole party. . . . It was under these unlikely circumstances that I was invited, almost too casually, to a dinner to be given the next night for Prince Mikasa, brother of the emperor and a reputed friend of the Jews. . . .

The American Club is the second best in Tokyo. The best one doesn't seem to admit Jews; most of the others are limited to correspondents, military officers, or nationals of a particular country. But it is a respectable place for thirty affluent Jews to invite the same number of important Japanese to dinner and a few speeches. The evening began at six and was over at nine, according to Japanese, not Jewish, *minhag*. The steaks were good, the speeches short, the mood cordial.

The idea for the get-together had apparently been formulated first by Koreshige Inuzuka, president, according to its latest name, of the Nipponese-Jewish Friendship League, a fairly new organization with about four hundred members all over Japan. . . . The Jewish community in Tokyo, disparate in background and religious inclination but united by business ties and other circumstances, is always glad to pay the bill for any parley that promises them a greater measure of security or prestige in a country where almost all Jews are aliens.

Inuzuka, a former captain of psychological warfare in the Imperial Japanese Navy, is a man of ability and charm. When saved from death in a clash with a German submarine during World War I, he had vowed to devote his life to some noble and private cause. That cause became the Jews. He told a *Nippon Times* reporter that his sympathies for the Jews were first excited when he watched the Russian Revolution from a battleship off Vladivostok and discovered in it a triumph of Jewish might and Jewish righteousness. Later in the 1920s, when he was a naval attaché in Paris, he identified himself with the French Jews and in fact kept a strictly kosher cuisine despite the incomparable blandishments of French cooking. During further assignments in Japan and China he showed numerous kindnesses to Jews.

In Shanghai particularly, which in 1939 was a refugee center, Captain Inuzuka found opportunity to help. Yet, as he states, his motives were far from purely disinterested. "I noted that the U.S. press was very much controlled by the Jews. Therefore, I expounded, if Japan remains friendly to the Jews in the Orient, it is possible to improve U.S. feelings toward Japan through the influence of mass media." A naive and plaintive blend of both philo- and anti-Semitism!

When the war ended Inuzuka was nominal commander of the occupied Philippines. He was called to Manila for questioning as a war criminal and was saved only by a letter from the Union of Orthodox Rabbis of America that described how he had saved hundreds of Yeshiva students from death. When Jews came in growing numbers to Japan after the war, he resolved to renew old and mutually profitable connections. . . .

The Jews of Tokyo are, in a more exact way than the Communists could know, both "cosmopolitan" and "Zionist": cosmopolitan in that they know many lands and many languages but are native to none; Zionist in that the sentimental center of their patriotism is the land of Israel. Because they are wealthy and at least temporarily well settled they will never go there, except perhaps a few for the six months necessary to gain Israeli citizenship.

In Tokyo they are a community apart, withdrawing from the native oriental simplicity, barred from the company of the snobbish European colonials. They are showy, unlettered, clannish, and insecure. . . . All in all, the Jews of Tokyo incarnate the wanderings, the perils, and occasionally the dignity of the Jew in an alien world. They are exiles even from themselves. . . .

I was flabbergasted at the high caliber of the Japanese guests. They included Foreign Office officials, the presidents of two of the largest banks (and banks to the Japanese, as to the Swiss, are supremely important), the directors of three of the great manufacturing companies, some professors from Tokyo's leading universities, and—perhaps most significant of all for Jewish needs—the director of the Immigration Bureau. I was seated—*nebach*—with the prince and the president of the community on one side of me, and former Admiral Yoshio Yamamoto with an interpreter on the other.

What had led the committee to seat me next to the admiral was surely the fact that I was a navy chaplain. The old man delicately ignored the slight implied by my very junior rank. One of Japan's great naval minds and a figure of importance in Japanese politics, he is now reduced by purge and senescence to the position of an elder statesman lacking both power and the will to power. . . .

Prince Mikasa dominated the entire gathering as soon as he appeared. . . . He is the youngest of four brothers, of whom the eldest is the Mikado. By custom as well as by inclination, this makes

Mikasa the scholar of the family. Imperial rule is reserved for Hirohito (who is almost never called by that name), sports for the late Prince Chichibu, diplomacy for Prince Takamatsu. Mikasa bears his role with grace, assuming horn-rimmed glasses and a scholarly manner to fit. . . .

I was asked to open the proceedings with an invocation. Forgoing any English remarks informing the Deity why and wherefore we were gathered, which would have required extensive translation, I limited myself to two Hebrew benedictions: the *motsi* for bread and the *broche* recited upon seeing a member of a gentile royal house. I am not sure anyone below a king rates it, but I had never been so close before and I was not going to take a chance. The prince later asked me for copies of the *broches*, which I wrote out for him in cursive script. He read them back to me haltingly, explaining that he did better with printed Hebrew characters. If he had done any better than he had, I would have fainted.

The first address was given by Leon Greenberg, a lawyer who had come from the States to try Japanese war criminals and never gone home. An ex-president of the Jewish community, he was probably chosen, as I was from among the three rabbis present, for his ability to speak English without accent. He paid tribute to the prince, to Captain Inuzuka, and to Professor Kotsuji, a doctor in Semitics from the Pacific School of Religion who, like the captain, had once been a great benefactor of the Jews in China. (He was now reduced to advisory work with the American navy.) Professor Kotsuji comes to all our holiday services in the navy chapel, but, despite a knowledge of Hebrew and Judaism equal to that of any of us, he has never pretended to be closer than a friend—unlike other and less learned Japanese nowadays who declare themselves to be Jews, half-Jews, or would-be Jews, though only a handful of them have actually been converted. Mr. Greenberg reminded the Japanese of their fine record of opposition to bigotry and hoped they would continue to befriend the Jews. We had evidence of this in their adamant refusal during the last war to hand over to the Nazis the one Jew remaining in the Tokyo area, a penurious *shammes* of the Yokohama synagogue.

Mr. Greenberg also remarked vaguely on some of the similarities between the two peoples, but he did not elaborate.

Prince Mikasa then spoke—in Japanese, of course. He was precise and eloquent, correcting an occasional mistake by the interpreter, who formerly might have had to commit hara-kiri for it but now satisfied himself with bows and blushes. The prince spoke diffidently, almost haltingly, but with great sincerity and persuasiveness.

Unexpectedly he began without the polite irrelevancies of the other speakers. He launched into an attack on the superstitious belief of many Japanese in the audience that their people was descended from the Lost Tribes of Israel. He deplored the theories, common here, that the Japanese and the Jews have some mystical affinity or spiritual identity apparent only to the initiated. The real relationship of the two peoples, more contrapuntal than identical, he considered to be more profound.

Then he spoke of himself, also unexpectedly and frankly for one upon whose words millions hang. He said that after the Western powers defeated Japan (he spoke of this more openly than I had ever heard any other Japanese do), he had had the *on*, the obligation, to Westernize himself. He had gone to school to Western culture. And, he said, in the six years of his study, he discovered one supreme fact—that the Jews were the key to Western civilization. The truth incarnated in Judaism, a truth of being rather than of theory, is the central meaning of history. I listened in amazement as he gave almost point for point the argument of Halevi's *Kuzari*, which culminates in the conversion to Judaism of the khan of the Khazars. History had brought him—Prince Mikasa—to the Jew, he said, and Judaism had brought him back to himself. For the Jew is not only the father of the West, he is the scion of the Orient. He is the holy bridge (a traditional and poignant Japanese symbol) between East and West. Through understanding Judaism the prince regained a sense of his dignity as a member of his people; he was again proud to be Japanese.

Prince Mikasa then became practical. He pleaded for an Imperial Institute of Jewish Studies in Tokyo, presumably financed by

Jewish money. He said that only an understanding of Judaism rooted in scholarly research would be of value. He offered himself as a student in that Institute.

Then he spoke of suffering. He said that Japan had only begun to suffer, that her pride and her might had been humbled for the first time in imperial history. But the Jews had often suffered and been degraded. The only hope for the Japanese was to learn from the Jews how to draw meaning out of their trials.

I flatter myself that I was one of the few appropriately touched by the words of Prince Mikasa. My fellow Jews seemed reluctant to follow his sensitive and modest reflections with sympathy. What they wanted was not praise but terms from Caesar. The other Japanese were either cool novices or ecstatic philo-Semites, therefore less deserving to be taken seriously than the prince in his middle way. For me, it was an unforgettable moment, a challenge, a vindication.

Then Captain Inuzuka spoke. He told of a mystic vision that had come to him in the night. As in some passages in Genesis, it was hard to tell whether God Himself or His angels had visited him, but in any event he had received a message from on high telling him that the hope of the world lay in an alliance between India, Israel, and Japan. I am not certain whether he meant the nation or people of Israel, or how literally he meant to bind us all. I am inclined to think his ecstatic pictures were merely part of an accepted Japanese way of expressing ideas on world politics. He said the atom bomb had been invented by Jews, that (though few knew the secret) the Japanese had invented a similar weapon. Like the Jew, the Japanese was both doer and thinker, an incomparable entrepreneur and a creative mystic. These two fabulous peoples—the only such—could, if they would drink also from the wells of Indian tradition, remake Asia and the world. His talk, though it continued in this vein, was interspersed with subtle remarks about the containment and defeat of communism.

After the close of the banquet I was borne under by expressions of Japanese *politesse*. Admiral Yamamoto, as he took his lonely farewell, heaped blessings on my head. The civil officials insisted I meet with them at greater length so that they could pursue their inclinations toward things Jewish. The shopkeepers and the businessmen invited me to buy wholesale.

It is the custom in Japan to offer one's host a gift. So I turned to the prince and offered to procure for him any Jewish books he might wish to read. He thanked me and asked me to answer a question that other Jewish representatives had been unable to do for him satisfactorily. "This is your year 5713," he said. "But 5713 years since what? The Christians count from the birth of their founder, we from our kings—and you?" I told him we began with the creation of the world. "Ah," he said, "it is the right way."

I went out into the foggy Tokyo night in confusion and pride. I wondered whether it was their recent defeat or the very truth of Judaism that had brought these strange people so close to us. And how their gate could be the mirror of our own. And for what a man might still be brought to royal estate.

[*Commentary*, April 1953]

JEWS AND CHRISTIANITY

YOU AND I received a Christmas card this morning. It was addressed to Rabbi Wolf and Congregation Solel. It has on its cover three crowns—and a cross. Its text reads: A Joyous Christmas and a Blessed New Year, in Jesus Christ Our Lord. It has no return address.

To the anonymous sender I express my (our?) thanks. I too pray that the New Year may be blessed for all of us. I wish too that this may be a joyous Christmas. If there is some scent of conversionism in your greetings, my anonymous friend, I accept that too with gratitude. I am proud that you think enough of my soul to want it saved.

And I like your taste. I too see Christmas as the Incarnation Day on which, according to my Christian neighbors, God became man. I too believe that Christ is the message of Christmas, and not anyone or anything but Christ. I believe that Donner, Blitzen, Santa Claus, and the Christmas tree are the enemies of that Christian Christmas. I believe that the "folk festival" of which so many of my friends talk is an enemy of the Glorious Day of the Incarnation. I believe that the Christmas card that features one's children instead of the Crown and Cross is a parody. Or perhaps it is the pagan worship of self which always prevents the authentic service of the King. I believe that the "American" Christmas is a fraud. There can be only one Christmas, the Christian Christmas.

I salute on that Christmas all true servants of the Jewish babe who became King. I wish that their magnificent Holy Day, the day of the Messiah and the Adoration of the Magi, of the Midnight Mass and *Adeste Fideles*, may not be betrayed or fragmented or commercialized. I believe that Christmas, a true Christian Christmas, can contribute to Peace on Earth, Good Will to Man.

[Congregation Solel *Pathfinder*, December 26, 1961]

RABBI IN NAIROBI

I AM the only Jew ever invited by the World Council of Churches to an Assembly of the world's Protestant and Orthodox churches, held every seven years. I attended the latest Assembly, which was held in Nairobi at the end of 1975, as the invited Jewish representative. For three long weeks I listened, talked to hundreds of delegates, was interviewed on television, lobbied shyly and cautiously for my people, and ate only vegetables and fruit to keep kosher. I found some Christians who had risked their very lives for Jews and some open anti-Semites in priestly garb, learned churchmen and ignorant bigots. The third world was the Assembly's scene and furnished many of its principal actors, but the script could have been as well produced in New Haven or Chicago. There were passionate (and demagogic) speeches aplenty, but the voting was always moderate and the Assembly usually acquiescent. I myself was surrounded by friends and supporters, but I felt very much alone. . . .

The large and brilliant group of Catholic observers are fraternal but also warily silent. In addition to me, one Sikh, one Muslim, one Hindu, one Buddhist were also invited as honored guests.

And indeed I was honored. I sat next to Margaret Mead, the legendary Pastor Niemoller, and the Indian ambassador (high commissioner) to Guyana. I was welcomed, feted, dined, and cherished, but the rules of their game forbade not only my voting but also my speaking except by invitation. Our invitations even to attend the Assembly were controversial, and many delegates ignored us or visibly evidenced the wish we had not come. Introducing us to the plenum just before the first vote to continue dialogue with "persons of living faith" (nee non-Christians) may itself have led to a backlash negative vote, which deeply dismayed the very leadership that had sponsored our invitations. I do not know if guests will ever be invited again. One should not make too much of the fact, but I was identified with a yellow badge. The kindness and wisdom of Dean Krister Stendahl of Harvard Divinity School, the chairman of the Commission on Relations with the Jews, and of Franz von Hammerstein, its heroic director, were constant; but there was some coolness elsewhere, and much embarrassment too.

Many delegates spoke to me in Hebrew: ministers from Cameroon and Ethiopia, even Metropolitan Nikodim of Leningrad, leader of the large, stolid Russian delegation. Many now live or had lived in Israel, but the only delegation from there called itself not "Israel" but "Jerusalem," so as not to commit itself on the status of that city or on personal and political loyalty. The canny Armenian archbishop of Jerusalem delicately negotiated between Egyptian hard-liners, on the one hand, and his own needs and those of his community, on the other. But the major distinction in reacting to the Jewish question was between those who had personally witnessed the Holocaust and those who had not. The Dutch, Germans, and some Americans watched all Jewish issues with deep concern; the Australians, most Africans, and the young were bored at best, hostile sometimes.

Arabs and Communists were seeking harsher denunciation of Israel than the third world in general would support. Some Asians felt there was just too much talk about Judaism and the Middle East, but here and there a powerful black or Indian friend was also heard. More Americans and Scandinavians than I would have guessed chose a safe "neutrality," sometimes masking unease. When Robert McAfee Brown mentioned Auschwitz (the only time), a German respondent regretted that the word was better known than *Kindergarten* (he is wrong; many non-Europeans really did not know what was being discussed), and an Egyptian Copt replied with charges of concentration camps in Israel, as if Auschwitz has its equivalent there, or anywhere. And then he said, "After all, Jesus was not really of the Jews."

Here began a most fascinating and crucial division of opinion. A black American bishop told me that I had no right to remark on Jesus' personal history, since I have explicitly rejected him as my Savior. A woman from Holland insisted that, after all, Jesus was a stranger also to his own people. Some Africans called for a Black Jesus, especially Canon Burgess Carr, the most impressive voice in all Nairobi. Many Europeans blushed at the sheer provincialism of a Jewish Lord. "Jesus Christ frees and unites" was the Assembly topic, but a historical Jesus was not at all what they meant. The Norwegian archbishop, who later led the fight against dialogue with other faiths, recalled that only the First Assembly (Amsterdam, 1948) talked principally about God. Since then it is only a churchly Christ who can, apparently, unite His church. And such a Savior must not be too narrow, too Jewish, or too remote.

Mission, conversion, became the major goal of the Assembly. To bring the whole world to Christ seemed often to overshadow the desire to feed the world or to join with others in redressing its injustices. The Assembly voted on Angola, Latin America, disarmament, and poverty (but not, of course, on minorities in China or Syria, and only obliquely on the USSR), yet its heart remained narrowly "Christian." The church has needs that no mere politics is likely to challenge or replace. Fine if it can speak for the oppressed too, but it is essential that it keep its own priorities clear. The mission of the church remains missions after all. Saving souls is an older and more popular goal than making revolutions. Dialogue runs a poor third. Christianity should talk to Jews and others only when and if it remembers whom it must always talk about. *Extra ecclesiam nihil salus* (no salvation outside the Church) was alive and well in Nairobi in December 1975.

The Assembly statement on the Middle East was a model of mealymouthed compromise, but perhaps the best that could have been expected from a group where every view was heard except that of the Jews. The policy statement called for Israeli withdrawal from the territories occupied in 1967, the right of all states, including Israel, to live in peace within secure boundaries, and for Palestinian

172 : Unfinished Rabbi

self-determination. It expressed hopes that Arab states (and the PLO) will now be willing to seek agreement with Israel on these principles. No one can cavil at these suggestions, I hope, but neither can anyone rejoice as if it were a breakthrough to higher political ground. A common American view that the World Council is in the hands of flaming radicals is simply not true; it is firmly controlled by a very bourgeois, left-liberal mentality, which is neither inimical to nor very concerned about the Jews. Mostly one feels the leaders do hope for peace in the Middle East, if only not to be bothered any longer by potentially disruptive issues. The real enemy of the WCC is neither Israel nor the Arab states but disunity itself.

Its statement on Jerusalem was almost entirely concerned with the protection of (especially non–Roman Catholic) church property and traditional denominational prerogatives. A superb example of *pro domo* special pleading, the statement nevertheless does not espouse any dangerous utopian scheme for Jerusalem that would be unwelcome to Jews. Israel is, perhaps, worth a church concession or two, and this statement asks no more. Jews can count on the churches to want prerogatives far more than political programs. We are always safer with the selfish; among Christians it is only the fanatical who might desperately attack Israel, and there were very, very few fanatics in Nairobi.

Some Protestant Christians, coming from countries where their religion is almost a monopoly (Norway, or an area like South Dakota), were inclined to be triumphalist; they are used to power and to victory. But others from multicultural places like India and New York or defensive enclaves like East Germany and Argentina are much more accustomed to moderation, if not to downright defeat. Some of them might have felt Judaism too remote for their attention, but they are not inclined to see mission as utterly overriding dialogue. They have to live in close association with Buddhists (Sri Lanka) or Marxists (Rumania), and tend to find Jews rather easier to confront. There was no unanimity at the Assembly about whether Judaism is indeed closer to Christianity than is Hinduism or secular humanism, and there was persistent unwillingness to single us (or me) out in any way. Yet, while that does violence to history, it may ultimately help to demythologize the Jewish question and thus be safer for us in the end.

The style of this twenty-day marathon was very different from many Jewish meetings. Christian patience, as well as a masochistic willingness to sit through nine hours a day of talking, seem to me incredible. When a morning was finally given to women, *seven* of them spoke successively, and all were applauded. Business sessions often debated twenty closely typed pages of proposals. Even the evenings were filled with committee meetings and homework. The WCC style is kerygmatic, proclamatory. I believe I heard five hundred Christian sermons in three weeks. But something was left out too. There were only a few hours given to study of the Bible, and none for any other text. This Jew missed the close attention to traditional sources our own faith demands. One felt almost that the World Council was sometimes improvising Christianity, speaking ecumenese instead of Hebrew, Greek, or Latin.

No trendy issue was left unvoted (racism, sexism, *et al.*), but none was much illumined by historical or revelational light. This came about partly because some powerful theological minds were absent (I think of the French theologian Jacques Ellul, the American John Cobb, and the German Wolfhart Pannenberg), and some who were present were hardly noticed (Jurgen Moltmann of Germany, for example). Those in charge were Christian statesmen, no mean breed, but their focus is tactical and not scholarly, much less devotional. General Secretary Potter himself sometimes seemed to transcend the merely contemporary by his personal courage and almost biblical wrath. But most of the deliberative sessions were technically professional, bureaucratic, and punishingly efficient.

Occasionally delegates said so. The longest applause greeted a young scholar from Oxford who listed the delegates among the world's oppressed. Indeed, many times we were worn down by interminable speechifying, only to be swept through debate on complicated issues in record time. But that was not precisely manipulation. It was rather a question of what I might call neo-Christian style. One met it at Vatican II and at clergy associations around the world. If Christians no longer study sacred texts, what can they do but proclaim?

And Christendom also remains firmly clerical. Not only the Roman Catholics: the Orthodox, the Anglicans, even the American and West European churches were represented in Nairobi by many bishops and clerics. The garb from Ethiopia and Hungary was stunning, but the effect of so many priests and metropolitans, who dominated the proceedings, was daunting to more than one Australian or Californian layman. Has the church of Jesus, a lay *Am-Haaretz* (plain-folks nonscholar) who had harsh words for clerical pomp, been delivered into the hands of a Sadducean hierarchy?

I was invited to go to Egypt after the Assembly with a WCC delegation, and gladly agreed. But the Orthodox Coptic bishop in charge of the visit explained to me in Nairobi that of course I would have to have a private tour, since they would not welcome an interfaith group. He was warmly hopeful I would understand, and I do— all too well! There remain great gaps between Christians and Jews, some of which seem to be widening. There are still huge Christian potentialities for mistrust and bigotry. But the World Council of Churches is more a wall of defense, I believe, than the battleground of our final destruction. There are in the WCC Christian statesmen and leaders who seek our weal; they dominate the Council, at least so far. But I am glad that, in the end, we put our trust not in their staying power but in the one Lord Who judges them as well as us.

[*Worldview*, March 1976]

SEEKING COMMUNITY: ADDRESS TO THE WORLD COUNCIL OF CHURCHES

PERHAPS IT IS not too bold to say that Judaism does not seek community but begins with it. Indeed, one of our central problems is the transcendence of our own deep concern with the Jewish people. But, in any case, we are born not single individuals who must consciously enter a religious community but children of a clan, members of a people, already integrated in a group described in the Bible as "children of Israel," "congregation of Israel," and even "nation of Israel," though perhaps none of these translations quite renders the nuances of the Hebrew descriptions.

A non-Jew may enter our community through conversion, which includes baptism and (for men) circumcision, but he or she is not encouraged to do so, since it is our conviction that God requires only of Jews the special demands of the Torah, whereas gentiles may attain salvation by decent, reverent lives circumscribed by the so-called seven Noahide commandments. Others need not enter our community for them to share with us human agendas and human fellowship, nor to participate fully in the Divine creativity which is every person's birthright. On the other hand, our community has no racial definition, and people of all colors and descent are members of it.

The Jewish community has sometimes been divided, for example, into priests and Levites and ordinary Israelites; but that distinction has fallen away since Temple times, and no important distinctions based on birth survive. We have no clergy in the usual sense, since there are no sacraments and can be no charisma. All Jews are commanded to observe the same Torah, and if there is any imputed superiority at all it is the superior wisdom of the scholar who understands the Torah best or of the pious person who observes it most gracefully and most joyfully. Worship is in the hands of laymen (or was, before some imitation of Christian, particularly Protestant, modes supervened), and no rabbinical prerogatives exist that are not bound up with plain knowledge. The rabbi is neither more nor less than a teacher; the community is chosen to study and practice in communion. Women are exempted from commandments that require a precise time for observance but are otherwise bound by all obligations both negative and positive. One of the great obligations is the commandment to provide for the needs of fellow Jews, whether those needs be for food and lodging (hospitality is a very important commandment) or for teachers and community organizations. The Land of Israel is sacred to the community, and in principle every Jew is obliged to live there provided no other obligation takes precedence. In any case, he must support the part of his community that lives in the Land every way he can. In the Messianic Age, the whole Jewish community will finally be united in its land and will live without divisiveness or separation from its God.

Judaism also takes seriously the human community. All men are descended from common parents and have a common "face," the Image of God. All persons are of equal status, and no ultimate distinction between them is possible. Judaism attempts to bring the human community closer together both by what it does and what it does not do. It emphatically does not try to Judaize mankind, nor to make invidious distinctions between faith communities or their commitments. If anything, it is too proud to engage in such contests. On the other hand, Judaism does require of Jews that they attend to the needs of other persons, not, of course, to the default of their responsibilities to their own families, clan, and country. Jews, like most people, have multiple loyalties, and sometimes these conflict, but more often, perhaps, they are congruent. We do not believe human community is achieved by subtraction from penultimate loyalties, especially since even these fall under the obligation to love only God with all our hearts and souls and wealth. A Jew can be loyal to his people, to his country, and to the world community which is coming to be, provided all of these fit into an architectonic scheme which not only culminates in but is everywhere informed by the love of the one God. The "neighbor" whom we are to love as we love ourselves is, in the first instance, our actual neighbor, then the next-but-one, finally all mankind. And "love" describes not an emotion but a task, a commandment which is laid out in detailed specificity by Jewish law and which leaves no one vague or unaware of his or her obligations.

Jews have lived all over the world and are therefore intimate with most of the world's religions. But our most obvious and most persistent relationships have been with the religions we are proud to call daughters, Christianity and Islam. The religion of and about Jesus, the Jew, as well as the teaching of Muhammad, a prophet schooled in Hebrew tradition and moved by Hebrew Scripture and example—these are naturally both very close to Jewish feeling and more problematic for Jews than more distanced communities, such as Buddhism, where there has been less competition with Judaism as well as less harassment of Jews. For all the latter, Christianity and Islam remain Torahnic religions with deep connections, sometimes obvious and sometimes subterranean, which both create and obscure conflicts between the several communities. For conflicts there are, and always have been. The Europe that destroyed six million Jews was, in many respects, an anti-Christian Europe, but even the neopagans had been nourished by anti-Semitism found in the documents of the church. Arab communities sometimes found what they took to be encouragement in the Quran for attacks on the Jews as Jews. Perhaps it is only our powerlessness that prevented Jews from using their own traditions against other persons, and today in an Israel that is powerful but insecure, such desires are not entirely absent. But, by and large, it is among the people of God wherever they are convoked that Jews have found their most trustworthy allies and their most sympathetic comrades. If the world is moving into a post-Christian epoch, it will also be a post-Jewish one, and Jews cannot await without trepidation new threats to the community's existence and self-understanding.

But in our view the future of mankind rests only partly in human hands. Man is obligated to do the Commandments, leaving to God the final decision about mankind's fate. About the latter we have no fear; but whether or not humankind will be obedient and responsible as it becomes more powerful is a question we cannot be sure how to answer. Our faith in God does not produce sanguine trust in any man or any community. But neither does it permit us finally to be fearful of mankind's future under God.

[Address to the World Council of Churches Assembly,
Nairobi, 1975]

PART EIGHT

Our Times

THE NEW ASSIMILATIONISTS

I AM in the mansion of the executive officer of one of the oldest and most important universities in the United States. A grandson of a president of the United States lives next door; as a dean, he reports to the provost, who is alone responsible for the day-by-day administration of this great university. The provost is a Jew. A generation ago, before World War II, a Jew could not even hope to be a tenured professor; now one of us is in charge, not only here but in a number of American universities. Why? Because of the triumph of the meritocractic principle? Or because, like the railroads, a threatened industry is forced to call in Jewish management? The former, I think. I am not sure.

But the provost is not only a nominal Jew, like so many intellectuals of our recent past. He knows. He speaks Jewish languages. He has headed important Jewish (and civil rights and other liberal) organizations. He is a philosopher of the law, a Jewish enterprise if ever there was one. He serves on the board of our B'nai B'rith Hillel Foundation. He has no desire nor need to suppress his origins nor to change his name. His wife writes best-selling novels about her childhood on New York's East Side and about Hasidism. Their home is filled with exquisite *mezuzot*, candelabra, Jewish art. To be sure, the *mezuzot* are inside the house to be seen, rather than outside to be ritually employed. But they are visible, symbolic, and extraordinary nonetheless. The provost is Jewish and everyone knows it, and he wants everyone to know it.

But what is "Jewish"? If it means religious commitment, the provost is private and noncommittal on this issue. Unlike many high administrators of Christian background, he is neither conspicuously a believer nor a skeptic. One has the feeling that faith is not the locus of his undoubted Jewish concerns, at least not in any theological sense, not in a "Christian" sense. He is comfortable in being Jewish and, if there is a problem, it is that he is perhaps too comfortable in being Jewish. . . . We have been accustomed to seeing our role as interstitial, marginal, alienated. But here is an (apparently) integrated human being. Do we miss tension, struggle, a Judaism that judges and in part rejects modernism? Or has the provost gone through these conflicts and come out the other side? In any case, Judaism seems alive and well in a home and an office where it has never been welcome before.

The generation that is in charge of the American educational establishment now includes many Jews, most of them far less "Jewish" than our provost, some of them deeply ashamed of their origins (our provost remembers City College fondly) or conflicted about their responsibilities (he sees them as fully congruent with where his heart is, and he may be right). That generation, my generation, had our hands full in getting advanced degrees from the best schools, finishing the dissertation or the professional internships, trying to stay married and raise a family—all this in the wake of the Holocaust which killed a third of our brothers and sisters and wounded every Jew of our generation. We helped create Israel, we helped build nearly a thousand new synagogues and schools, we worked out our own Jewish life alone and in communities of fellow seekers. We succeeded; we failed. But, I believe, it is the next generation, our children's, that will finally face the issue of commitment and/or success more squarely and more fully than we. We look like them, but our heads are often those of our parents and theirs before them. We never fully assimilated; most of us never meant to in the first place. We are, after thirty years at the university or at the hospital or in court, not very different from what we once were. *They* are profoundly transformed.

We are told in Hansen's Law of sociology that the third generation remembers what the second generation tried hard to forget. Thus assimilating Jewish parents, themselves children of immigrants, may have children who return unexpectedly to *kashrut* and Zionism. But the return is often complicated. The third generation can be, indeed, proudly and fearlessly Jewish, but the themes to which they return have been utterly transformed by their experiences in the American milieu. They return not to what was but to their image of what was, to their special version of the millennial Jewish situation which has been greatly transformed, if not wholly reversed. The third generation *does* remember, but often in the way it has been taught to remember by the culture of the American university.

For Jewish tradition, the highest virtue (*k'neged kulam*) is disinterested study of the Torah. To study and restudy God's word (Pentateuch, Bible, all of the religious tradition, ultimately) is what human beings must do when they aspire to insight and obedience. Study is the study of sacred texts in a sacred community, with the goal of serving a holy master. But many young Jews now understand a wholly different goal of education: study is goal-directed; it is, in fact, the royal road to power in our meritocracy. . . . There are no sacred texts, but there are magical ones (law books, business school protocols) which open all doors, including the sealed gate to our redemption. Redemption, of course, no longer means oneness with God and with a messianic world, but oneness with those who rule on earth already.

Israel is also a value to these new Jews, but in complete transvaluation. What was once perceived as a Holy Land, full of need and full of the power to bestow grace, the land of the prophets and sages, the land where God's commandment requires us to live, the land where Jewish self-definition is most plausible and most rewarding—that land has become a very different kind of paradigm. Israel now means power, particularly naked military power. Israel is still a task, but it is now the task of protecting the Jewish community in its own land by attaining power in other lands (particularly in the United States) where Israel's future will be decided. Jews must assimilate in order to become expert in managing violence, in order to protect valid Jewish interests in Israel and around the world. . . .

The Holocaust is also transformed under the reconsideration of third-generation perspectives. In Jewish thinking it always looms very large: as theodicy, as martyrdom, as tragedy, at once terrifying and problematic. But for our young, the Holocaust serves almost exclusively as a warning: if Jews are powerless they will be killed; hence they must never be powerless again. . . . The point is to become powerful, and the way is by becoming more assimilated than the assimilationists, more American than old American families. Poor Jews, separatist Jews, cannot protect the Jewish people. Only we, the university educated, well connected and successful beyond any previous generations of Jews, can do that. We honor the Warsaw Ghetto fighters and the victims of Auschwitz best by refusing to become victims ourselves, and that means by refusing categorically to be interstitial any longer in the American polity. The true answer to the Holocaust is found, finally, at the Harvard Business School and Exxon.

Jews were often left-liberals in the past because they were poor, say our new assimilationists, and because they continued to identify romantically with the poor even when they moved up the economic-social ladder. But we, the new assimilationists, will have no time for these romantic illusions any longer. They are dangerous and regressive. It is time we identified openly with the upper-class party and the upper-class club and the upper-class ambition that fit our present situation. Judaism teaches first and foremost, "If I am not for myself, who will be?"; it requires of us that we forsake any pseudo-ideals that obscure our self-interest.

I doubt that our young careerists speak the whole truth. Not only did Hillel the Elder add, "But if I am only for myself, what am I?" but the whole meaning of the key phrase is quite different. Professor Ephraim Urbach has pointed out that the meaning is: If I do not perform the *mitzvot* myself, who can do my job for me, and if I do perform them only for a reward, what reward have I, and if I do not begin now, when shall I? Left-liberalism among Jews is conditioned not only by a transient sociology but by a pervasive, millennial interpretation of Jewish piety and prophetism in the everyday obligation of politics. Of this our young assimilationists know nothing and care nothing. If our sole obligation is to move up in the gentile world, old-fashioned Jewish ethics must be transcended. For the sake of the Jews, we may be required to stop being so Jewish. For the sake of saving our necks, we must finally learn to stop worrying about other people's skins. Egalitarianism is a handicap in any meritocracy; so it is time we cease pretending we are about others and start moving to the top where we belong—not only, of course, for our own sakes but for the sake of an embattled Western world and a vulnerable Jewish folk.

It may be true that the military-industrial complex has long been a hotbed of anti-Semitism, but its elite must know by now that they need Jewish leadership, our young careerists believe. They cannot continue to exclude Jewish brains from top positions unless (like the Soviets) they are willing to pay a tremendous price, ultimately an unacceptable price. The third generation (often, already, the fourth) of American Jews is ready at last to enter the sacred precincts of American capitalism and to begin to take over key roles. We are needed, they say, and no one can keep us out any longer, especially because the "we" that is going to move in is a much more acceptable "we"; Choate and Yale and Stanford Law School have done their task for hundreds of us. We are now *salonfähig*, acceptable everywhere. What our former masters may not know is that though we look very different, we are as proudly (if not as "religiously") Jewish as any previous generation. We are not only a fifth column in the corporate world but also heirs of the Rothschilds and Warburgs. We are where we belong, at last.

Thus, say our ambitious young men and women, we can surrender a Jewish style which was only transitional in any case. It is no loss to give up lox and Yiddish. Woody Allen has already demonstrated that such a Jewishness was sexually debilitating and personally counterproductive. So have more profound critics more profoundly—writers like Hannah Arendt and Jean-Paul Sartre. We are ready to slough off immigrant habits and feelings in order to take our place in American social life. We shall, of course, not need to become Reform Jews (that measure was, in any case, too little and too late)—theology is neither a stumbling block nor an advantage; it is merely irrelevant. But we *shall* need to dress somewhat differently and talk differently and experience differently. That's all, and that's enough for our neo-assimilationists.

But, are Jewish modalities really so completely separate from Judaism? Is our "style" nothing but East European shtetl memories, or is what we are determined by Jewish fate, if not also by Jewish faith? Can we dismiss as mere nineteenth-century cultural baggage what seems to embody an essential way of being in the world? Jews can, of course, easily give up lox and funny-looking clothes. But how about our sexuality and parenting and philanthropy and even our style of learning? Is it obvious that we have nothing to lose by changing these crucial modalities of service and survival? Is the way we pray utterly irrelevant to how we live, our Bible and Talmud to what we have become? I do not believe that those who choose to assimilate in order to serve the Jewish people will remember how to do that, much less how to serve the ancestral God. If we buy into American (or Soviet or Israeli) society without reservation, we shall inevitably have sold out something once precious to us and to God.

The Jewish hero was once upon a time the scholar-saint. Later he was the scientist and the student of Western culture, the soldier and the *kibbutznik*. Is he or she now to be the aging preppie, the successful meritocrat, the Marrano manager for General Motors who cleverly masks his or her Jewishness with a Jewish mask? In the Enlightenment period we were advised by Jewish thinkers to be Jews at home but human beings abroad. Now, apparently, the roles are to be reversed; outside we shall flaunt our Jewish colors, our loyalties to fellow Jews, our fearlessness, to be what we want. But at home, inwardly, we shall have transformed ourselves into something quite other. There will be no real Jews left to protect, not in a Jewish state, even one that is strong enough to survive and conquer but not finally to embody the millennial dream, nor in a Diaspora that will win every game but the last and most important. Some already call this success, but to me it is death of the Jewish spirit and the last assimilation of all.

[*Conservative Judaism*, Summer 1980]

ELECTIONS

TO MY RECOLLECTION, I have never used this column in the service of partisan politics. The reason, I hope, is not that I was afraid. It was rather that I could not find much point in any so-called political issue. The real moral decisions of America are made, I believe, within the parties and above the parties, but almost never between the parties. I could not agree with friends who were able to see profound moral differences between an Eisenhower or a Nixon, on the one hand, and a Stevenson or a Kennedy, on the other. I did not see how any man could programmatically choose the party of Dodd and Eastland, on the one hand, or of Tower and Hicken-looper, on the other.

But I believed all along and believe now that religion and politics are inseparable. My only reservation was that national "politics" is subpolitical. That is, the great issues of American policy (peace, civil rights, automation) have never been voted upon in any national election. When and if they were, religious men would have a duty to vote for peace, for the Negro, and for the poor. I believe the time has finally come.

Whatever Senator Goldwater's personal virtues, and I believe that he has a number, including courage, charm, and sincerity, I think that every religious man must vote against the senator this November. Whatever the senator's reasons were (and they become less clear as the campaign continues), Goldwater voted against a test-ban treaty, against the Civil Rights Act, and against the War on Poverty. He has spoken continually against the Supreme Court's defense of the individual American, and against the right of the federal government to assume responsibility for some of her citizens who are in serious danger, and against close civilian control of military policy, and against international negotiation. These are not partisan issues; they constitute the basic consensus of the American policy. Goldwater rejects out of hand not only bipartisan foreign policy but bipartisan domestic policy too.

In every single deviant position, Senator Goldwater has opposed absolutely not only the American consensus but also the religious commonality. No religious body in America, no serious church leader, no responsible congregation would today dream of sharing his dangerous nationalism, his economic primitivism, or his incredible appeal for good feeling rather than plain justice between the races. No Protestant, no Catholic, no Jew. Goldwater has placed himself squarely against the whole ecumenical struggle of the American churches to find a better way to live together.

Goldwater cannot make me a conventional Democrat. But he can remind me that in any party in any year in any country, a political movement can assume power which repudiates my faith and threatens my life. I believe that religious men and especially Jews, and most especially members of this congregation, of whatever party and whatever conviction, should take it upon themselves to name Goldwater their enemy and to do everything they can to reduce him and his antireligious program to obscurity. He will not be the last threat to our American integrity, but he is the clear and present danger, and we should fight him while we still can.

May God help us to elect Lyndon Johnson president!

[Congregation Solel *Pathfinder*, October 21, 1964]

IT COULD NOT have come at a more inconvenient time: Erev Kol Nidre, at noon. But that was when Walter Mondale was in New Haven, to address Yale students and some ethnics whose votes were in doubt. And for lunch (*milchig*, at a kosher-style downtown restaurant), he proposed to meet with our Jewish leadership, self-styled and/or self-appointed. Some thirty of us spent two hours or so with Mr. Mondale, asking a lot of silly questions and getting a lot of silly answers. I have known Mondale slightly for some years. Seven or eight years ago he addressed my congregation in Illinois wisely and courageously about Vietnam and Israel. This time he contented himself with such platitudes as: "Harry Truman was my idol [*sic!*]; Hubert Humphrey was my mentor; you have nothing to fear from Walter Mondale." In political Jewish, I suppose that means that Truman was the first to recognize Israel, Humphrey has been on the take from Jewish organizations for years, so you Jews can expect me, Mondale, to do what I can for you, especially if I become vice-president. The fall of a good senator into a tired, vapid office-seeker, if perhaps also still the best of the four presidential and vice-presidential candidates, was to me shocking and sad.

His big job was, apparently, to convince us that Jimmy Carter, that born-again Paulinian, would also be good for the Jews. "The first thing Jimmy wanted to discuss with me was Israel. It was at the top of his agenda. We talked about moving the American embassy from Tel Aviv to Jerusalem. He made no promises, but I know what he would like to do. You can trust Carter, because he really believes the Bible, to be alert to the interests of the Chosen People."

What, of course, we can really expect, at the very best, is that President-elect Carter (victorious since our meeting with Mondale) will do what he thinks is best for America, keeping us strong and yet not belligerent, free and just at the same time—and the most we can hope is that such success would not be bad for Jews in Minnesota or Leningrad or Haifa. What we cannot expect and should not desire is that in order to win Jewish support, presidents will ever do what they believe works against the legitimate interests of their country, and we should not look like we do.

But we do! Otherwise why would an intelligent man like Mondale think he must tell us that Israel's expanded borders are a prime concern of his ticket, or Ford that Mr. Rabin loves him even better than he did Mr. Nixon or Mr. Johnson? The candidates make us look like that is how we decide whom to vote for, and thus place us in the position of less than loyal Americans as well as something of simpletons too. . . . Why did so liberal and thoughtful a Democrat as Mondale not think Jews would be concerned *as Jews* about unemployment, minority rights, or the compassionate programs of succor for the elderly and the disadvantaged that his opponent has been ruthlessly vetoing? Does he think we are jingoist Israelis, we who are surely not jingoists in our American loyalty? Could he not guess that we have many different views about the Middle East, and that we would welcome a thoughtful, modulated analysis of the problems of the Palestinians, of the Lebanese disaster, of how American power should and should not be deployed in the interest of world peace? Apparently he could not.

I believe that we Jews are communicating a dangerously erroneous view of our real commitments. We look like bad citizens, ethnocentric partisans, and often also fools. The truth is that the American Jewish electorate is far more sophisticated than we have been made to appear by those who seek our votes. . . . We deserve to be seen as the most thoughtful, best educated, and perhaps most humanely responsive of all American political blocs, if indeed we are a bloc at all. But we permit ourselves to be cajoled and manipulated by greedy candidates who play on our most atavistic moods and our most inhumane self-righteousness. That does neither them nor us any honor and cannot produce a single clear gain for our fellow Jews across the world. The Israeli attitude to campaign promises is on the whole realistic. They know full well that come January the main outlines of policy will be found to be substantially the same under Carter as under Ford. The Jews of America, on the other hand, have allowed themselves to be used in this election because all we have required of candidates is a loyalty oath to the security of Israel. The oaths have been given, but they are devoid of political content and are therefore useless in enabling us to respond to

American pressure for an overall settlement that does not correspond with current Israeli policy.

[Breira *interChange*, November 1976]

"RABBI ELAZAR said: Anyone who praises a place more than the prophets and sages did, is uprooted from the world. . . . Anyone who prays prematurely is described in the verse, 'For He will not hold guiltless the one who takes His Name in vain.'"

During the 1984 presidential campaign Mr. Reagan was guilty of these terrible sins. His triumphalist boosterism in a country that is filled with contradictions and suffering (as well as successes and hopes) was both tragically mistimed and self-serving. The religious right misunderstands the nation and the deontological nature of faith. God is not available to endorse our most pretentious claims to moral superiority and to invidious aggressiveness. Mr. Reagan called up the deepest atavisms of a nation whose heart is devious, as all hearts are devious, and for whom self-satisfaction overrides repressed terrors and the will to self-transcendence. Mr. Reagan is a postclassical, faithless man of faith.

But the triumph of the right is a symptom of the gutlessness of the left, personified by Mr. Mondale's inanities and pandering. Could he really have believed that religion is only a personal matter with no important consequences for political action? But then, could he possibly have believed all the incompatible ideas he spouted? All the constituencies he sought must have doubted that he could have meant what he said, even if, by accident, he had understood what he meant.

Fritz Stern, in an important essay, "Germany, 1933: Fifty Years After," says that an important precondition for the Nazi counterrevolution was a prior "silent secularization" of the center and the left. In short, fascism grows on the soil of national unbelief and personal narcissism. . . . "In confronting National Socialism," writes Stern,

"Germans responded to something far deeper than a political choice. For many of its adherents or sympathizers, National Socialism was a promise at once of immediate melioration and of satisfaction of a deeper yearning, a longing that had expressed itself before in sudden eruptions of the spirit. . . .

"After the *Kulturkampf* [of the 1870s], Protestant Germany, where in the 1920s and 1930s National Socialism won its decisive triumphs, experienced what I would call 'silent secularization,' a term adapted from the medical vocabulary which describes an unnoticed heart attack as a 'silent' one. Secularization was largely 'silent,' a protracted transformation characterized more by concealment than by confrontation, more by pretense of continuity than by an acknowledgment of a profound break. . . . In Protestant Germany, the death of God remained an unacknowledged secret, disguised, transmuted, denied—denied at times by the very voices that warned against the secular wave, the godless world."

The truth is that "religion begins in mysticism and ends in politics." The hysterical yet gentle moderation of a Mondale is no more acceptable than the fatuous duplicity of a Reagan. The Republicans chanted "USA USA" as if our nation were a football team. Democratic orators, including the highly praised Jesse Jackson and Mario Cuomo, were short on ideas and long only on nostalgia. Radical seriousness about religion is not their *metier*, nor are they serious, either, about the life of politics and its terrible commitments.

All of us, left and right, have broken the profound connection between faith and act. We have trivialized our beliefs by making them wholly personal. We have vulgarized our politics by making it realistic and self-seeking. "Realism" is the death of political vision, as it is also, inevitably, the death of religious insight. Silent secularism breeds fascist imperialism. If we do not learn how to pray and to obey the commandments, we probably will not know how to stop the bomb or feed the hungry. The ethical legacy of our moribund faith is just about exhausted by now. Mr. Mondale was its last legatee. Mr. Reagan, threatening Central America, joking about the end of the world, churchless, inhumane, and devout-speaking, is the image of the future. No real religion and no serious politics add up to no American future at all.

[*Sh'ma*, February 8, 1985]

THE SHOAH

LAST MONTH something happened at Solel that will, I believe, be a footnote in Jewish history as long as men remember. It happened during our annual memorial to the European Holocaust which we undergo each year on the anniversary of the battle of the Warsaw Ghetto. For two days and two nights this year, our young people read the names of those who died in the camps and ovens. They did not, of course, read six million names, but they read hundreds of names, most of which have never been pronounced anywhere in the years since the Nazis burned their bodies. The kids stayed up all night, praying and reading in shifts, eating whatever was brought in, thinking, asking, remembering—*remembering*.

Many sad and glorious things happened during the *Shoah* (Hebrew for devastation or "Holocaust") Weekend. Seven hundred children and two or three hundred adults accepted the agony of recollection. The little kindergartners spoke touchingly about the sad times of life and the most mature high school students read out loud the diaries of the dying ghettos. We sang the songs "The Last Road" and "Ani Maamin." We wept with the child who never again saw a butterfly, and we revolted with the Zionist partisans, and we asked God over and over again how it could be and what we must do.

But most telling of all was the simple recitation of the names of the dead. One by one we brought them back to our own, very different world. One by one we gave them "hand and name" (Isa. 56:5) as the Bible tells us we must do. One by one we recovered the martyred dead of our people. One by one, in tears, in silence, in awe, in

God knows what depth of soul, we found the lost, we found ourselves.

[Congregation Solel *Pathfinder*, May 11, 1966]

THE LONG-AWAITED Holocaust Museum is rising rapidly on the Mall in Washington, D.C. That worries me, as it has for a long time. The name is wrong—what happened in the *Shoah* was no "holocaust," no sacred sacrifice to God. The place is wrong. The commission in charge has had too many resignations, including that of Elie Wiesel as chair. The cost is wrong in an era when Jewish and human needs are so enormous. The portrayal of Jews as mere victims is dangerous and incomplete. By the way, the honorary chairman is Ronald Reagan, the sage of Bitburg.

But lately I have been thinking of Native Americans. They were the victims of the one true genocide committed on the American continent. They must feel bewildered to see our European *Shoah* commemorated and their local murder ignored. I believe we, as Jews, should take the lead in helping to create a Museum of Native American Experience, including a vivid description of how they were expelled, betrayed, and murdered by successive American governments. If we "deserve" a place of memory, so surely do they.

It is our duty to remember the *Shoah* and to teach it to our children. Not to give us Jews special rights or special roles, but to make us sensitive to the outrages that marred all of Western history and to the tasks of human rescue and succor that still remain. For this, more than a museum on the Mall will be required: no less than a true renewal of the heart.

[KAM Isaiah Israel Bulletin, March 31, 1993]

OVEREMPHASIZING THE HOLOCAUST

ALMOST twenty years ago, Congregation Solel in Illinois, where I was a rabbi, began a yearly weekend of Holocaust commemoration. We read the names of the martyrs, studied the work of Raul Hilberg and Leon Poliakov, debated Hannah Arendt and Bruno Bettelheim, dramatized Elie Wiesel and Anne Frank, made replicas of the camps and charts of the six million, wept, agonized, reflected, pondered. I have no regrets about having been among the first and the most persistent teachers of the Holocaust, there and later at Yale, but I do have serious doubts about what has happened to our study in those twenty years.

I recently attended a session led by children of survivors who told the story of how they had been raised with secrecy, shame, and silence about what had been done to their parents, and how they slowly, painfully recovered their own heritage and have since become active and involved Jews. But they were, unfortunately, not telling the truth. They are not, in fact, active Jews. They are victims of false consciousness who, like many of us, simply because we feel the tragedy and talk about it, believe ourselves to be "good" Jews. The *Shoah* has become a surrogate instead of a reminder.

In the several years since New Haven has had a public edifice commemorating the European tragedy (the first anywhere in the United States), most Jewish community events have taken place around the memorial statue. No matter the nature of the convocation (defense of Soviet Jewry, anti-Palestinian, fund-raising), the memorial became the normal place for Jews to get together. Needless to say, that gave a rather strong negative slant to the nature of

Jewish unity and made it more charged than it need otherwise have been. The Holocaust is, in more than one sense, the center of our Jewish self-consciousness. One wonders, inevitably, what that kind of centrality signifies to our younger children who, living in apparent freedom and affluence, sense their community's growing preoccupation (if not monomania) with Hitler's Europe.

Inevitably enemies of the Jews, or even normal rivals, become assimilated to the Nazi image. Arafat is Hitler; Brezhnev is Hitler; even Black Power advocates Rap Brown and Stokely Carmichael turn into Eichmann or Himmler. The danger in this kind of thinking is that we blind ourselves to real and rational dangers by equating them with a currently unreal and/or different one. We have come to think of the PLO as nothing more or less than the SS and cannot understand why most others see it as a rather fanatical but quite typical "liberation" movement, not much different from Begin's *Irgun* (which also murdered innocent people). We are not seeing Palestinian nationalism but Nazi genocide and therefore meet a serious challenge with blind and hysterical misperception.

If we are led to think that the *Shoah* is incomparably the most decisive and instructive event in the four-millennial history of the Jews, it will necessarily color and contaminate all our views. The Book of Deuteronomy, Rabbi Akiba, the *kibbutz* must all pale in relative insignificance in the attention of the Jewish school or synagogue. One does not now learn about God or the *Midrash* or Zionism nearly as carefully as one learns about the Holocaust, and one surely does not care nearly as much.

Several of our best theologians have become concerned about the *Shoah* to the virtual exclusion of any other kind of problem. Richard Rubenstein has drawn the logical conclusion that Judaism as a religion is finished and that only a neopaganism, freed from the pretensions of *heilsgeschichte* (sacred history) can now save the Jews. In a kind of Nietzschean super-Zionism, he turns the tables of the Torah over and substitutes a religion of terrified blood solidarity for one of the covenant and Messianism. If the Holocaust is absolutely decisive, as it is not only for Professor Rubenstein, how could we

198 : Unfinished Rabbi

possibly still wait for Redemption or obey the commandments? The purpose of Judaism, Rubenstein claims, is to teach Jews how to survive their enemies, in the process of which we shall, of course, have to become more like them than we have ever been. The Jewish religion is a survival kit for Rubenstein's traumatized survivors; who of us feel no need of that?

Emil Fackenheim, once our most subtle and learned philosopher of Judaism, has given up speaking about anything but the threat to Jewish existence, a crusade which came to seem necessary to him, especially after the Six-day War. What that event taught him is not that the State of Israel is relatively safe and powerful but that our people remains as alone and undefended as it was in the days of Hitler. We must, accordingly, forget our trivial differences of theology and practice, which are no longer really worth debating, and merge into one single self-defense unit against our enemy, the whole non-Jewish world. . . . Jews are not only all survivors now, but also all potential victims, into the endless future. How could anything else (like Kantian and Jewish ethics or the philosophy of the *Midrash*, about which Fackenheim has written exquisitely) be mentioned in the same breath with the eternal war against the eternal Amalekite, a perpetual conflict with a whole world that, in Cynthia Ozick's phrase, wants the Jews dead.

Despite their very real differences, these two most influential constructions of the Holocaust share a basic conclusion. We must turn Judaism into what it has never been before, an instrument of warfare against our enemies. What was always a way for Jews to serve God must now become a self-interested use of faith to insure that we are not undone by our enemies.

Many Christian theologians have become preoccupied with the Holocaust, with very mixed results. Instead of confronting the basic issues of Christian complicity, as Rosemary Radford Reuther has done, most of them prefer to work out some complex, obscurantist theodicy, with the consequence that the dilemmas and passion of their work are transferred to extraterrestrial realms. I do not believe the alleged silence of God is nearly as pressing an issue as the all too active deeds of men. God gives us freedom, Judaism insists consistently. He permits evil, even the most dreadful evil. Suffering of the kind that Auschwitz symbolizes is not an accusation against God; it is a warning about human sin. In one sense the Holocaust is a trivial issue, easier to "understand" than cancer or a typhoon. God could not prevent Auschwitz and still leave man free to do good. In another, anthropological sense, it is the supreme question of history. Not why did God let it happen? Rather, why did people make it happen? The hard question for Christianity and for all of us is not the death of God but the relentless continuing cruelty of mankind.

The personal consequences to Jewry and to other people of what we have made of the *Shoah* are dangerous indeed. If we seem to ourselves and to others as victims more than anything else, or, in order not to be victims, as oppressors, then we dangerously construe our future in the light of a one-sided view of our past. A Jewish child, bombarded by images of dying children, with no clear message of the life Jews live, *did* live even in Hitler's Europe, might well opt out. No healthy person chooses to be a perpetual victim; no good person would willingly spend a lifetime fighting against others who might someday be, though they are not yet, our enemies. A Christian world that sees Jews as perennial sufferers and nothing else will not see much wrong with going on doing us in.

There is a strong neo-assimilationism in our midst. It takes the *Shoah* as the model for Jewish destiny and, in struggling against it, takes arms against all humanity. It accepts all the worst accusations of the anti-Semites and builds upon these canards a new, angry, and militaristic pseudo-Zionism. In order to survive, we shall assume power in the only ways power can be achieved—at the end of a gun barrel or by Machiavellian manipulation of other groups for our own interests. There is no shame in proclaiming ourselves to be our ultimate concern. "Never again" means nothing more or less than "Jews first—and the devil take the hindmost."

Sensitive and religious Jews are appalled by this option, and often drive deeper into a hermetically sealed privatism in which they are protected against choosing to be either victims or persecutors. They see that politics can be murderous, so they choose to be apolitical. They fear that Israel must either colonize a million Arabs, support Nicaragua's Somoza, the shah, and South Africa, or be destroyed, so they create islands of softhearted non-Zionism in the belly of Jewish America. They fear the Holocaust is always now, so they surrender a terrifying present for a timeless and a historical mysticism.

Politically the consequences of our Holocaust-centered life are even more dangerous. Every small dissent is built into a life-threatening danger. We believe no one has suffered as we have (but where are the gypsies and the Armenians? or the millions of dead in Cambodia and Indonesia?), and therefore our claim on the conscience of mankind is limitless. Chauvinism is the preferred alternative to acquiescence, and no third way is even imaginable. American Jews are asked to choose, once and for all, between abject assimilation and the blanket endorsement of intolerable reaction.

The reticence of our greatest minds to write about the Holocaust is, I believe, emblematic. Heschel, Agnon, Buber—all survivors—wrote about the *Shoah* almost only by indirection. Their silence speaks volumes of tact and agony and love. So too does the patient historical work of Raul Hilberg, Yehudah Bauer, and the new generation of scholars at Yad Vashem. They resolutely de-mythologize the Hitler period. Thoughtful Orthodox rabbis in the Agudat Yisrael forbid even the use of the term *Shoah*, preferring *hurban* (a term for destruction, used of the Temple in Jerusalem, pogroms, and martyrdoms) *Europa*, which firmly sets the terrible events of our century within an authentic and millennial Jewish framework. Insisting on the utter incomprehensibility and uniqueness of Auschwitz, as Elie Wiesel does, makes it impossible ever to deal with or to transcend. There are many ways to avoid a painful issue; one of them is to be tempted by it into triumphalism, paralysis, hysteria, or suicide. . . .

[*Sh'ma*, November 2, 1979]

PART NINE

Psychotherapy as Judaism

PSYCHOANALYSIS AND RELIGIOUS EXPERIENCE

THE TRANSCENDENT implications of religion and psychoanalysis have been studied intensively in recent years. We cannot yet infer the meaning of this attempt to reconcile two enormous systems at their deepest levels. Perhaps the reconciliation itself is impossible or premature. But it might be well to examine parallels between what analysands and religious people *do*, at the simplest possible level. In the comparative experience of psychoanalysis and faith, we might find a new and proper beginning place.

The overarching difficulty in such a comparison is, of course, the essentially private nature of the religious and of the analytic experience. What happens in these several activities is, by definition, ineffable. Both religious and analytic experience are immediate, personal, and thus incommunicable. A person who describes his experience of God violates it or betrays it. A patient who tells everyone he meets about his analysis has, we may be sure, never really been analyzed. The true analysand, like the true man of faith, is necessarily reticent about what has happened to him. He hides the truth because it is too private to share and too important to reduce to mere conversation.

He also hesitates to discuss his experience because it is objectively absurd. From the outsider's point of view, the man on the couch and the physician on the chair behind are quite ridiculous. Hence the countless jokes about the doctor and his patient. Unless we were one of them, it would seem that they both were silly. Ridiculous too is the man of faith, except to a man of faith. Nothing could be more idiotic than belief—if there is no One to believe in. No man could be more absurd than a person in prayer—unless he is praying to a real God.

The Hasidic rabbis tell of a dance in which many joined with wholehearted delight. They abandoned themselves to the music and its beauty. But along came a deaf man, and to him they all seemed senseless animals moving without reason and without dignity.

Like love, to which both have been frequently compared, the experience of psychoanalysis and the experience of religion are meaningful only from within.

In addition, these experiences do not issue in objectively useful truth. They do not communicate information. They are, from the philosophic point of view, without content. A man does not come from an experience of the numinous (encounter with the holy) with new facts about the world. He does not issue from prayer more learned than he was, if by learning we mean something that can be communicated rationally to other men. Saints are not *eo ipso* scholars. Prophets are not philosophers. The God of Abraham, Isaac, and Jacob may (*pace* Pascal) be the God of the philosophers, but this is because of Who God is, not what they were. Abraham was a knight of faith, not an epistemologist. The only thing God reveals is Himself, as Franz Rosenzweig understood.

So, too, analysis does not teach a man new facts about the world. It does not instruct him; it changes him. It does not inform him; it modifies him. It does not elucidate; it empowers.

What "truth" comes from analysis is, like religious truth, personal, paradoxical, existential. Such truths as man wrenches from confrontation with himself prepare him for the world's truth, but they do not contribute to his store of knowledge.

Freud understood clearly the incredibly embarrassing parallel between psychological and religious (or, as he calls it, "mystical") apprehension.

> . . . Certain practices of mystics may succeed in upsetting the normal relations between the different regions of the mind, so that, for

204 : Unfinished Rabbi

example, the perceptual system becomes able to grasp relations in the deeper layers of the ego and in the id which would otherwise be inaccessible to it. Whether such a procedure can put one in possession of ultimate truths, from which all good will flow, may be safely doubted. All the same, we must admit that the therapeutic efforts of psychoanalysis have chosen much the same method of approach.[1]

This kind of psychic insight both requires and produces a relentless honesty. The patient must say *everything* he thinks in order to learn and to be healed. The religious man must be bravely open in his experience with God. For, as the rabbis say, the "seal of God is truth." Neither business nor science, neither the law nor the forum requires the infinite yielding of faith and of psychoanalysis. The method and the goal are the unwinding of self before the other, without which there can be no meeting and thus no help.

This unwinding of truth produces a kind of self-suspicion peculiar to the man of faith and to the analysand. Each suspects his own motives, drives always deeper into his own nature, and, at the same time, inevitably learns tolerance for other men. They are fellow creatures, fellow sinners, fellow sufferers. They only do what he has dreamed. They only act out his wild, demonic wishes. They can be forgiven, as he must learn to suspect and also to forgive himself.

Prayer requires both humility and pride on a grand scale. It requires the humility to acknowledge one's absolute dependence upon an Other, the humility to confess one's sins and confront one's unworthiness. But prayer also implies a gigantic pride, the pride that makes of God a "hearer of prayer," in the Hebrew phrase. God, for the praying man, is so close that He can hear, so concerned that He wants to hear.

In analysis, too, both humility and pride are required. Without that pride of self sometimes called ego strength, the ultimate therapy is too difficult. Without humility in the shape of one's sense of being imperfect, the motivation for cure is lacking. The patient

1. Sigmund Freud, *New Introductory Lectures on Psycho-Analysis* (New York, 1933), p. 11

must conceive of himself as sick, as needy, in order to recover. He must believe himself worthy of health and competent to grow, or he cannot be treated. He must come to a specific doctor whose judgment he trusts and whose person he respects. He must undergo the discipline of specific practice, most of which has no objective justification. He must honor the method and the practitioner with a very striking humility. But he must also have enough pride to believe that the analyst's task is to cure *him*, or to help him cure himself. He must be narcissistic enough to spend years elaborating his own symptoms, investigating his own history. For this pride is in the service of the humble result that he may be free to grow beyond those symptoms.

The paradox that regular speech produces spontaneous action is unique to religion and psychoanalysis. *Keva*, the fixed liturgy of Judaism that is shared by the daughter religions (Christianity and Islam), is indispensable. The Sabbath cannot be Thursday. The morning prayer cannot be recited at dusk. The Passover cannot be celebrated in the winter. Each word must come when it comes and not at another time. The words are fixed, the hours of prayer are fixed—but the result is spontaneous.

Kavanah, a gathering together of the spirit, constitutes the complementary and polar need of the religious man. He must not only speak the words required at the time required but must finally learn to speak his own word in his own time. By regular attentiveness he learns how to express himself more fully. By *keva*, fixity, he comes to *kavanah*, intention.

So, in analysis, the patient comes at fixed hours to unravel himself by the already traditional methods of dream analysis and free association. By punctilious attention to the analytic calendar, he comes to a freedom in which he can learn to say all he means. He cannot be cured just by coming to a regular place at a regular time for a regular purpose, nor only by "expressing himself." He needs the tension between the fixed and the spontaneous to make him well.

He comes, in metaphoric terms, through bondage to freedom.

He moves, by transferring the heavy burden of his neurotic past to another's stronger back, at last to taking up freely the proper, weighty labor of a man. He replaces the pleasure that was his former standard, a pleasure he could only imagine or half-remember but never achieve, with the standard of reality. He gives up Eden to discover God's world.

Psychoanalysis is thus precisely what Judaism means by *Torah*: direction, way, education for life. True, the experience of God is without objective content, but it is not without implication. So also analysis, which appears anomistic, leads to specific decision and command. The doctor does not say to the patient, "Do not drink!" or "Do not commit adultery!" But the *analysis* makes it very clear that to be himself he must stop drinking. The law issues from the experience. The Torah comes from the dialogue. It is a personal law couched, like the Ten Commandments, in the second person singular. It does not say, "Drinking is wrong," but only, "You have to stop drinking." It is a word, like all religious words, to the single man, but for him it is decisive. God help him, he can do no other!

It is decisive, or it is nothing. Either/or! Religion is either man's deepest experience, or it is a joke. Psychoanalysis must result in either the profoundest kind of transformation, or it was a waste of time and money. While we no longer make the absolute distinction, healthy/sick, we cannot ignore the reality that underlies the spectrum of actual example. It is different after analysis, or there was no analysis.

For the analysand, there can be no question of doing it partway. The taster, the eclectic, the hobbyist cannot be analyzed. One cannot make up the rules; he can only discover the rules he must follow. He must do what he can do. To play with analysis, to make of it a two-hour-a-week or a five-hour-a-week hobby, is to render it useless. To evaluate, to pick and choose, is not to choose at all.

> . . . A kind of buffer state has been formed between analysis and its opponents, consisting of people who will allow that there is something in analysis (and even believe in it, subject to the most divert-

ing reservations), but who, on the other hand, reject other parts of it, as they are eager to let everyone know. What determines their choice is not easy to guess. It seems to be a matter of personal sympathies. Some take objection to sexuality, others to the unconscious; the existence of symbolism seems to be particularly disliked. The circumstance that the structure of psychoanalysis, although unfinished, nevertheless already possesses a unified organization from which one cannot select elements, according to one's whim, seems not to enter the minds of these eclectics.[2]

The person who toys with the church or synagogue is also unable to meet the God of that church. A universal man who sees "good" in every faith has never known the meaning of any of them. In such matters absolute truth may be unavailable, but a man can walk only one road toward truth. Where Freud believed formal religion to be a universal neurosis, we may rather say that private religion is invariably neurotic. So is private "self-analysis." Without the discipline of other men and historic insight, the patient is left to wallow in solipsism and despair. To select among is to avoid; to discriminate is to evade; to do-it-yourself is not to do it at all.

It is hard work to be religious. It is hard, slow work to be analyzed.[3] Not because it has to be hard, but because we resist the truth. God is really there, and therefore it is not hard, in principle, to meet Him. But *we* are not always there. We build walls around our souls, defending ourselves against a fearful Other. The hard work of religion and of analysis is breaking the resisting walls. For this reason, the religious experience available to every man is found among few. Psychoanalysis, which hopes to treat the ills of mankind, is a rare phenomenon. In principle, both are universal. Because of human resistance to truth, both are rare. Because we make them so, they are hard work. And, as Spinoza said, "rare" and "difficult" are finally synonymous.

2. *Ibid.*, p. 189.

3. *Ibid.*, p. 213: ". . . psychological changes only come about very slowly; if they occur quickly and suddenly it is a bad sign."

Indeed, both are infinite in their scope. "The deeper we probe in our study of mental processes, the more we become aware of the richness and complexity of their content."[4] "The reward of a commandment," says the Chapters of the Fathers, "is a commandment." An experience of God promises us only: another such experience. Freud wrestled all his life with the problem of the interminable analysis. In truth, such work is never done. We achieve by insight only and ever the possibility of new insight. Health and faith are both asymptotes toward which we infinitely tend.

Thus religion and psychoanalysis share a proximate pessimism about self and life. The man who has experienced either the Almighty power or the depth of self has no illusions.

> Why have we ourselves taken so long to bring ourselves to recognize the existence of an aggressive instinct? Why was there so much hesitation in using for our theory facts which lay ready to hand and were familiar to every one? One would probably meet with but little opposition if one were to ascribe to animals an instinct with such an aim as this. But to introduce it into the human constitution seems impious; it contradicts too many religious prejudices and social conventions. No, man must be by nature good, or at least good-natured. If he occasionally shows himself to be brutal, violent, and cruel, these are only passing disturbances of his emotional life, mostly provoked, and perhaps only the consequence of the ill-adapted social system which he has so far made for himself. . . .
>
> Unfortunately the testimony of history and our own experience do not bear this out, but rather confirm the judgment that the belief in the "goodness" of man's nature is one of those unfortunate illusions from which mankind expects some kind of beautifying or amelioration of their lot, but which in reality bring only disaster. . . .
>
> We are now led to consider the important possibility of the aggression being unable to find satisfaction in the external world, be-

4. *Ibid.*, p. 127.

cause it comes up against objective hindrances. It may then perhaps turn back, and increase the amount of self-destructiveness within. We shall see that this actually occurs, and that it is an event of great importance. It would seem that aggression when it is impeded entails serious injury, and that we have to destroy other things and other people, in order not to destroy ourselves, in order to protect ourselves from the tendency to self-destruction. A sad disclosure, it will be agreed, for the Moralist.[5]

Psychoanalysis is indeed a "sad disclosure for the Moralist." But not for the religious man. The moralist believes that abstract rules can chasten history, that telling makes men to do good. But the religious man knows how intractable is his own resisting inclination. He is beyond the ethical realm where only despair prevails. He attempts to be changed not by hearing or trying but by the holy dialogue with God. So, too, the patient, hiding no evil, finds forgiveness even for the unforgivable. To go from where we are to higher ground, ethics does not suffice. We require not good ideas ("God does not give advice," says Rabbi Baeck) but transformation. The moral problem is not to know what is good, but to do what is good, and that is not a moral problem. What keeps us from good is our evil inclination and what we have made of our fears and needs. Analysis cannot make us angels, but it can help us to be free. This is both sacred and risky work.

Along with the pessimism for today, psychoanalysis shares with religion a sure optimism. Knowing how sick mankind is, it nevertheless strikes out for its cure. The only word for this kind of utopian behavior against all evidence is "Messianic." Hopeless, it lives in the promise that now is not forever. Like religion, it abhors the present but works toward the prophetic kingdom of the future.

The religious confrontation with God is analogous, but only analogous, to the relation of analyst and patient. The analyst is a person, like God, but he is not God. Their meeting is a true meet-

5. *Ibid.*, pp. 142, 144.

ing, but it is not the ultimate one. And yet, does God not participate wherever two are gathered in His name?

Healing is surely in His name and for His sake. It is, in the Jewish tradition, a *mitzvah*, a command of God. . . . Just as the leper had to cleanse himself before he reentered the camp of Israel, so any sick person is obligated to heal himself that he may come toward the holy place. Analysis foreshadows salvation.

Phenomenologically, the event called psychoanalysis and the event called religious are remarkably alike. This suggests that their deeper currents may indeed somewhere run together.

[*Journal of Religion and Health*, October 1962]

PART TEN

Personalities

ABRAHAM JOSHUA HESCHEL

HIS REAL NAME was Abraham Joshua Heschel Heschel; he was precisely named for his illustrious ancestor (the Apter Rebbe, Abraham Joshua Heschel). When his friends called him "Heschel," they were calling him by his first name. I never heard anyone call him "Abraham" or "Abe."

I first met Heschel thirty years ago at the Hebrew Union College. He had come there in the late thirties, almost at the last possible moment, because HUC was in the business of rescuing European Jewish scholars and nobody else much was. He was most uncomfortable in a Cincinnati Reform milieu that expected him to teach without a *kippah* and pray publicly in the anemic style of classical Reform. The student body was largely composed of secularizing liberals, with literary fellow travelers constituting the intellectual leadership. They despised Heschel and ridiculed him, though in the end they finally were to honor him for his anti–Vietnam War stand, and some of them even got religion. A small group of us were his disciples: Sam Dresner, who later followed him to the Seminary; Gene Borowitz, whose graceful *hesped* (eulogy) for him in *Sh'ma* was the best I've seen; maybe three or four other young pietists. He took walks with us and tried to show us his vision of a restored and inspirited American Jewry, but it was hard for us to imagine a new Jerusalem in Burnet Woods.

I once missed an examination in liturgy with Dr. Heschel (as we all called him at HUC), so I went to his office for a makeup test. He sat me down and asked: What passages in the *Siddur* do you find philosophically unacceptable? I listed them: resurrection, personal Messiah, all the liberal *bêtes noires*. He smiled, he "explained" what these ideas really meant, he refuted every possible objection. Shaken, I left him knowing I was no longer just a Reform Jew.

After six years Heschel went to JTS (the Conservative Jewish Theological Seminary in New York), hoping for the kind of acceptance he could never find in Cincinnati. Instead he was isolated, ignored by some, attacked by others. He was permitted to teach only a few rabbinical classes; he was never considered as a candidate for president, and not only because he was older than those who were. His reputation grew both for his scholarship and for his activism, but his books were not reviewed by important scholars very often and his social activism was an embarrassment to the Conservative movement and to men like Seymour Siegel and Wolfe Kelman who remained his closest disciples. If one wonders why the Jewish community has so few fine teachers, one might reflect on how this man, one of her greatest teachers, was at once lionized and effectively destroyed. We were all his followers, but he had no home. No home in the Hasidic world which he had left behind; not in the Conservative movement which had another agenda than his; not in the Christian community which thought of him as a prophet but never quite understood what he was driving at; not in the peace movement which used his voice or in the civil rights movement which used his face, both of which had trouble with such a Jewish Jew who was a believer at that. We all admired him, but none of us knew what to do about him, and we still don't.

When Heschel died, his family asked Bill Coffin, chaplain of Yale, to say the *hesped*, but that was not to be. His Hasidic *landsmen*, who had kept far from him in life, reclaimed his body in death. They buried him like a *tsaddik* (major rebbe) in Galicia. They wept and they stormed and they took him home, while we, his more assimilated admirers, stood off in awe. Radical groups and mainline Jewish organizations publicly mourned him and continued to write tributes. But who will follow his way? Who even knows what it is?

Heschel had his faults. He was too proud of his humility. He was too eager to give an old talk for a new fee. His (English) books are overwritten; some pages are painful to reread. Heschel posed, he postured, he dramatized himself. But his faith was all too palpable, and many hated him because he honestly believed what they dishonestly could not. He was all Jew, and so he loved the blacks and Vietnamese as himself. He would not always say in public what he said in private (about Israel, especially), but he knew right from wrong and did not spare any of us who considered ourselves his party and his hope. . . .

Heschel taught us about Shabbat and about prayer, about violence and faith, about our past and our present. Heschel, like Buber, thought of answers before we even posed the questions. He was everywhere, and everywhere he made a difference.

The last time I spoke with him was at Lake Forest College some time before he died. He told me about his final months in Germany, of how that community had been galvanized and transformed, and not because of Hitler alone. Jews were finally learning, Jews were doing *t'shuvah*, Jews were finding themselves. It had happened in Germany, this prototypical Polish Jew was saying to me; it can also happen in America. But, and Heschel lowered his voice as he always did when he wanted to emphasize a point, but *there is very little time*.

Now there is less time. Now he is gone.

[*A Critical Insight into Israel's Dilemmas*, a journal
published at Washington University, 1973]

MORDECAI M. KAPLAN

WHEN Mordecai Kaplan was sixty, we celebrated his birthday in Chicago. I attended the celebration as a kid, and I will never forget what was said. My uncle and teacher, Felix Levy, gave the principal address. He told us that he had wrestled with Kaplan and against Kaplan for years, but that he came to honor the man who, more than anyone else, had raised and clarified the question of how to be a Jew in the modern world—raised issues honestly and clearly, and that even though some of us could never accept his answers (religious naturalism, ethical nationalism, liturgical surgery), we would be influenced all our lives by his questioning.

Soon after, the Reconstructionist movement, which he had founded earlier, produced a seal to symbolize its goals and ideals. As a young rabbinical student I wrote Dr. Kaplan that I thought the seal showed a fatal flaw in Reconstructionism. In the center of the symbol was not God, as I thought should be, but the Jewish people. I think I was right then and I think I am right now, that no religious community can put itself at the center of its commitment without serious danger of falling into the position that whatever the community does is sacred. God as a judge and as a limit seems to be more necessary in the twentieth century than ever before.

Kaplan responded to my objections, and we continued a dialogue for a whole summer. As I look back almost forty years, I wonder if any other eminent Jewish leader would have troubled to write letters (in longhand) to a student about what both were concerned to argue. Would anyone else of his stature really care about me, or about whether or not I thought he was right? I doubt it.

When Kaplan was ninety he tried at the Eden Hotel in

Jerusalem to convert my wife to Reconstructionism. He spent a vigorous morning of argument, using all his undoubted powers of persuasion—with not much result, but leaving ineradicable memories for my family. Would anyone else have been able to do that at ninety years of age? Would anyone of his learning and importance have been willing to try?

There seems to be a resurgence of Reconstructionism in recent years. Not only institutional successes, based in Philadelphia and led by neo-Reconstructionists, most of whom did not know Kaplan, but also a refined theoretical interest in Durkheim and in Kaplan, his American Jewish epigone. Group-centered faith, religion as the expression of a national ethos, is again in vogue.

I cannot endorse this trend now any more than I could forty years ago. Nationalism unleashed still seems to me the most dangerous temptation of our age. Kaplan was well aware of the deficiencies, moral and political, of political Zionism, but his system had no way of transcending the needs and claims of the people or of imposing a principled, regulative ethics upon it. He may himself have unwittingly contributed to unleashing the moral whirlwind.

Still, what I remember of Kaplan is his honesty and his persistence. He was a failed ideologue (who isn't?). He never plumbed as deeply as the Frankfurt school, or as a Yeshayahu Leibowitz or a Rav Soloveitchik among the Orthodox. He was, rather amazingly, all too American. That means he asked good questions, wrote some good books (and some potboilers), and kept at his task for almost three generations. He never converted me or my family, but we never came to love a Jewish teacher any better, nor remember anyone with more gratitude and admiration. We are no Reconstructionists and never will be, but we are all his children, nonetheless.

[*Sh'ma*, December 9, 1983]

MORDECHAI MARTIN BUBER

THREE YEARS AGO I took my two sons (then nine and eleven) to the modest house in Jerusalem where Martin Buber lived. The beautiful old man ushered us into his study and turned immediately to my boys. With a charm and candor denied in him by those who assert he could only *talk* about dialogue, Buber completely enchanted us all. Finally he asked the children, "What would you like to know?" It was a truly cosmic question. I felt that if they could ask about the mysteries of Creation or Messiah or how to bring world peace, *anything*—the sage would have been able to answer them.

But they did not know what to ask. I did not. Our whole generation did not know how to put the question to its greatest thinker, its most exquisite spirit. And now it is too late.

We asked him about power, but he only knew about peace. We asked about customs while he knew about Torah. We asked how to win Jews, and he just told us to serve God. If we had only known what to ask for, he would have understood how to give it to us.

For there was so much he knew. He knew *Tanach* (Bible), not with the cold objectivity of the university professor nor with the confused passion of the ghetto recluse, but with clarity, insight, and respect. His books on Moses, prophecy, and interpretation are among the great *Midrashim* of all time.

Hasidism he not only knew; he invented it. Or, at least, the kind of neo-Hasidism that can be relevant to suburbia and not only to *Meah Sh'arim*, the Hasidic neighborhood of Jerusalem. Of course, for him knowing meant selecting. His Hasidism was not *glatt kosher*. But, despite Gershom Scholem's criticisms, it was not whimsy either. It was what Hasidism wanted to be, if perhaps never became.

Buber was a socialist, the least doctrinaire socialist of the century and perhaps the most prophetic. He was a pacifist, more subtle and brave even than Gandhi. He was an existentialist more human than Kierkegaard, more precise than Sartre. He was a Zionist to the end, even when he unwillingly had to denounce what Zion seemed willing to become. He was a Jew, not Orthodox, not Reform, not Buberian, a full-time Jew who could never see himself thereby less a man.

I and Thou began a revolution. The Buber-Rosenzweig Bible was the first and greatest modern translation. His Hasidic books transformed Jewish life in Europe and then in America. Heschel, Herberg, Arthur Cohen, all of us who are working in Jewish ideas are unthinkable without him. Jewish thought since Maimonides will someday be divided into a pre- and post-Buberian period.

But he was more than his books. More than his politics. More than his ideas. He was a whole man, a man so modern he embraced the ancient, a man so profound it will be the work of a thousand years to follow out his every lead.

We live in a dangerous time, when God is often eclipsed. But through Martin Buber the Holiness shone, the sparks were gathered, and, for a time at least, we all were saved from despair.

[Congregation Solel *Pathfinder*, October 7, 1965]

YESHAYAHU LEIBOWITZ

THE THREE most important living Jewish thinkers, Emmanuel Levinas, Joseph B. Soloveitchik, and Yeshayahu Leibowitz, are remarkable combinations of traditional and highly original thinkers. Perhaps only the combination of rigor and imagination, of *halakhic* structure with *aggadic* spontaneity, makes possible creative thinking among Jews. Be that as it may, no writer has more distinctive and, to my mind, important things to say to us than has Professor Leibowitz, whose work is finally being translated into English but who personally has been kept from the American scene by a combination of fear and inanition. It is time we listened hard to this uniquely passionate and learned scientist, scholar, and believing Jew.

The Torah is, of course, the basis of Judaism (says Leibowitz), but the Written Torah is created (not merely interpreted) by the *Torah She-b'al Peh* (Oral Torah). The Bible is a code which rabbinic interpretation cracks. It is a primitive, remote, inaccessible book which the rabbis humanize and make available. The Torah provides no reliable information, not about God and not about the world. It is literal nonsense. But the oral interpretation, which is human feedback to Divine obscurity, uproots literalism and translates doubtful history and second-rate literature into Law.

Judaism is nothing more or less than obedience to the Law. It is *avodat Hashem*, slavery to God, "Islam" (Surrender to God, pious resignation). It is all getting there, all road and no destination, no goal, no rest. It is all means with no end (as God, too, is *En Sof*). It is all content, detail, form, never merely shell. God is only in the details; there is no essence. Judaism seems objectively absurd; it fills no human need. But it creates Israel, a community of observance and obedience. Judaism wisely permits all opinions, but it mandates *halakhic* behavior.

The *halakhah* is a prosaic precis of a divine poem which we cannot comprehend. It is not ethics or philosophy or ideology; it is a praxis, almost in the Marxist sense, an outcome of ratiocination which annuls and uplifts all prior theoretical speculation. *Halakhah* is infrastructure; theology is superstructure. The Law is no escape from our mundane predicament. *Haolam k'minhago noheg*; the world goes on as if nothing and no One had happened. The Law does not redeem from sin; right after the Day of Forgiveness, *Yom Hakippurim*, ends, we immediately recite, at the beginning of the evening prayer: He is merciful and will forgive sin. We are sinners even in the hour after *Ne'ilah*. We are and always will be. The *halakhah* is a law for sinners.

There is no final redemption in this kind of world. Therefore the commandments remain valid. The only result of obedience is an infinite task of adding commandment to commandment. Joy must be intrinsic; there is no reward other than the doing of the command. Of course, as the rabbis say, one who performs under orders is greater than one who freely does right. Judaism is about slavery, not option. It is a conscientious giving of self, not an auto-emancipation.

The *halakhah* is at present in trouble, Leibowitz teaches, because of the disobedience of *halakhic* authorities and their want of courage. In a world with a Jewish state, the *halakhah* must be reconstructed again, as it was so many times before. What once was Temple sacrifice became prayer (*avodah*). What once was High Priestly ritual became the most central act of a people's reconciliation (the Day of Atonement). Now we must again perform similar acts of transformation, but always and only by the standards of *halakhic* method itself.

God is unknowable, but the *mitzvot* are clear and present obligations. The good is platonic and mysterious, but we know what is "good and right in God's eyes" because He told us. Judaism is *keva*, a decisively fixed obligation into which *kavannah*, spontaneous piety, can be poured. It is a task which human beings, Jews, can perform and, because they can, must. We know exactly what we must do, and if we do not do it, that is only because we refuse to do it. If we do the Law, the Law will enslave us to freedom. What is written on the tablets (*harut*) is liberation (*herut*), only because God alone is our single chance to be. Enthralled by Torah, we turn our gaze toward the Giver of the Torah. Nothing changes, but everything is different from what it was.

Though an Orthodox Jew, perhaps because he is one, Yeshayahu Leibowitz is angry at the *dati* (religious) establishment in Israel. Since the siege of Jerusalem in 1948, they have consistently separated themselves from the community, seeking special privilege instead of communal standards. The state uses Jewish symbolism, like "Rock of Israel" in the declaration of independence, for political purposes. Equivocation reduces religion to a kind of "public utility." Instead of struggling for values, the religious parties have engaged in clerical politics, fake coalitions, and partisan deals. From the responsibilities of state-building, they have sought exemption (*heter*), not accepted the onus of leadership. They want to keep Shabbat or eat kosher while other Jews man the security stations on Saturday and eat what is left over. They want the privilege of studying Torah instead of serving the people, while other Jews must always serve and never study. But the *halakhah* applies to all Jews. Only contemporary Orthodoxy makes a smaller claim than that.

Religion in Israel "only interferes with values that the secular state might otherwise develop." Religious Jews have become a mere sect (*kat*) instead of a model. Therefore the established synagogue must be disestablished. "Church" and state must be clearly separated, once and for all. Religious Jews should undertake all civil responsibility, without exception, that their siblings who are less devout must. They should not act as if the Jewish state were Poland or Iraq, where evasion and duplicity were necessary to keep Judaism alive. The present task is not to suffer for Torah but to act vigorously in its spirit and by its direction.

The question "Who is a Jew?" is a *halakhic* question which only the rabbis can decide. But the question "Who is a citizen?" is a political one which only the state can decide. Talmud and Codes were documents of exile. The real question now is: What would a Roman procurator do if he (and civil government) lived by the Torah? A new situation calls for a new enactment *al pi ha-Torah* (following Torah methods). Times ask changing questions, which the *halakhah* must continually address.

Above all, this means that the Jewish state must not be an immoral state. Victory in war never can produce religious insight. Expansion of territory has created a parasitic Israel, dependent on American arms, a concubine of Western nationalisms, a pawn of foreign strategies. Many incidents, like *Kafr-kassem* and *Qibya*, were military violations of the *halakhah*. Where was the religious outcry? When the synagogue gives approbation to conquest, it is heretical, Sabbatean. The Six-day War was like the wars of Jeroboam, which the Prophets (at least) denounced. Security is a mask for ambition. In a pre–World War III world there is no security, and Israel has not made mankind more just or more safe.

The State of Israel should become more neutral than Switzerland, more harmless than any other, if it is not to violate Jewish law. Unlike the Soviet dissidents, Israeli intellectuals are silent, if not also silenced. Their voice for peace is almost unheard. The religious and the thoughtful collaborate with militarism and acquiesce in sin. But "nothing of value is achieved by mere unity. Everything of value has been achieved only by severe internal struggle." Dissent should always be permissible but is now considered disloyal. Without dissent we are inevitably lost in our own pride and insularity.

The state should disengage from the occupied territories. "We must at once, this very night, get out of the territories inhabited by a million and a half Arabs, barricade ourselves in our Jewish state, and invest our entire strength in maintaining it. There is another possibility, a remote one, that a settlement will be imposed on us by the great powers. . . ." We must evacuate the territories without determining who will rule, for the sake not only of the Arab Palestinians but of believing Israeli Jews.

Yeshayahu Leibowitz has been saying these things for years. Why have we not heard? When shall we begin to listen to our greatest thinkers and teachers? "Blessed be He Who shares His wisdom with those who fear Him" (a traditional blessing recited upon seeing a great Torah scholar). And they with us.

[*Sh'ma*, May 29, 1981]

JEAN-PAUL SARTRE

JEAN-PAUL SARTRE, the most wide-ranging and brilliant mind of his age, died with a broken heart. His final despair, which he bravely resisted with the help of a study of Judaism, began long before, during the occupation of France. As we now know from recent studies of Vichy France, it was a terrible place for humane radicals, or anyone else. Most of the French supported the anti-Semitism, the prerevolutionary brutality of Pétain and his henchmen. To be a resistance leader and one of its foremost publicists, as Sartre courageously was, meant not only to risk torture and death at the hands of the Nazis but to be hated by one's own countrymen. Sartre was a true survivor. Like many European Jews, he fled the boot and the poison of a France debauched by occupation and collaboration alike. He could never forget the bitter lessons of the forties, an epoch when he already began to grow old.

He was also disillusioned by the "god that failed." Never a Stalinist, Sartre nevertheless once placed extravagant hopes in the Russian revolutionary government. He was a classical fellow traveler who wanted no enemies on the "left" and, at least sometimes, ignored the gulag and the knout of a police state that claimed to be the preeminent democracy of the working class. Marxist utopianism was doomed to disappoint an honest man, and Sartre saw through most of its pretensions early on. His existentialist "angst" may never have been as real to him as it was, for example, to Kierkegaard, but it clearly reflected an early loss of faith in the Communist revolution. An ex-Communist, Sartre never became a dogmatic anti-Communist, but he supported every attempt at revolution in the revolution. Still, the memory of lost hopes must have haunted his old age.

He was also disappointed by a literary and philosophic career that seems to most of us not less than spectacular. He knew what every writer knows: the purpose of writing is to produce master-pieces. Since he never finished many of his projects, revised all of them, and doubted most, Sartre died unfulfilled. He knew that he was "not Shakespeare, not Hegel," that world literature would accord him respect but not the final honor reserved for genius. Novel-ist, philosopher, biographer and autobiographer, social critic and political spokesman, he tried too much and finished too little to meet his own standards, and so he died in disappointment, in-evitably.

He was also undone by the world of the 1980s. As he reveals in the great final interview with Benny Levy (in *Le Nouvel Observateur*, March 1980, translated in *Telos*, Summer 1980, and in *Dissent*, Fall 1980), Sartre is terrified by the rightward swing of most Western governments, by the Soviet invasion of Afghanistan, and by the in-creasing likelihood of atomic war in Europe. Whatever he expected of postwar political structures, his expectations could not have been more dour than what in fact occurred. Any hopes for international-ism, for a more civil conflict resolution, for steps toward world ac-cord, have been dashed by the renewal of the cold war under the auspices of American and British intellectuals as well as of Russian militarists.

Sartre understood that "the life of man manifests itself as a fail-ure." It is in the nature of mortality that it leaves all things unfin-ished. Even sick, even at seventy-five, frail, blind (or half-blind), Jean-Paul Sartre clung to life, expecting five or ten years more in which to work. "The eye is never satisfied with seeing, nor the ear with hearing," and no one's life story is ever fully told. Death comes always as an interloper; the threat of nonbeing is always real and de-cisive for all human pretensions, and closes, at last, every open door.

This, of course, is because, as Sartre came painfully to understand, we are not God. Our deepest wish is to be self-caused, self-defining, omnipotent. But we are not, really not God (maybe, Sartre sometimes thought, even God isn't), and in that limitation lie the seeds of our tragedy. From the nausea of his early work to the resignation of his last interview, Sartre taught that "hope is necessarily disappointed." Inevitably, with mathematical certainty, the life of man is too short, too full of failure, too small—simply because he is only man after all.

Sartre dealt with his loss of historical hope by painfully acquiring another kind of hope. He replaced both existential dread and Marxist utopianism with a Jewish messianic patience. In the final interview with his friend and associate, the unlikely *baal t'shuvah* (returnee to Judaism) Benny Levy (formerly Pierre Victor), he reports his discovery that "the messianic idea is the base of the revolutionary idea." For many months before he died, Sartre studied Salo Baron's voluminous, magisterial work on Jewish history, and, with Levy, came to a new-old view of the human prospect.

Sartre finally reads messianism, in Steven Schwarzschild's felicitous formulation, as permanent revolution. The human community is not a fact, as he once dreamed it might be, nor a lie, as he later feared, but a goal. It is not where we once were or now are, but it is where we someday shall be. Hope is not extrapolated from events but always and inevitably imposed upon history. It comes despite, not because of, "reality." It is always hope against hope. The expectation of redemption is not itself historical. Man must do his duty. Someone else will have to redeem the world. Sartre, the most persuasive nonbeliever of our century, nonetheless says, "I hated in humanism the certain way man has of admiring himself." Sartre found humanity less than admirable. But he believed, at the end, that we need not be admirable to survive.

Marxist revolution is not the goal; violent insurrection is not the way. For the final Sartre, world community is the goal, and patient obedience to duty is the way. In the most striking formulation in the final interview, he says, "Intention is transhistorical."

Which brings us back to man, the root of radicalism. "The primary relationship is man to man . . . which we must now rediscover." As if he had invented Buber and the Bible, Sartre now proclaims, "We belong to a single family." Of course, "the unity of the human enterprise is yet to be created," still, proleptically, "what I have is yours and what you have is mine. If I need, you give to me. If you need, I give to you. That is the future of morality." What would sound simpleminded in a less complicated writer, here sounds from the depth of William James' "second naiveté," like a chastened and exhausted rediscovery. As Schwarzschild puts it, the apocalypse of revolutionary terrorism must give way to the ethical possibility of Jewish messianism if we are to fulfill the goal of a humane social order.

In the end, Sartre became a kind of "Jew." Already in the resistance of 1940–1945 he had risked his life against fascism. In *Les Temps Modernes*, at the very time of the Six-day War, he published what remains the most balanced and useful collection of essays on Arab-Jewish peace and declared his solidarity with Israel. He did not accept the Nobel Prize for literature, giving reasons that are well known. But he did accept an honorary degree from the Hebrew University in 1976, reminding the Israelis how deeply he shared their dreams and telling them that the more he cared about them, the more he cared also about the Palestinian people.

"In order to understand the Jew from the interior, I would have to be a Jew," Sartre told Benny Levy (himself worth a story, one which might be titled, "From Mao to *Masorah* [tradition]"), and he tried hard enough to achieve that very goal. Studying Jewish history, like many thinkers before him, he caught a vision of the messianic hope: survival, obedience, and loyalty to humanity itself.

"The Jew lives. He has a destiny. The finality toward which every Jew moves is to reunite humanity. . . . It is the end that only the Jewish people (knows). . . . It is the beginning of the existence of men for each other."

In the last days and in the last words of Jean-Paul Sartre, "our chief contemporary" (Mauriac), "an author who belongs to the future" (Barthes), a "fighter on all the battlefields of intelligence" (Audiberti)—in those last days and uniquely in the final interview we find a brother and a teacher in Israel. More than a man, Jean-Paul Sartre achieved a stature and significance that can only be called symbolic.

"Blessed be *Adonai*, Master of space and time, Who gives some of His wisdom to mere flesh and blood" (the traditional blessing recited upon seeing a great scholar of secular wisdom).

[*Sh'ma*, April 2, 1982]

THE THEOLOGY OF
"YITZ" GREENBERG

IN TRADITIONAL Jewish thought, or at least in one version of our central tradition, Jews are responsible for doing the *mitzvot*, and God is responsible for protecting the Jews. Irving Greenberg comes close, in his important recent essay "Voluntary Covenant," to reversing these roles. A series of papers written by him and published by the National Jewish Resource Center (later called CLAL), which he founded and heads, have become a kind of semi-official theology for the United Jewish Appeal and more thoughtful members of the Jewish establishment. No wonder: Greenberg is learned, persuasive, and personally both charming and forthcoming. The conclusions of his latest manifesto require and deserve serious critical attention.

Irving Greenberg believes there has been a profound transformation in the conventional relationship between God and Israel. . . . God early on required of Israel that it serve as His surrogate, "ministering to all nations and connecting them to the Divine." God remained "active" with Israel in order to prevent its defection from this central and necessary responsibility; circumcision is a perfect sign of the once involuntary, irrevocable nature of our chosenness. . . . That pact worked pretty well for many hundreds of years.

Most of Greenberg's paper is devoted to the revolutionary deconstruction of the original covenant relationship, in which God's providence fully guaranteed both Jewish survival and Jewish loyalty. Already the fall of the first Temple, and, more poignantly, the destruction of the second Temple, marks a conscious withdrawal of the

Divine Presence from Jewish history; after that no more prophecy, no more sacraments—a new kind of human partnership with a God Who is increasingly unavailable. The *Shechinah* (Divine indwelling) is hidden from then on, so Israel itself must learn to assume much of the providential role formerly played by God.

"The mixture of authority and modesty of the Rabbis is also consistent with the unfolding of the covenant model." The rabbis, according to Greenberg, basing himself upon a passage in Tractate *Shabbat* of the Babylonian Talmud, asserted that Israel took upon itself the renewal of the covenant after the pact had, in a way, lapsed because of God's removal of Himself from personal responsibility for the Jews. It was, from rabbinic times on, the task of the people and its leaders to name the specific terms of their loyalty and to define the responsibilities of Jewish peoplehood. God had once given the Torah, but its interpretation later fell entirely to human beings, scholars, *poskim* (judges). Orthodox ideology, which "offered a juridical view of the covenant," missed the full radical implications of covenant renewal, implications only fully manifest in our own time. But rabbinic Judaism is already on the way to a "voluntary covenant," "developers and conservers at the same time."

The old idea of covenant was shattered once and for all at Auschwitz. Greenberg quotes Elie Wiesel: "When God gave us a mission, that was all right. But God failed to tell us that it was a suicide mission." There can be no question of reward and punishment or Divine providence any longer. There can be no sense of shared loyalty and mutual love or responsibility between God and Israel. He left us in the fatal lurch. Worse, He sent us on a "suicide mission," thus permanently revising the terms of His own covenant. We do not owe Him anything, really, after the Holocaust, that we do not wish to pay.

On the other hand, many Jews have voluntarily renewed the covenant simply by refusing to die as a people. We can have no more obligations in the old sense, but we can choose, and many of us have chosen, the dream of redemption. We have, as a people, volunteered to carry on. Our covenant (according to Greenberg's citation of Rav Soloveitchik in note 63—a reference which by no means seems to me to say what he thinks it does) is no longer a covenant of doing but of being. We are loyal simply by remaining Jews, whatever we do about our affirmation in the future. The final meaning of the fall of both of the Temples, the meaning even of human free will as such, certainly of the progressive alienation of God through history culminating in the Holocaust, is a voluntary covenant whose terms are finally set only by the human party. This inevitable "redistribution of power" is what political Zionism really means. If Messiah didn't come to Auschwitz, he can never come. We must redeem ourselves and/or our world. God permitted the Holocaust; we must, and only we can, overcome it forever.

The implications of the idea of a voluntary covenant are, of course, political and theological at once. "It makes no essential difference if the Jews involved consciously articulate the covenantal hope or express a belief in the God who is the ground of the covenant." They are expressions of that covenant whatever they may think or do. By being ready for martyrdom, they fulfill the essential obligation that remains for them to fulfill. Other *mitzvot* are, in a way, optional. Pluralism endorses various alternative formulations of duty. Reform must waive its dogmatically modernist criteria; Orthodoxy, its univocal demands. After Auschwitz all differences between Jews become trivial, even in relation to God.

"[The] State of Israel is the central vehicle of Jewish power, self-defense, and redemption building; its needs should be given greater religious weight, perhaps rated as a matter of life or death." Greenberg believes, theoretically more than in practice (to judge by the rather one-sided series of publications of the Resource Center), that there can be many interpretations of the new, human, Israel-centered covenant. He does not want the Jewish state to become an idol. But "Yom HaShoah (Holocaust commemoration day) and Yom Ha-Atzmaut (Israel independence day) must become central holy days of the Jewish calendar"; Jewish survival must be the center and not merely a part of Judaism. All the days of the week can finally become as holy as Shabbat. A new covenant ceremony can and should coexist with circumcision (the old sign of the old involuntary covenant).

There is a principle behind this radical revisionism by an "Orthodox" rabbi. It is, I believe, the great, novel heresy of the twentieth century, of what he fondly calls the Third Era: Analogous to this concept of voluntary covenant, Greenberg asserts that "greater is the one who is not commanded but voluntarily comes forward than the one who acts only out of command." This is a bold denial of a central Jewish view. Here unravels the whole tapestry of Jewish self-understanding. *We* are the center of the covenant. *We* have the primary task of self-protection. (Do the Palestinians too, even if they have not yet suffered a Holocaust?) We are the makers and unmakers of the *mitzvot*, since our existence is already a fulfillment of them all. We define the terms on which we are willing to survive. We do what we choose, not what God chooses; of course not what the United Nations or the peoples of the world might expect. The biblical God has shrunken to near invisibility; we are just about all the God there is left in the world. Greenberg has systematically deconstructed Judaism in favor of a political teleology whose consequences are clear enough: voluntarism means liberation from duty.

Irving Greenberg says more than I have said he says. Some of his views are almost antithetical, perhaps he would say dialectically related, to these. Above all, he insists (like Bonhoeffer, who was also profoundly affected by the Hitler period) that God's self-alienation is to be perceived primarily as the liberation of humanity, that the new covenant is, in a sense, our own coming of age. What has been unfolding for centuries and emerges in the Holocaust is not just Divine withdrawal but Divine love for an increasingly responsible humanity. God is educating us to take over His world.

God is therefore not so much unavailable as invisible. The covenant has reached a new level of redemptive power. Even Auschwitz may be a kind of Exodus. That something precious was in fact broken does not mean it was ended; in Greenberg's view, it has become more adequate than ever before. God may have endangered us, but He also shared and still shares our endangerment. He may no longer be able simply to redeem humanity, but He longs for our redemption as passionately as He ever did. He may even be more present than ever, though less markedly visible, may be more involved even though distinctly less immediate, more important in a mystical sense if less commanding and less demanding than He was before.

The reader will have to decide whether this indeed represents a true mystic vision or rather, as I believe, mere obfuscation, a mystification in the Marxist sense. Greenberg believes that less God is more. I believe that less God is always less, and that a secret divinity can hardly shape our ends or call us to true self-transcendence.

I believe that Israel is still chosen, still obligated; and by no merely voluntary covenant. I suspect Greenberg's complex theological dialectic of being a cover for the new Jewish chauvinism, and Greenberg of being a victim of his own mysticism. The old covenant is, of course, problematic, not less after Auschwitz. Still, it not only empowered but also confronted Jews. The voluntary covenant, I fear, is a product of our natural inclination to evil more than it is a new revelation. In any case, Irving Greenberg has raised questions that Jewish history cannot evade, even if, as I think, he himself is sometimes evasive and often dangerously confused.

[*Sh'ma*, May 13, 1983]

NETTIE S. WOLF

ON THURSDAY, April 27, the Jewish Community Center's Senior Adult Division will install my mother in its Hall of Fame, an honor bestowed on only a few men and almost no women. She deserves it. Born in Coshocton, Ohio, in 1890, she has been at various times a labor liaison worker who figured in the famous Hart, Schaffner and Marx strike, a girlfriend of vaudevillian Ted Lewis, a mother to dozens of orphans at Marks Nathan Jewish Orphan Home, a fighter for reform candidates and for peace, a friend of people of many races and religions, and a mother and grandmother like they used to be. I don't say this because she is my mother, but because it is true.

Nettie Schanfarber Wolf was liberated before there was liberation. She worked in men's worlds, but she always came to a woman's task. She raised me without a husband to help, and she got what we needed without making a man's salary; and, though twice a widow before her forties were finished, she never gave up on life and she never betrayed her woman's calling. She was brought up and lived all her life as a Reform Jew, but that never meant to her not keeping Sabbath or not knowing what Judaism is all about. On the contrary, she learned to communicate in Yiddish and to understand traditional Jewish practice, because nothing any Jew ever did was alien to her; still, she never thought it necessary to pretend she was something other than what she was. Her idealism is always hard-nosed, and her realism always tempered with a deep messianic hopefulness, which still sustains her now in her eighties. I am not the only one who owes her more than we could ever possibly repay.

[Congregation Solel *Pathfinder*, April 19, 1972]

PART ELEVEN

My Life

FRAGMENTS OF MY LIFE

MY FATHER DIED when I was seven years old, and from then on I needed desperately to find a father who would not die. My own father was a gentle, elderly man whose career was in business and politics. He was an alderman and a court clerk in the Republican administration of Mayor "Big Bill" Thompson in Chicago in the early part of the century, representing a newly important South Side Jewish community who were loyal to the party of Lincoln. His death changed our family permanently, although my mother coped with this (her second widowhood before her forty-second birthday) with great courage and intelligence.

My father's family was thoroughly assimilated. His grandfather had left Germany about 1848, and the several marriages of that man's son, my grandfather, had produced many children from three different wives. Most of them married non-Jews; one of my uncles was a Christian Science reader. My father himself was reputed to have gone to the horse races on Yom Kippur before he married my mother, whose background was quite different. Her people were pious, observant Reform Jews, currently an endangered species.

My mother was a Schanfarber from Ohio. The Schanfarbers had been Americans since the early nineteenth century, and their family prestige meant a good deal to her. Her uncle, Tobias Schanfarber, entered with the first class at Hebrew Union College. Rabbi Schanfarber once told me that Isaac M. Wise had visited his rather modest, even impoverished home and had more or less kidnaped the twelve-year-old Toby to become a rabbinical student in Cincinnati, an event about which Toby had lifelong regrets or, at least, ambivalence. He served as rabbi and later emeritus of KAM Congregation:

Kehilath Anshe Mayriv (as they mistakenly termed it, instead of the more accurate transliteration Maarav) until the early 1940s. More than fifty years later, I am now his successor there. Toby was a hearty, deaf man with no children. He lived with us during some of the winters of his retirement. He posed endless questions about Pirkei Avot and Amos, teased me about my childish desire to become a rabbi, and gave me some of his Hebrew books (Brown, Driver, and Briggs's Biblical Concordance, Enelow's editions of Hebrew ethical works, and the like). He taught me to love the Chicago White Sox with a lifelong passion, which I have passed on to my children.

My mother's family were committed and even important Reform Jews. Her brother was a national officer of B'nai B'rith and a synagogue president. One sister married Felix A. Levy, a president of the Central Conference of American Rabbis and a major influence on my life. I studied Hebrew from my eighth or ninth year, though our family did not believe in the Bar Mitzvah ceremony, holding that thirteen was too young for any important decisions or for acquiring sufficient knowledge to be an adult Jew in any intelligent sense. Felix Levy's youngest daughter, who grew up with and went to school with me, later married Wolfe Kelman, the executive of the Conservative rabbinate during his whole career; two of their children are Reform rabbis in Israel.

Felix Levy took me under his tutelage when I was thirteen years old. He read the Hebrew classics with me: The Book of Jonah, *Rashi*, Maimonides' *Book of Commandments*, Ahad Ha'am's essays, the many volumes of *Golah V'nekhar* by Yehezkel Kaufmann (the pioneer biblical scholar of the Renewed Land of Israel).

Felix Levy was a unique and seminal figure in the development of American liberal Judaism, casting the presidential vote that broke a tie in favor of the Columbus Platform of 1939 which marked the end of classical Reform and the beginning of a more observant and obedient liberal faith. He was the first Zionist to be elected president of the CCAR and the first to propose Reform *halakhah*, a legal discipline to give detail and rootage to our religious ideals. He knew a dozen languages. Professor J. H. Breasted at the Oriental Institute in Chicago had taught him Egyptian. He read Cassuto not only in modern Hebrew but also in Italian, and introduced his work to America. He and his wife spent every summer in Europe and communicated with Buber and the other luminaries of German Jewry in their own language. His reading was continuous and immense! He spent most of every day and evening studying some theological or philosophic work, though he wrote very little himself, out of modesty or because of some inner constriction that he could not overcome.

The time that Rabbi Levy gave to me was almost incredible. When I was a university student, a vacationing rabbinical student, and later his assistant rabbi from 1948 to 1955 (with two years' absence in the Far East as the only Jewish chaplain in the U.S. Navy there), he would spend *all* of every weekday morning with me, reading and discussing classical Jewish texts. No rabbi today could devote so much time to study and teaching one student (or occasionally two, when Samuel Dresner was able to be with us).

I was admitted to the Hebrew Union College in 1942 after only two years of study at the University of Chicago, because of the exigencies of World War II. I was eighteen years old, but I had prepared for the College much of my young life.

Some of my classmates have written about our wartime years at HUC (particularly Richard Rubenstein in his autobiography titled *Power Struggle*). While the greatest catastrophe in the history of the Jews was devastating our people, and while young Americans were fighting and dying on battlefields all over the world, we chosen few were both privileged and protected in our academic tower. I was inordinately happy to be sharing my studies with other young men (there were a few women, but they were not encouraged to believe they would be candidates for ordination) who shared in varying degree my lust for Jewish knowledge and my powerful desire to be a rabbi.

I had good teachers from whom I learned as much as my active outside life would permit. Partly because of guilt at being isolated from the tragedies of that time, I spent many hours as president of Cincinnati Young Judea (a Zionist youth movement) and as codirector of a Reform Jewish high school. I am not sure whether that was noble work that still needs no defense or a mere holiday from the lonely task of mastering Hebrew thought, a goal which has partly eluded me all my life despite a continuing dedication to study and a considerable expenditure of intellectual energy. My fellow students were diverse and sometimes even hostile to one another. Two of them threatened to kill me, one by drawing a real (but unloaded) pistol and promising to avenge my "teasing" of him. Student meetings were long and taxing, but they were also the training ground of some of the most important leaders of American Jewry in the postwar period.

My closest friendships—with Eugene Borowitz and Steven Schwarzschild—were initiated at the College. Our backgrounds could not have been more different: Gene came from a successful, hardworking, Yiddishist immigrant family; Steven from a German Jewish elite that had been forced to become refugees and to begin a new, hard life in America. I was the Yankee among us. But, amazingly or not, perhaps paradigmatically, background was no barrier to our becoming brothers of the spirit. We early recognized a potential in one another that many of our class did not. We helped one another to study Martin Buber and Hermann Cohen, Christian theology and socialism, all of which our teachers could not, or would not, teach. We criticized one another's ideas and debated one another's choices, though they inevitably more and more converged. Nothing in my life has been more important to me than these two friendships. I think of Steven every day, especially since his premature death, and I think of Gene every day because of his enormous influence on me and because of my admiration for his accomplishments, a few of which I helped to initiate and all of which I have been proud to applaud. He has become the premier teacher of liberal Judaism in our generation, and in his radiant scholarship I have been honored to share. We have occasionally disagreed; we have even been remote from one another at some periods of our life, but we could not be what/who we have become without each other and each other's love.

The students of the College were divided, roughly, between left-liberals (even including some fairly orthodox Communists), who saw their mission as fighting for social justice in America, and others, including some refugees from Europe, who were attempting to recover traditional elements of Judaism and Zionism. My friends and I could not, and still cannot, see why these two missions had to be separated. For us, at least, the rediscovery of Hebrew, *halakhah*, and Jewish nationalism in no way precluded our struggle for world peace and for equality and racial justice in America. We wanted to make liberal Judaism turn more intensely inward and, at the same time, to radicalize the claims of Reform in the service of social causes.

We were influenced by some important predecessors like Felix Levy; Judah Leon Magnes, who founded the Hebrew University and earlier had struggled as a learned Reform rabbi against the smug bourgeois leadership of his community; and Stephen Wise, a Zionist leader of enormous influence who also spoke out for the poor and the exploited in American society. For us, the great rabbis were usually on the left politically and on the right theologically: men who wanted both a more observant Judaism and a more courageous social agenda.

Our teachers, however, were mostly old-line classical Reform thinkers. President Julian Morgenstern began each academic year (during the Holocaust) with a denunciation of Jewish nationalism and a reiteration of "prophetic" Judaism, a program which seemed to us outmoded and dangerously irrelevant. The HUC curriculum was centered on Bible, which meant a critical study in a German style that was already beginning to be superseded by the new biblical theology coming from American universities and from followers of Karl Barth and Martin Buber. For me, that meant writing a rabbinic thesis on Jeremiah's theology, which my adviser Sheldon Blank successfully defended against Morgenstern's accusation that I was a closet fundamentalist because I would not carve the prophetic text into discrete authorships of varying authenticity. I was not the only student who anticipated what would later be called canonical criticism, and, despite President Morgenstern, I was not really precritical but postcritical; that has remained my position to this day. The Bible for us was not merely a text for historical reconstruction but a document of Jewish spirituality which had to be confronted and even obeyed. The Bible was, as our friend Jakob Petuchowski would write, the Bible of the synagogue; we are not German Protestants but Jewish "students of the wise" for whom it is Torah and for whom rabbinic interpretation remains indispensable.

Abraham J. Heschel, who taught at the College until he left for the Jewish Theological Seminary of America in 1945, was at the center of these issues. Young and then still unheralded, not a very good classroom teacher, his eye always on a celebrity status he would achieve twenty years later, Heschel nevertheless understood our questions and spoke to our needs. Some became his *hasidim* and left with him to become Conservative rabbis. Others, social justice supporters, ridiculed his piety and his attempt to recover Jewish theological categories. They were later to follow him to Selma and to Washington in the struggle for civil rights and peace in Vietnam.

I was a student of Heschel's, his secretary for two years, and his critical admirer until he died. At the least he was a resource for my own attempts to imagine a postliberal Judaism that had room for law and scripture, for both Maimonides and the powerful philosophy of Franz Rosenzweig (which I hardly understood but already knew to be a milestone in twentieth-century Judaism).

Several times Gene Borowitz and I ran for the office of editors of the Hebrew Union College Monthly, and each time we were defeated by candidates more concerned with political agendas than with what we considered religious ideas and programs. In the interdenominational National Religion and Labor Foundation, whose seminary vice-president I became, I found that other seminaries were producing candidates who agreed with my preliminary attempts to reconcile social criticism with theological sophistication. They too became my teachers and my friends.

On ordination I accepted the post of assistant to my uncle and teacher, Felix Levy, in Chicago. I considered this a great privilege because of his enormous learning and his willingness to teach. But there was also something questionable about my choice to return to the very congregation where I was remembered as a precocious but rather willful child and a somewhat wild adolescent. In any case, by the time I returned from service in the Korean War in 1953, another rabbi had ingratiated himself with the congregational leadership, and he succeeded to the pulpit upon Rabbi Levy's retirement shortly afterward. I went back to graduate studies in Semitics at the University of Chicago's Oriental Institute, and to a small congregation which welcomed my family with truly open hearts and which I was loath to leave in 1957.

In that year a new congregation was opening in the suburbs of Chicago's North Shore. It had begun as a branch of KAM (where I am now serving) and a fan club for KAM's rabbi, Jacob J. Weinstein, a memorable writer, a Zionist, and, especially, a leader in the movement for integration, beginning with his own neighborhood which is still a model of interracial harmony. When neighborhood stability was threatened in the fifties and sixties, many of Weinstein's followers had left for the suburbs. They invited him to turn their branch of his synagogue into a new, independent congregation which would continue the bravely liberal tradition of the mother congregation. Rabbi Weinstein prepared to move, and I was eager to replace him, some twenty-odd years earlier than I actually did. But the political leadership of Chicago could not spare Jacob because they saw him as crucial to the narrowing possibility of racial harmony. Instead I was invited to lead the nascent congregation on the North Shore. My psychoanalyst convinced me to accept the pulpit, abandoning some of the happiest years of study and modest rabbinical experience I would ever have. The new community was intellectual, political, and exceedingly innovative and radical in its intentions.

We took the name "Solel," which signifies "pathfinder," though it also has some less favorable connotations in rabbinic literature. For us, the name symbolized a new way in American Jewry—more serious, more egalitarian, centered on study and prayer, not on sisterhoods and bowling leagues. We were pretentious and ambitious but not complete fools. Some of our agenda made a difference to our five hundred families (perhaps the first congregation with a long waiting list). We studied the Bible together in a twenty-two-year seminar. We carefully read Heschel and Rosenzweig and Herberg and other luminaries of twentieth-century thought. We sent every graduate of our Hebrew program (there was no Bar Mitzvah) to Israel, at the congregation's expense, for a summer of study and of living in a community or a *kibbutz*. We had no fund-raising or plaques or honorees. We built a million-dollar building without fanfare or special gifts (even from some fabulously rich members, who got away with contributing much less than they should have). We were lay-led and lay-constructed; our democratic impulses literally knew no bounds. We represented liberal causes and had both Martin Luther King and the Chicago Seven speak from our pulpit. We were almost as innovative and important as we pretended to be. Solel became a symbol of an alternative future for American Judaism.

For me it was the best of times and the worst of times. My marriage failed, my moods swung wildly, my personal time diminished. But I managed to produce a textbook for teenagers which introduced the newer Jewish thinking to America—for almost the first time, surely the first time in a confirmation textbook. I edited *Rediscovering Judaism*, a collective attempt to summarize the new Jewish theology, sometimes called existentialist. A number of us younger Jewish thinkers had been meeting regularly at Oconomowoc, Wisconsin, and later in the Laurentian Hills of Quebec. Across denominational lines and differences of ideology and law, we nevertheless validated each other's struggle for a convincing Jewish philosophy for modern (though not untraditional) men and women. Among us were Schwarzschild and Borowitz; Elie Wiesel; Zalman Schachter (the only true genius among us, although a wild one); Maurice Friedman, who made Martin Buber available in American English; Emil Fackenheim, who began to distance himself from us as the

Holocaust more and more consumed his attention; and "Yitz" Greenberg, who ultimately fashioned his own transdenominational version of Jewishness, both of the latter under Wiesel's charismatic influence.

For all of us, the Holocaust lay deep in our consciousness. I had helped create a *Shoah* weekend of remembrance each year at Solel, the emotional center of which was simply the reading of names of those who were murdered, a continuous recitation that lasted for forty-eight hours. Still, some of us were, and are, unwilling to accept the death of God or the necessity for a radical revision of Jewish tradition because of the Holocaust. What died in World War II was not the idea of God, much less God's Self, but rather the idea of human perfection or even of perfectibility. My own essay in the collection *Rediscovering Judaism* was about the rabbinic doctrine of the evil inclination and its relationship to Freud's metapsychology. Our common project in modern Judaism was neither optimistic (as classical liberalism had been) nor pessimistic (as some neo-Barthians were) but resolutely messianic, in the spirit of Hermann Cohen, as well as of Talmudic and Maimonidean eschatology. We were heirs to an ethical meliorism that coexisted with a realist view of human potential, chastened by war and Holocaust, uplifted by faith in God and hope for the ultimate redemption of the world.

I went to Yale in 1972 as Hillel rabbi at a time when students began to turn far more conservative and cautious than they had been in the sixties. My goals were both personal and rabbinic: I wanted to serve a community of Jews of all stripes and to practice a more traditional personal life, keeping Shabbat and *kashrut* more carefully than I had done, and praying daily not only with liberal Jews but also in the Orthodox *minyan*. Some students felt that I was using their community to practice on; they were not entirely mistaken. But I also tried to reach my own kind of neotraditionalism, with some success. Just as at Solel we had produced several rabbis, both Reform and Conservative, so Yale men and women I taught went on to each of the rabbinical seminaries.

I taught college seminars for credit at Yale in twentieth-century

Judaism and Christianity, in the problem of Jewish chosenness, as well as in the leading texts of modern religious philosophy. Limited to fifteen seminar members, I had to choose from a hundred or more who regularly wished to join. It was a time for reflection on our several traditions and for a tentative rediscovery and reconstruction of Jewish (and Christian) faith. William Sloane Coffin was a beloved colleague, talented beyond measure, a deeply believing Christian though a less disciplined political activist, whose support for the peace movement I could share but whose flamboyant style and message were not always my own. Yale was itself tightly wound and often narrow in its Ivy League superciliousness, but I met some of the finest young men and women of my life who shared their hopes with me and helped me to rebuild yet again my own version of Jewish responsibility and doctrine.

In 1973, during the Yom Kippur War, a group of younger rabbis and dissenting professionals in the Jewish community founded Breira: A Project in American Jewish Responsibility. I was chosen to be chairperson after others refused. Our name betokened our desire for an alternative (*breira* in Hebrew) to the intransigence of both the PLO and the several governments of Israel. We proposed what has come to be known as a two-state solution, now more than ever the chief possibility for a peaceful, long-term resolution of the Middle East conflict. Our "annual" convention (held only once before our dissolution) featured General Mati Peled, an Israeli dove, and Irving Howe, an American Jew of secularist but deeply and passionately held Jewish convictions. We hammered out a multiplank platform for the reform of American Jewish institutions, democratization of Jewish life, and support for the small but honorable Israeli peace movement.

Our organization dissolved within a few years under the enormous pressure of the Jewish establishment (which attempted to get me and other Breira leaders fired, though rarely with success) and because of our own personal incompatibility. I learned from the difficult years of Breira that it is a long way from a theoretical Jewish ethics to the politics of American, not to say world, Jewry. Nahum

246 : Unfinished Rabbi

Goldmann and Martin Buber, themselves founders and teachers of Jewish communities around the world, were my models of Jewish work on behalf of peace. I was and am, like them, a Zionist (my Zionist sermon in the HUC chapel in 1947 was the first of its kind to win the annual sermon prize), but, more and more, I have subsumed Zionism under the judgment of a stern if compassionate God. Breira was a failure that, like others in my life, was also a premature but paradigmatic sign of successes to come.

In 1975 I went to Nairobi, Kenya, as the first delegate to the World Council of Churches to represent world Jewry. How I could be chosen by our major denominational self-defense and civil rights organizations remains a mystery to me, but I went to speak as best I could for the survivors of the *Shoah* and for legitimate Jewish claims in Israel and throughout the world. Reverend Krister Stendahl of Harvard was my mentor and colleague; we often found ourselves on the same side of disputed issues, usually in dissent. When I reminded the delegates that their Lord was born not in Nairobi (or in Kansas City) but in the Land of Israel, the Primate of Norway arose to denounce my narrowly Jewish view (confirmed, I had thought, by their own gospels). Jesus Christ, he insisted, is born in the hearts of those who call him Savior and only there. Christendom, I concluded, cannot decide whether to be a world-transforming or a world-denying faith, whether to be Judaists or Hellenists, whether to look to Rome or Jerusalem. I do, however, sympathize with their dilemmas; we have unfinished business of our own.

I was determined not to die in New Haven, but at the age of fifty-six in 1980 it was not clear where I could or should spend my final rabbinic years. By the purest of chances I was invited to meet with a rabbinic search committee of KAM Isaiah Israel Congregation, back in Chicago. They had heard I was available, if somewhat controversial, so they asked me to say something "controversial" to them. I answered: I believe in a PLO State in the West Bank and Gaza. Yes, a man responded, that is indeed controversial. A few years later my not very subtle comparison of Israeli and Soviet politics made some of them regret having chosen me as their rabbi. But it has been, on the whole, a wonderful marriage. My parents had met in the Temple; my granduncle had been its rabbi. I had once served on its staff, and my children began nursery school in our present building. Not much in life is preordained, but some things are, and I feel as if my own life has come full circle. This is where, finally, I belong.

I have been a part of a small but decisive school that changed American Judaism during our lifetime. We represented a convergence of liberal and neotraditional streams, a struggle to recover rabbinic categories, a suspicious view of the modern (or modernist) enterprise represented decisively by Mordecai Kaplan, and an attempt to bring the most profound European Jewish theology to America. From one point of view, Steven Schwarzschild Americanized Hermann Cohen, Eugene Borowitz Americanized Martin Buber, and I (along with others) brought the views of Franz Rosenzweig onto the American Jewish agenda. For example, in my contribution to the famous Commentary Symposium (1966), I basically reproduced Rosenzweig's view of Jewish law in my own American imaging.

I have had the privilege of teaching at major institutions like Yale, HUC-JIR, and the University of Chicago Divinity School, but my life has always centered on being a rabbi in the communal or congregational sense. Marshall Sklare wrote about me in Highland Park (in his Lakeville Studies) that I didn't really want to be a rabbi and that Solel didn't want to be a congregation. That is not quite accurate: we both wanted to be what we were, but in a new way, which perhaps would also be a more old-fashioned way. Nothing, in my judgment, is more radical than naked tradition.

On the other hand, it is also true that as we grew older, Steve, Gene, and I all returned to our "Reform" roots, insisting that nothing is permitted in Jewish thought that is unethical, no matter how otherwise convincing or pervasive. Liberal Judaism means, in the end, the view that ethical standards ("*hatov v'hayashar*," as the rabbis put it) construe Jewish theology and law fundamentally and always. That approach has led to terrible errors, in which modern liberal political views are crudely and simplistically identified with Judaism-as-social action, but it remains true that Judaism must at least match these standards as well as judge and refine them.

My life has mellowed in recent years in the accustomed ways: a fortunate and important marriage, children who have helped improve the world as well as their family, the first grandchildren, and an intelligent and striving congregation. Much of this I have not especially deserved; no one can deserve so much good. I am already almost twenty years older than my father was when he died. I have had a fascinating and varied career and can boast many wonderful students, though true discipleship is perhaps no longer relevant or even possible.

Martin Buber once said that the way to remain young is to continue to innovate. That seems right to me. As long as God gives me the power to do so, I will try to make old truths new and new truths holy. I have had good teachers and friends, good models to whom I have tried to be faithful all my life. Conscious of my grave failures, knowing only a few partial victories, I leave to those who come after me a messianic task which will never be completed, in historic time at least, but from which none of us has the right ever to desist.

[*Jewish Spiritual Journeys*, ed. Lawrence A. Hoffman and
Arnold J. Wolf, 1997]

MOMENTS IN MY LIFE

FIFTEEN YEARS AGO, when I was trying to finish my doctoral studies at the University of Chicago, I got a call from the rabbinical selection committee of some crazy new congregation in the suburbs. They wanted to talk to me about becoming their rabbi, an idea which seemed to me as unlikely as my becoming third baseman for the White Sox (a pitcher would have been *more* probable). But I came, and they snowed me, and I snowed them, and I have never once been sorry that I was impressed by people who knew about Buber and cared about Jewish education, or that they liked a rabbi who answered "I don't know" to most of their questions.

Now, 3 books and 60 articles, 700 sermons, 400 *Pathfinder* columns, 2,500 adult study sessions, 1,500 religious school classes, 750 hospital visits, and God knows how many personal conversations later, I have decided I should leave. I go with affection and relief, with satisfaction in the small successes and the noble failures we have achieved together, and with enough memories to fill out my rapidly approaching senescence richly. You have not always been generous to me or to one another, but you have been unfailingly interesting and often you have been uniquely creative as well. You have forgiven my impatience, my errors in judgment and in timing; you have often been a real and holy congregation, a rarity for suburban America in the fifties and sixties, a miracle in the seventies.

But enough already! You may have noticed that many of our noblest works are almost ten years old by now: the twenty-two-year Bible class, which looks like it will get through the *Megillot* at least; the confrontation with black rights and Black Power; the experiments in curriculum and anticurriculum for our kids; the Sabbath morning modern *minyan*; theological dialogues; original lay-produced liturgies; Hebrew school graduates' summers in Israel; funny congregational meetings; the million-dollar building designed not to look like it; teenagers who cared; our risky, bold, and not always fruitless struggle to bring Judaism into a world we share. You may have noticed that we have become rather less courageous and somewhat more conventional of late, and that my voice has accordingly grown more shrill, my encouragement more panicky. The golden young I have loved and taught with so much joy these years now frighten me sometimes by how callous they seem and how American. After fifteen years on the North Shore I feel more a stranger than ever, and I escape back to the city with something very like relief.

Solel is a success, while I personally do better, I think, as captain of sinking ships. Not that Yale is exactly endangered, but it is surely clear that American Jews have done less and done more poorly for their college young than for anyone else supported by their great agencies of communal weal. Something guilty or self-righteous in me (or maybe even a trifle saintly) relishes a deep salary cut and a funny old office bordering academic slums. Something in me needs to be desperately needed, and it is easy to intuit how little most of you need me to fulfill your own Jewish agendas. Another rabbi will be more useful now in raising new questions and eliciting new commitments. I cannot hide from the fact that my style and my convictions have cost our educational and religious program a lot of money. If I had been more careful, the millionaires who left us or who stopped giving (some never started) might have helped our tutorials or our scholarships escape their perennial distress. I have the distinct impression that my strange blend of traditional theology and radical politics is no longer in.

One thing more: I am not sure I am a Reform Jew any longer. I find denominationalism repugnant and go with joy to a Jewish community that eschews any such divisiveness. I will be rabbi to the traditional and humanist, to freaked-out and scholarly Jews, to a congregation of more kinds than the Reform in which you and I grew up. Now I can have a kosher home and share my ideas with people who disagree with them in more ways than you ever have. I can pray every day and not ride on the Sabbath and try to write some more and try to figure out what is next to do.

But of course, the Solel years can never come again. I came to you a young man, and I leave deep in middle age. My children were in nursery school then, and now they are in college and *kibbutzim.* You gave me an ear and a hand and a heart; you paid me almost enough to live like you, and criticized me almost enough to convince me you were right. You introduced me to the finest people I have ever known (some are dead, some are gone away, some have remained close for all these fifteen years). You have shared my joys and my anguish, and some of you have made the joy more joyful and the pain more tolerable. You have seen me manic and brilliant, confused and compassionate, burning and ice-cold. You have seen me grow and slip, know and forget, struggle and surrender. We have looked deeply into each other's hearts, and sometimes it seemed also into the Heart of the world. I go from you, knowing I must, but with pride in what we have built and in what we have tried in our several ways to become. Yours were the best years of my life; together we have become a footnote in the history of the Jews.

In love and hope,
Arnold Jacob Wolf

[Congregation Solel *Pathfinder*, March 6, 1972]

OPENING DAY at Comiskey Park reminds me again of how Jewish baseball is. Each player is alone, but they all play for the whole team, and only the whole team can win. The game is fun, but it is also very demanding and sometimes dangerous.

The game has no time limit; one never knows whether the game will be long or short, though there is a general time frame for most games. Each player must hit, field, and run, but each one does it in a slightly different manner and some with much more care for detail than others. The game is nonviolent but very energetic, and it calls for stamina during the long season.

Age, size, IQ, race are all pretty much irrelevant. Unlike basketball, which is only for tall persons, or unlike even swimming, which is for the young, baseball is a universal sport.

The most important truth about the game is this: much of it is boring. You wait and you wait—sometimes for almost the whole, long game. But finally—and no one knows exactly when it will be— you will be the only one who can catch a fly ball or the only one who can drive in the winning run. Everything will depend on you. For that single moment, no matter how slowly it comes, the player must always be ready. There may be no second chance.

[KAM Isaiah Israel Bulletin, April 27, 1988]

A SERMON FOR ROSH HASHANAH, 1991

[delivered September 10, 1961]

WE WERE very young when we began, so young that it is hard to remember. It did not seem too difficult for us to build together then the congregation that we all desired. We had great imagination and great need. We had the pliant modulations of our body's health, the soaring innocence of souls that seemed to fly. We had one another, and we were young.

It was a time, thirty years ago, when people spoke of New Frontiers, of new ambitions, new accomplishment. It was a time when nothing could be kept from man—when we were like children of the ancient gods, glorious and powerful and pure. Our women shone like girls. Their bodies would move across the greens and courts and dancing floors like magic children's, and they knew no fear. Our men were powerful and moving too—toward new accomplishment and new power. Our whole country, too, seemed on the edge of destiny, seemed newly come to great estate.

It was no surprise to us that we could do great things as well. Our congregation grew in number and in wealth. We put the building in the forest, and we put our name in countless mouths. We called ourselves pathfinder and innovator, we experimented in prayer and in instruction. We found success growing like crabgrass all around. For we were young, the masters of our soul.

Now we are growing toward the edge of life. The face in the mirror is no longer mine but my father's face. The women that I see look funny in Jamaica shorts and drink too much and wonder where the children went when they grew up. The Temple isn't new anymore. Someone else's is newer and cost more, and lots of people have forgotten our name. And some of our friends have moved and some have died and some forgotten us and some were never friends at all. And no one told us what it's like to get old, and no one made us ready.

Lots of things that once were far away run through our minds now constantly. The barbarous and tasteless funerals, the recitations of death. Somehow, as we go more often, even these begin to fit into our lives. The old books that we thought we had outgrown find their way into our hands now. Yes, sometimes we fall asleep over the Bible; you cannot learn to read it now, at our age. But still it feels a little friendlier than those huge novels that nourished our middle years. Sometimes we go to pray at Temple, not with much success (God has more on his mind than old men and old women), but we find some comfort in the repetition and the people. Our congregation's creativity is spent, the sermons wind interminably around an old irrelevance, but something is still there. *Sh'ma Yisrael! Yisgadal vyis'kadash!* In the beginning God created the heavens and the earth! It hardly matters now that we do not understand the words. We have heard too many words. The law courts and the stock exchange, the Congress and the beauty shop have been filled with words. And we are filled with words and sick of words that try to mean something. So now we would rest a time in meaninglessness, in old words and a foreign tongue, in words whose resonance is kind and will not ask too much of us.

Where are the words we used to know? Where are the sounds: Play Ball! Encore! I love you! Where have the young words gone by which we sought to mold our time? Where the brittle laughter of our little children? Where the sounds of our passion and achievement? Where the glasses tinkling with wine, the orchestras playing in a hundred shows and clubs and parties? When did the laughter turn too shrill, the passion melt and temper and dissolve? When did they stop inviting us? When was it we were alone first of all? When did the other ones come up to take our place in partnerships and love affairs and politics? When did the men at the place start talking louder so that we could hear, the women at the market turn the aisle to avoid us? When was it that everything we had became strange to us: the paintings from an old-fashioned taste, the furniture a little funny, the jokes a little stale?

And the words, the words! The beautiful words, the words of tenderness and acumen. The words we molded till they looked alive. The words we used to make the deal and cement the partnership, the words we used to make the children behave our way or send them off when we had other things to do, the words we spoke in public to God and in private under His very nose, the big young words, the proud words, the titles, honors, judgments of our universe. The science words, the poetry, the words that made the world our world! What has happened to us, that our garrulous generation has fallen silent?

It was that night, some thirty years ago, that we reflected on the achievement of our time. That year the Russian and our men had gone away from earth. That year the whole world had seemed to be ready for a mysterious departure and redemption. The hand of man was great with power then, his mind spanned galaxies and gathered stars in a radar screen. We all felt power then, the power to do new things which could be great. The world was no longer a prison which kept us in but a launching pad from which we would spring out toward better places and rewards. The ancient dream of flying free, unfettered by our body's weight, was true. The dream of leaving this world for a better one was true. And who was master of it all but us? What breed of angels would we find out there to share our secret and to fill our space with good?

We never met anyone out there at all, did we? The space was empty but for other worlds not like ours. Moons were all too cold and suns too hot for man, and the other planets too much like ours. The men we peopled worlds unknown with were our own selves, born of inner dreams and needs. And space is empty after all. Only man is here, we know now. Only we, and maybe God.

So we came back again to earth, chastened and uninstructed by our flight. We'll go again, of course. Man will always go and come and go again. But, as with Columbus, the Indies of our dreams are home. America was only Europe finding itself. The other planets and the worlds are at the end of our driveway. Younger men than we will go. They still believe the myth. They still follow the stars. For us the old untidy earth is at last enough. Or, if it is less than that, it will still have to do.

It is not easy to be old. Some of us are sick and some defeated. Some are bitter and lonely. Sometimes we pray for release. Sometimes we cling to a hope for somebody's affection that does not come. Masters once, we are outcasts today.

We ask for reverence, but we do not receive it; we hope for attention, but it passes us by. Our children look at us with confusion, fear, and apathy. Our very age is a kind of defeat. The wise doctors helped us reach our age. But instead of blessing, men look at us as if we have a rare disease called life. We who sought the beauty parlor and not the hospitals, we are ashamed of our grey hair, which once was the mark almost of wisdom. We do not tell our age for fear our friends would flee. Our fear is mirrored in other men's contempt. Having worshiped youth, we cannot ourselves be gods anymore.

Somewhere we made the wrong turn. Somewhere we forgot the plain grandeur of being human. Somewhere we turned merciless because we forgot to honor the old. Even Eichmann loved children, but our generation's fear of age was a measure of a spirit frozen and decayed. We are men who do not dream anymore. Outliving our usefulness by standards we ourselves have set, we must apologize for being alive. Because we have defined our lives as function, the function now at last curtailed, we ourselves are empty. Our preoccupation with games and hobbies has not built for us any inner strength. Success was our God, accomplishment our duty. Now what remains for age to celebrate?

We are afraid of being useless. Having treated other men as means, we cannot regard ourselves as ends. Man had more to give than what other men are able or willing to accept, but we have forgotten what it is. We considered life only production and consumption, and now we are too old to make, too weary to enjoy. But man is more than what he does. Mankind is needed—just to be, isn't he? And does not Someone somewhere need us, Whose name we have not called?

Is our life, then, significant? Has all our work been trivial, our reading killing time, our celebration mere entertainment? Have we even found a meaning hidden in the heart of things? It is hard to know. We wish to be needed, to believe that something is asked of every one of us. We wish to use time and not fear it. But we have run away from time, we have forgotten the old men and the old generations, and now it is our turn to be forgotten. We have preferred the new book and the new play, the new friend and the new joke. And so we ourselves have made ourselves obsolete. We live with memories of moments we have missed. We tried to conquer time with space and only emptied ourselves of life.

Yet "time is the presence of God in the world of space. Just to live is holy; to be, a blessing. The moments all are marvels," wrote Heschel. All that time needs is God, a person, a moment. And this, though old, we still have left.

All our lives we gave to our children, everything except ourselves. We nurtured them and bought them things and worried about where they were going. But did we share ourselves with them, sharing being the only gift that people can accept? Did we represent the past of all generations to our sons, or only the pace of future time? Did we bring our own mothers to our girls, or subtly turn away from them and give our daughters no inheritance? Did we so need our children that we tried to buy them off? Or were there times we shared in truth, when one with one, all with each, we knew our love and made it live?

Our children cannot make our lives worthwhile. We must be for them the inspiration, the bequest. We are the tradition which we did not know; for them, we are the exaltation and the meaning. We are the scroll that they will have to unravel all their lives. We are their blessing and their curse. If only we have not caricatured our souls! If only we have been true to our commission!

Is it death we fear? Death, the old and bearded angel? Death with its release and promise both together? How can we fear our brother death, with whom, unknowing, we walked every street, lived every moment? Not ending, but beginning, is our fear.

We have believed that heaven and hell are within, the place one lives himself eternally. And now we are not satisfied to be ourselves forever. The burden of beginning is too much. The little deceits and the grand betrayals weigh us down. O God, we pray, release us from what we have become, make us more than we have been able to be. We, the aging tennis players and the grey *grandes dames*, the clerks and the tycoons, the fathers without sons, the mothers without peace. Heal us and we shall be healed. Turn us, O Lord, and we shall repent in perfect reconciliation. Love us, O God whom we have not loved. Forgive our sins and make us whole.

For the sin of pride we atone with humiliation. For the sin of forgetting we atone with remembering too much. For turning our back upon the poor and the outcast, we old men are cast out from our own place, despised, unknown. For harsh words, silence. For bitterness of spirit, the gall of other men's contempt. For blasphemy against Thee O God, Thou hast hidden Thy face from us. Now turn, O God, unto us Thy frightened children, and give us what we have not deserved.

We have sinned openly and in secret. We have contemned our heritage. We have exploited those weaker and lied to those stronger than ourselves. We have broken the chains of community. We have been selfish and smug and blinded to the blessing. We have been callous and cruel and bored to death. In all that we have done, O God, Thou are righteous and we are old and wrong and scared.

Once we were boys, tracing the alleys of our city, playing childhood games and holding our father's hand. Once we were children with our noble hopes and fragile aspirations. And You were there. You saved us from the flying stone, the angry word, the darkened bedroom, and the fear of growing up. You watched us grow toward manhood. When war broke over our heads, You were a shield about us, protecting us from death. You blessed our marriage couch and our children's crib. You made our plantings grow and made us full. You gave us food to eat and homes to live in that were good. You gave us friends and love and rare meat and good liquor. You spread Your wings about our houses and our congregation. You brought us back to Thee, unwilling and slow. You waited out our petulance. You mollified our plaints. You strengthened our weaknesses. You straightened our road when it was turning off. And You were always there, even when we ourselves were gone.

Now we are old. We have lived the threescore years and ten allotted to man, yes, even by reason of strength the fourscore years. As dusk descends, a calmness at last comes over us. We soon shall join the caravan of ancestry, to see again, but not with eyes, our parents' face, to be a part of endless time. The world will go on without us; it still has You. Our children will, we pray, fulfill Your will, not our confusions. Our country and our folk will live out its promise by the deeds of other men more resolute than we have been. And men will still seek You, lose You, find You after all.

O God, do Thou bless our little lives and call them good. We perishable earth and immortal soul, we finite matter and infinite spirit, we children of the dust and stars, are ready now for You. We have heard You calling in the sleepless night, and we shall come. A last look only at our generation. A final farewell, a touch of someone we have loved, a last drink for the road. "O Lord, what is man that Thou art mindful of him, or the son of man that Thou considerest him?" Yet Thou hast made us but little lower than Thyself. Thou has crowned us with glory and honor, with anxiety and hope, with death and with life everlasting. We come, our Heavenly King. We shake from our feet the dust of earth, and mount the staircase of time which leads to Thee. We come to Thee, our Heavenly Father, bemused, remembering—and unafraid.

[*Best Sermons* Magazine, January 1966]

INDEX

A NOTE ON THE AUTHOR

Arnold Jacob Wolf was born in Chicago in 1924, the only son of Nettie Schanfarber Wolf, a social worker, and Max A. Wolf, a Jewish Republican activist and owner of a tailoring business. In his youth, Arnold was introduced to the study of Judaism and the Bible by his uncle, the prominent Reform rabbi Felix Levy. He also appeared frequently as a child radio actor on WGN and Mutual Radio, usually in soap operas and children's programs.

Arnold graduated from Lakeview High School, then studied at the University of Chicago, where he received an A.A. degree. In 1945 he was awarded a B.A. in philosophy from the University of Cincinnati; three years later he was ordained by the Hebrew Union College in Cincinnati, where he had studied with Abraham Joshua Heschel.

From 1951 to 1953 he served in the U.S. occupation forces in Japan as the only Jewish Navy chaplain in the Far East. In 1957 he was the founding rabbi of Congregation Solel in Highland Park, Illinois, a pioneering Reform synagogue which combined religious traditionalism with political activism. He marched in Selma, Alabama, for civil rights; FBI agents attended and recorded his 1967 sermon against the Vietnam War. From 1972 to 1980 he served as Jewish chaplain and Hillel director at Yale University. Since that time he has been rabbi of Kehilath Anshe Maarav Isaiah Israel Congregation in the Hyde Park neighborhood of Chicago. He has also written *What Is Man?* and *Challenge to Confirmands* and has edited *Rediscovering Judaism* and *Jewish Spiritual Journeys.*